Philippe Kruchten · Steven Fraser ·
François Coallier (Eds.)

Agile Processes in Software Engineering and Extreme Programming

20th International Conference, XP 2019 Montréal, QC, Canada, May 21–25, 2019 Proceedings

Editors
Philippe Kruchten
University of British Columbia
Vancouver, BC, Canada

Steven Fraser
Innoxec
Santa Clara, CA, USA

François Coallier
École de technologie supérieure
Montréal, QC, Canada

https://doi.org/10.1007/978-3-030-19034-7

Preface

This volume contains the research papers presented at XP 2019, the 20th International Conference on Agile Software Development, held during May 21–25, 2019, at the École de technologie supérieure in Montréal, Québec, Canada.

XP is the premier agile software development conference combining research and practice. It is a hybrid forum where agile researchers, academics, practitioners, thought leaders, coaches, and trainers get together to present and discuss their most recent innovations, research results, experiences, concerns, challenges, and trends. XP conferences have inspired the successful evolution and adoption of agile practices by teams and organizations, not only in the software industry and academia, but also beyond. Whether you were new to agile or a seasoned agile practitioner, XP 2019 provided an informal environment to network, share, and discover trends in agile for the next 20 years.

Submissions of previously unpublished research papers related to agile and lean software development were invited for the XP 2019 Research Track. The submissions received addressed a variety of agile software development topics of concern to researchers and practitioners alike. Submissions based on empirical studies and including practitioner and academic collaborations were encouraged. We received 45 submissions. After the first screening by the track chairs, 38 submissions were sent for peer reviews. Each submission received (on average) four reviews from Program Committee members. Based on reviewer comments, 15 papers were accepted presentation and publication in these proceedings.

The success of the XP 2019 conference and the Research Track should be attributed to the passionate and hard work of many people. We greatly appreciate the contributions from authors, the Program Committee, the volunteers, and our sponsors. Last but not least, we would like to express our sincere thanks to the XP Conference Steering Committee and the Agile Alliance for their ongoing support.

April 2019

Philippe Kruchten
Steven Fraser
François Coallier

Organization

Conference Chair

François Coallier	École de technologie supérieure, Canada

Program Co-chairs

Steven Fraser	Innoxec Innovation, USA
Philippe Kruchten	The University of British Columbia, Canada

Research Workshops Chair

Rashina Hoda	The University of Auckland, New Zealand

Doctoral Symposium Co-chairs

Casper Lassenius	Aalto University, Finland
John Noll	University of East London, UK

Industry and Practice Co-chairs

Alex Sloley	Construx, USA
Dennis Mancl	MSWX Software Experts, USA
Yang Wang	Bosch, Germany

Experience Reports Co-chairs

Rebecca Wirfs-Brock	Wirfs-Brock Associates, USA
Steve Adolph	cPrime, Canada

Educator Symposium Co-chairs

Craig Anslow	Victoria University of Wellington, New Zealand
Martin Kropp	Fachhochschule Nordwestschweiz, Switzerland

Research Posters Chair

Philippe Kruchten	The University of British Columbia, Canada

Agile Montréal Liaison

Martin Goyette	Agile Montréal, Canada

Institutional Partners

École de technologie supérieure, Canada
Agile Montréal, Canada
Agile Alliance, USA

Tutorials and Workshops Co-chairs

Robert Chatley	Imperial College, UK
Shane McIntosh	McGill University, Canada

Open Jam Facilitator

Ansley Nies	Acorn Consulting Enterprises, USA

Panels Chair

Steven Fraser	Innoxec Innovation, USA

Sponsor Liaison

Phil Brock	Agile Alliance, USA

Logistics and Registration

Tarah McMaster	Agile Alliance, USA

Press and Media Sponsors

Pam Hughes	Agile Alliance, USA

Student Volunteers Coordinators

Roberto Erick	École de technologie supérieure, Canada
Lopez Herrejon	École de technologie supérieure, Canada

Local Arrangements

Patrick Cardinal	École de technologie supérieure, Canada

Agile Alliance Liaison

Jutta Eckstein	Independent, Germany

Steering Committee

Juan Garbajosa (Chair)	Universidad Politécnica de Madrid, Spain
Ademar Aguiar	Universidade do Porto, Portugal
Hubert Baumeister	Technical University of Denmark, Denmark
Philip Brock	Agile Alliance, USA
François Coallier	École de technologie supérieure, Canada
Jutta Eckstein	Independent, Germany
Steven Fraser	Innoxec, USA
Casper Lassenius	Aalto University, Finland
Erik Lundh	IngenjörsGlädje, Sweden
Michele Marchesi	University of Cagliari, Italy
Maria Paasivaara	Aalto University, Finland
Seb Rose	Cucumber Limited, UK
Nils Wloka	Codecentric, Germany

Program Committee

Scott Ambler	SA+A, Canada
Daniel Amyot	University of Ottawa, Canada
Craig Anslow	Victoria University of Wellington, New Zealand
Hubert Baumeister	Technical University of Denmark, Denmark
Jan Bosch	Chalmers University of Technology, Sweden
Joanne Boyd	Flextronics, Canada
Nanette Brown	SEI, USA
Frank Buschmann	Siemens AG, Germany
Fabio Calefato	University of Bari, Italy
Renato Cordeiro Ferreira	IME-USP, Brazil
Robert Crawhall	Innoxec Innovation, Canada
Manuela Dalibor	RWTH Aachen University, Germany
Torgeir Dingsøyr	University of Science and Technology, Norway
Yael Dubinsky	StepAhead, Israel
Sarah Elder	North Carolina State University, USA
Hakan Erdogmus	Carnegie Mellon University, USA
Neil Ernst	University of Victoria, Canada
Steven Fraser	Innoxec Innovation, USA
Alfredo Goldman	University of São Paulo, Brazil
Lorenzo Granai	Cisco Systems, Switzerland
Peggy Gregory	UCLAN, UK
Eduardo Guerra	National Institute of Space Research, Brazil
Orit Hazzan	Technion – Israel Institute of Technology, Israel
Rashina Hoda	The University of Auckland, New Zealand
Helena Holmström Olsson	University of Malmö, Sweden
Nasif Imtiaz	North Carolina State University, USA
Deepti Jain	AgileVirgin, India
Nico Jansen	RWTH Aachen, Germany

Philippe Kruchten	The University of British Columbia, Canada
Casper Lassenius	Aalto University, Finland
Ville Leppänen	University of Turku, Finland
Lech Madeyski	Wroclaw University of Science and Technology, Poland
Rezvan Mahdavi Hezaveh	North Carolina State University, USA
Sabrina Marczak	PUCRS, Brazil
Shane McIntosh	McGill University, Canada
Judith Michael	RWTH Aachen University, Germany
Tommi Mikkonen	University of Helsinki, Finland
Alok Mishra	Atilim University, Turkey
Nils Brede Moe	SINTEF, Norway
Juergen Muench	Reutlingen University, Germany
Daniel Méndez Fernández	Technical University of Munich, Germany
Lukas Netz	RWTH Aachen University, Germany
John Noll	Lero, Ireland
Ipek Ozkaya	Carnegie Mellon Software Engineering Institute, USA
Maria Paasivaara	Aalto University, Finland
Cécile Péraire	Carnegie Mellon University Silicon Valley, USA
Ken Power	Cisco Systems, Ireland
Akond Rahman	North Carolina State University, USA
Pilar Rodríguez	University of Oulu, Finland
Daniela S. Cruzes	SINTEF, Norway
Viviane Santos	Federal University of Pará, Brazil
David Schmalzing	RWTH Aachen University, Germany
Bran Selic	Malina Software Corp., Canada
Helen Sharp	The Open University, UK
Darja Šmite	Blekinge Institute of Technology, Sweden
Simone V. Spiegler	University of Stuttgart, Germany
Stefan Wagner	University of Stuttgart, Germany
Xiaofeng Wang	Free University of Bozen-Bolzano, Italy
Hironori Washizaki	Waseda University, Japan
Michael Whalen	University of Minnesota, USA
Joseph Yoder	The Refactory, Inc., USA

Contents

Agile Adoption

Agile Practices in Practice: Towards a Theory of Agile Adoption and Process Evolution

Brendan Julian(✉), James Noble, and Craig Anslow

Victoria University of Wellington, Wellington 6012, New Zealand
{Brendan.Julian,kjx,Craig.Anslow}@ecs.vuw.ac.nz

Abstract. As teams and organisations make the difficult shift to agile ways of working, there has been relatively little investigation of how they adopt and use agile practices. To aid those teams looking to move to agile we should examine how others have done so and what practical value they found. We studied teams which adopted agile practices across a spectrum from taking on a whole methodology to a couple of practices at a time, and then committed to continuous assessment and improvement of their ways of working. Those teams favoured adapting agile-based, team-oriented practices suited to their particular needs over technical practices and defined methodologies.

Keywords: Agile adoption · Agile software development · Continuous improvement · Grounded Theory · Industry applications

1 Introduction

Agile practices have had a marked impact on the technology industry around the world, supporting increased communication, quality and productivity in teams and their products when implemented successfully [5,23]. Yet adopting and effectively using agile ideas and practices still presents a significant challenge to teams and organisations [12]. There also seems to be a disconnect between extant literature discussing what agile is and the comparatively smaller amount of research into how agile is applied in industry [6]. In order to aid those teams looking to make a change to agile it is important to examine how others have already done so and to share their experiences with the wider agile community.

We sought to understand agile use and evolution in multiple teams around Wellington, New Zealand by analysing the changes they made to their processes over time. We wished to identify trends in how teams adapt and modify their process to fit their work, and to understand the success of those changes.

In this paper, we present a Grounded Theory study of the adoption and evolution of agile practices in several local organisations. We conducted semi-structured interviews with twenty-two agile practitioners in twenty organisations, each with varying levels of expertise across different roles and types of work.

P. Kruchten et al. (Eds.): XP 2019, LNBIP 355, pp. 3–18, 2019.
https://doi.org/10.1007/978-3-030-19034-7_1

Based on this data, we present our theory on the motivations and means of agile adoption and the ongoing process of adapting and improving on agile practices to suit the specific needs of the teams and their work.

2 Methodology

2.1 Grounded Theory

Grounded Theory (GT) is a socialogical research method proposed by Glaser and Strauss in 1965 [10] and formalised in 1967 [11]. Rather than verifying an existing theory, GT seeks to build a theory from data where little to no established theory exists. GT is a commonly used method for qualitative data analysis, including in the software development industry [1,16,17]. GT assumes the researcher is unfamiliar with the area of interest to aid discovery of a theory, so to account for our own prior knowledge we instead chose to adopt Charmaz's Constructivist Grounded Theory (CGT) variant [3]. CGT theories are co-constructed by the researcher and participants through investigation of the area of interest, rather than discovered. CGT promotes using prior knowledge and experience as a means of more effectively examining data that may require esoteric domain knowledge, as we already have experience with agile practices we considered CGT to be well suited to our study.

2.2 Data Collection

We conducted twenty-two interviews with participants from twenty different organisations, nineteen within the tech industry and one outside it. Interviews were 30 to 90 min in length and followed a semi-structured format. After each interview, the data was coded [18]. Codes were then used to inform further interviews and modify questions as part of constant comparative analysis [9]. Table 1 gives aliases and roles for the participants.

Among those interviewed in this study, most working in small-mid sized teams were using or have used some form of Scrum [24]. Few, if any, were using "pure" Scrum. A number were using some form of Lean such as Kanban [27], or a combination of the two, referred to as Scrumban [20]. We also observed some use of scaled agile frameworks such as Scrum of Scrums [28] and SAFe [21].

2.3 Theory Development

Through a process of constant comparison, we used previously gathered data to inform further data gathering, and used that new data to aid in interpreting previous data. We took the codes drawn from the interview notes and grouped them into general descriptive categories of observed practices and modifications via card sorting [29]. We further developed the theory by grouping cards by categories of changes and the driving factors behind them, focusing on identifying changes in participants' methodologies. For example, the initial code of

Table 1. Interview participant aliases and roles

P#	Role	P#	Role
P1	Product Owner	P12	Project Coordinator and Logistics
P2	Scrum Master	P13	Facilitative Team Lead
P3	Team Lead	P14	Technical Business Analyst
P4	Intermediate Developer	P15	Consultant/Agile Coach
P5	Consultant	P16	Team Lead/Business Director
P6	Mobile Developer	P17	Lead Developer
P7	Full Stack Developer	P18	Management Consultant
P8	Release Manager	P19	Client Delivery Manager
P9	Scrum Master/Agile Coach	P20	Test Consultant/Account Manager
P10	Project Manager/Scrum Master	P21	Solutions Architect
P11	Scrum Master	P22	Digital Producer

"buy-in" developed further into concepts such as "willingness to make changes", "capacity for change" and "commitment" as we gathered more information. Our information gathering continued until we were confident we had reached a saturation point, a point at which little to no new information was being uncovered. Through the twenty-two interviews we began to reach saturation at around 18 interviews, past which interviewees were providing their own perspectives on concepts we had already previously identified. These changes allowed us insight into how and why teams chose to develop their practices over time, from adoption through to constant evolution.

Once data collection was complete and theory development was well underway, we began to compare our findings to other similar studies and ideas. In particular we noted several similarities between our discoveries and the proposed Agile Fluency Model by Larsen and Shore [2] with regards to teams assessing their ideal level of agility, as well as several interesting comparisons and contrasts to Hoda's work on agile adoption [14]. We discuss this further in Related Work.

3 A Theory of Agile Process Evolution

In the teams we studied through interviews we identified two general means of adopting agile practices which we termed the "big bang" and "gradual" approaches. With a big bang [22], teams begin by adopting all of a by-the-book process to learn the practices and then begin to modify them. In contrast, teams following a gradual approach take on and integrate a couple of agile practices at a time alongside their existing, non-agile ones through a longer transition period. These approaches describe two ends of a spectrum wherein some teams performed a wholly big bang adoption across the whole organisation while others simply added stand-ups and issue tracking to their existing work, and many variations in between.

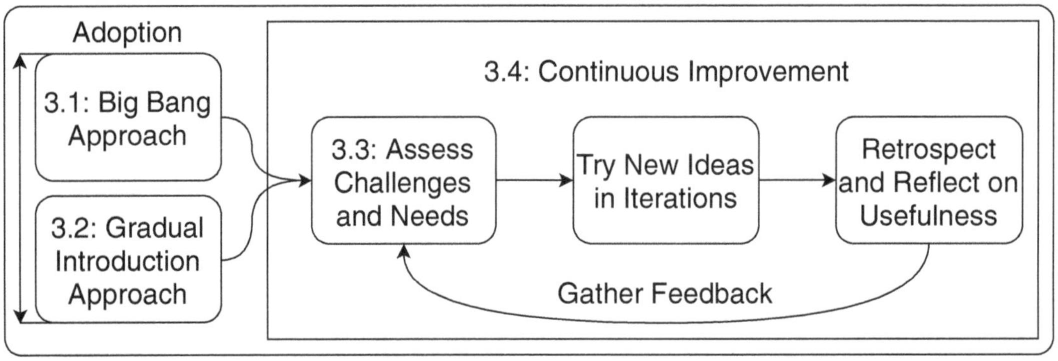

Fig. 1. Our model of Agile Process Evolution. Adoptions of agile methods by teams sit along the spectrum between a "big bang" or "gradual" approach. Following adoption, teams shift to a focus on continuous improvement, iteratively reflecting on and modifying their practices to better fit their current work.

As teams developed expertise and understanding beyond adoption, they focused on continuous improvement, iterating on their process over time to ensure it fits their needs. Adopting agile was not seen as a one-off event by interviewees, rather it requires a willingness to change and commitment to improving *how* a team works. We present a model in Fig. 1 which visualises this process, demonstrating how teams which adopt agile through either approach tend to develop towards the same goal of adaptability and continuous improvement, making adjustments as needed to ensure that their practices fit their work.

3.1 The Big Bang Approach

Those in leadership or consultant roles (such as P1, P5, and P9) often shared the idea that newer teams should start with an established framework that has extensive literature and successful examples behind it.

> *"That's what I always recommend to people; start with Scrum and then evolve it"* - P1, Product Owner

In a big bang adoption a team starts out following the same large set of general practices from day one. Even if there is an initial productivity hit while learning the practices, it was seen as being better to get it out of the way:

> *"You need to start a project the way you mean to carry it on... In terms of that basic agile structure you want to have that in place but you want to be agile with that. It would evolve some change over time but you want to have an understanding of the method and roles as close to day 1 as possible."* - P18, Management Consultant

The team should gain aim to experience with all of the practices involved in a chosen framework, learn their value, and understand why they're used, and then begin to assess which practices work well and which could be improved or replaced.

> *"[Scrum] is the best one to start with, because it gives them a bit of discipline. It's a framework they can hang on to and follow the rules, and it helps them get into an iterative, fast feedback style, and they can then learn to break the rules."* - P5, Consultant

Proponents of big bang felt that the core practices of frameworks such as Scrum were valuable guidance for teams looking to adopt agile, even if they weren't completely suited to their needs, and that attempting adoption without some guidance was needlessly difficult. For example, one organisation (P10, typically Scrum-oriented) explicitly attempted to build an agile framework from the bottom up with no starting practices, rather adopting practices as they felt they would be needed. Quickly, they found that although they were able to identify issues with or gaps in the methodology built so far, the lack of structure made it difficult to identify how to best rectify the issues that arose:

> *"We have tried putting nothing in place and taking on things as we need them. That hasn't worked out so well. There was a lack of structure, structure is really important. Without that, things start to fall apart, things get lost. Some people think agile means you've got no structure, but really I think you need more rigour, discipline and structure to actually make it work."* - P10, Project Manager/Scrum Master

3.2 The Gradual Adoption Approach

In contrast with the big bang approach, P2, P4, P8, P12, P13, P14, P15 and P19 spoke of integrating agile processes into an organisation's existing, non-agile, methodology and gradually making changes to more agile methods. The first practices to be introduced were almost always iterations, stand-ups and retrospectives, accompanied by some form of task tracking and visualisation. For some teams (P8, P12, P13) those practices alone were well suited to their needs. Others (P2, P4, P14) continued to adopt practices to become fully agile teams, usually transitioning into something akin to Scrum or Kanban.

P19 shared their experience of a transition and felt that for an organisation lacking in agile expertise, attempting to take on too much in one go could be overwhelming, and instead the organisation looked at adopting and expanding their practices over time.

> *"It was small bits at a time and I don't think that was for any other reason than if you try and do it all in one hit it just becomes overwhelming and it fails. Where if you can do a bit, perfect it and that becomes the norm then move on to the next bit. First of all it was breaking into squads and then you were part of a squad of a business unit and then you do things like daily stand-ups and you just go through it."* - P19, Client Delivery Manager

P15 related the adoption method back to a team's capacity and needs. A team may not be capable or even have a use for fully adopting Scrum up front, but they may find great value in simply getting everyone in the same room every day for a stand-up to improve communication.

> *"What I really try and help teams do is feel out a good sense of... what they're capable of in any given time. An organisation might say "We're gonna have a digital transformation, an agile transformation". For me it's figuring out what their purpose is, their overall purpose. You start to look at and observe tiny moves, suggesting small things. Will a stand up every day serve?"* - P15, Consultant/Agile Coach

Although fostering a commitment to the practices and driving change among team members was sometimes difficult, interviewees (P5, P6, P9, P10, P13, P14) noted that over time, and with greater experience, commitment increased. One noted that team members began organically making use of the task tracking board that put in place without prompting.

> *"The biggest put off is the idea of having to have everything sorted and we're in an environment where things can change on the day so you've got to be flexible. So I wanted something that was flexible but also visual... Within a few weeks or so of us [maintaining a Kanban board] as a regular activity, my colleagues started putting up stuff as well, which was great because they were taking ownership of it"* - P13, Team Lead

Simply having progress be visible and traceable allowed team members to more effectively plan and organise their work as the team organically embraced the board over time. Along with this tracking board, this team had adopted stand-ups and regular iterations in their non-tech, part-time environment. While a full agile transformation would be surplus to requirements, simply improving communication and visibility of information was incredibly valuable.

3.3 Challenges to Adoption

Resistance. In trying to drive a transformation, experienced individuals (P1, P2, P5, P6, P9, P10, P11, P14) noted it was often difficult to effect widespread change if either the people or environment were resistant to it. They recognised an "if it's not broken, don't fix it" mentality, that a process that isn't actively hindering progress is good enough, even if there is an opportunity to improve. This attitude was seen as particularly prevalent in government departments, where existing processes are inflexible and change is looked on with suspicion.

> *"The business don't understand the DevOps and agile model here. Basically, we play the agile game totally for the teams...but then, the upper parts of the business haven't really bought in. They're coming around but they still see it as kind of a fad"* - P2, Scrum Master

It was felt (P2, P5, P9, P10, P13, P14) that some team members may need to see the effectiveness of a change in order to accept it, but making effective changes without some level of acceptance was difficult. Those same practitioners observed significant differences in attitude over time as newer adopters who had been previously resistant learned the effectiveness of a new way of working.

Outside Forces and Regulatory Compliance. Those working in or with government departments or highly regulated organisations (P2, P8, P12, P14) showed frustration at trying to implement agile in an existing rigid framework.

> *"One thing was a resourcing problem. They wanted development and testing done at the same time, which is fine, but they didn't want to bring developers over to do testing because the pay gap is so different, but they also didn't have enough testers"* - P2, Scrum Master

This team could fully adopt agile at their level, but required a translation layer, ala "Agile Undercover" [15], to document and demonstrate work as required by the existing process. Alternatively, they could try and implement what agile practices they could (such as, iterations and issue tracking) within the existing framework while still fulfilling their obligations to their overseeing body.

> *"Often, depending on the organisation, there's the governance structure, and in government that can be quite heavy. At the moment there are two forums that things have to go through to be signed off [on top of the team's iterative processes]"* - P12, Project Coordinator.

Neither solution was considered perfect, but at least implementing more flexible practices helped improved team morale and effectiveness on some level, even if such efforts were hamstrung by existing, rigid processes.

Needs of the Work. Interviewees focused on the importance of team practices over technical ones when it came to adopting agile ways of working. While technical elements such as pair-programming, test-driven development and more were mentioned and valued, the primary motivations were almost always about improving communication through practices like daily stand-ups and end-of-iteration retrospectives and achieving a regular, fast delivery cadence that would allow them to frequently check their work against their clients' expectations.

Regarding existing frameworks such as Scrum, Kanban etc. participants found them to be useful guidelines rather than rules. Every organisation has different needs and will find value in different practices. Frameworks should be taken as a valuable source of ideas rather than followed blindly.

Participants 5, 6, 9, 10, 11 and 15 considered it vital to understand the purpose and potential usefulness of a set of practices to make better decisions about their applicability to the team's context. Through using the practices, teams gain experience and understanding of how applicable they are to their work and enable them to make informed decisions about how to modify the practices from there on. Gaining some experience and context would then allow teams to make more informed choices and have better discussions about what works well or what might need changing.

> *"Then they can have a meaningful, evidence-based discussion about what they can achieve... We're trying to build a self-organising team, capable of*

setting their own priorities. It's quite amorphous, you've got to avoid just following the process, avoid a cargo cult. It does need a certain prescription result at the beginning to build up that muscle memory, this is why we have stand-ups, this is why we have retrospectives, sprint planning." - P15, Consultant/Agile Coach

The primary boons of conducting stand-ups and retrospectives were facilitating open communication and gathering feedback from every member of the team. Having everyone in the same room, at the same time, discussing the same project would allow everyone to stay informed and discuss their current work while retrospectives were used to reflect on work completed as well as the practices used to do so, as one interviewee put it "what went well, what didn't go well, and what fell to shit." - P9. Several interviewees noted that over time, doing the same kind of stand-up or retrospective could become stale. They proposed that teams should seek to mix it up and try different styles in order to keep interest up, and ensure high quality and consistent feedback.

"You've got to change it up now and then, otherwise people pretty much become bored with it and don't participate as well" - P9, Scrum Master/Agile Coach

Different teams would hold planning meetings at various scales, some with the immediate team each week all the way up to three-monthly department-wide planning sessions.

3.4 Focus on Continuous Improvement

Post-adoption, all teams moved into a overall practice of continuous improvement. Teams recognised that no set of practices is ever perfect and committed to regularly assessing how they work, often as part of retrospectives, in order to ensure their methods were well suited to their work and to improve and develop over time as a team.

Nature of Work Determines the Process. More mature teams, those who have been employing agile successfully for a significant length of time (P1, P2, P3, P6, P9, P10, P11), tended to focus on ensuring their practices are adapted to the work, rather than trying to force their work to conform to their established practices.

"If something like the definition of done or the definition of ready isn't quite working for us, then maybe we look to improve that. It's a constantly evolving process. It's about making the process work for that team." - P6, Mobile Developer

For example, one large organisation (P9 and P11) operates an overall scaled agile framework on a four-week release train. A particular team was operating on a two week Scrum schedule, however, they switched to a four week Kanban schedule to align with the cadence of the rest of the organisation and account for irregular releases from their supplying vendor.

> *"So Scrum doesn't really suit us, because we're getting stuff fed in, Kanban makes it easier to limit our work in progress so we can try and get through things as efficiently as we can"* - P9, Agile Coach

Almost all teams used estimation in some form when planning and prioritising their work, though specific methods differed. Several interviewees (P9, P21, P22) shared that they were moving away from their earlier hours-based estimation to more abstract points which allowed them to more accurately prioritise work relative to other work rather than attempting to time-box it.

> *"Lately we have made a concerted effort to move away from hours-based estimations in favour of story points. Largely the motivation here was that hours-based estimates were proving difficult and often inaccurate or unreliable."* - P22, Digital Producer

Changes can also be related to how a team performs a particular practice such as issue tracking. P9's team found that using the digital solution Jira suited their purposes better than their previous on-paper solution as the team had distributed elements which didn't have access to the physical board. While the physical solution was great for those who could interact with it, it was impossible for off-site members to actively contribute. On the other hand, P16's organisation moved initially from a paper solution for tasks and BitBucket for tickets to Jira, but later switched back again:

> *"It was originally in Jira but it made a lot more sense to take the stories out of Jira and give them their own identity. Jira is shit really, it's fine for low level tickets and capturing screenshots but the other thing that we've used which is working really well is [a spreadsheet based Scrum board]"* - P16, Team Lead/Business Director

Especially when working with distributed teams or off-site clients, it was generally considered to be better to adapt the practices employed to account for difficulties rather than try to push through them with existing processes.

> *"We get down to [vendor] at least twice a week to do refinement sessions. I'm not sure that's a strict Scrum ritual, it's a thing you're supposed to do but Scrum doesn't seem to guide you on how to do it, so we [visit vendor fortnightly] and spend an hour going through our draft stories."* - P1, Product Owner

Organisations working in fields with significant regulatory components must factor in the time needed to complete the necessary testing and documentation into their release schedule.

> *"Probably the biggest impact for us is regulatory. The documentation alone is massive... We break it down quite granularly... We can treat it a bit more agile... We can shuffle things around to keep ahead of the game"* - P8, Release Manager

Each of these examples demonstrates the pragmatism found in agile practitioners we interviewed, and their focus on doing what works for them.

Despite differences in methods of adoption, most interviewees (P1, P2, P3, P5, P9, P10, P11, P13, P14) felt it was important to constantly adapt their practices and continuously improve on how they performed their work.

> *"You need to adapt... That's what's good about agile in general, 'cause the principle is never stay static. You've always gotta question the process and adapt the process to fit your environment, your people, your way of working."* - P1, Product Owner

Change was a universally accepted fact of the working world, for better or worse, and a means of assessing shortcomings and rectifying them was considered highly valuable. Attitudes to changes varied quite widely, as did opinions on drivers for those changes. Through the interviews, participants were prompted on specific changes they made to their work-flow processes, though they were highly specific to the team and project at hand. Suffice to say time should always be taken, often in retrospectives, to examine aspects of the current process that may not be a good fit, and to not be afraid to try something else that may work better.

Most of the interviewees attested to using a form of Scrum or something Scrum-like (P1, P2, P3, P6, P7, P8, P9, P10, P11), but none were using pure, by the book Scrum. While teams made use of sprints, daily stand-ups, end-of-sprint retrospectives, start-of-sprint planning, and some means of issue tracking, they often deviated by dropping some practices or bringing in others.

> *"The most important thing is the values and principles. We use Scrum largely, but the values and principles always help us find what isn't working."* - P10, Project Manager/Scrum Master

Commitment to "Being Agile". The phrase "Don't do agile, be agile" and the concept of agility are not exactly new [4,13,30], though it was explicitly brought up by nine of the twenty-two participants.

> *"Agile is a mindset...Doing agile is only half of it, the rest is being agile"* - P6, Mobile Developer

The core idea here is to not simply follow the motions of the process for the sake of doing so but to employ the agile ideals to assess how you work, as much as the work you do. As P9, an agile coach, noted: "If it's not working, why the hell are you doing it?" A practice doesn't necessarily have to be bad to warrant changing or tweaking. Agile practices are just practices like any other and therefore are only as useful as their practitioners allow them to be. Simply performing the rituals will likely not produce successful results without a commitment to making proper use of them. As an example from P11, retrospectives are largely useless if those participating are unwilling or unable to provide constructive criticism of the work completed and the process used to do so.

> *"Agile might potentially allow you to expose weaknesses in a better way. Agile might give you an option to break down [issues]. The guy that was a grumpy old bastard last week under Waterfall is still the same grumpy old bastard this week, you've just changed the methodology. [Agile] required a change in culture, people and mindset as much as a change in methodology"*
> - P11, Scrum Master

Effective implementation of agile ideas requires a commitment to make the most of the practices put in place, with a view to continuously improving on and modifying those practices to best suit the work at hand. Just as no team examined was using pure Scrum, rather some variation which they found better suited them, no one process will necessarily fit a given team on any given job.

4 Evaluation

Glaser's Criteria. Glaser provides four criteria for assessing the validity of a theory [8,19], which is tied to the soundness of the research method and the data gathered by that method:

Fit: We adopted a CGT methodology in order to employ our previous understanding of what agile methodologies *are* to help investigate *how* they are employed in industry. The categories we developed were based on the data gathered, using our previous experience to interpret the data.

Work: By evidencing the theory, we have formed a clear link between interview results and our developed theory, which explains the data we have gathered, shows general patterns and provides new insights. Opinions shared by participants were generally very consistent. Even though they may adopt agile differently, they all focus on the concept of continuous improvement of their work and processes. The work criterion describes a theory that provides a solid explanation for identified phenomena. Owing to the consistency between out twenty-two participants, we consider this to be the case with out study.

Relevance: Our questions were predominantly aimed at how teams decide to adopt and adapt agile. The responses we gathered show how teams who adopt agile through different means trend towards the same end goal and find similar value in their different practices.

Modifiability: We developed our theory with each interview adding new perspectives and information, and it is open to further refinement.

4.1 Threats to Validity

There are two key limitations we encountered in this study:

Scope: We interviewed twenty-two participants from around Wellington, New Zealand. While this provides a good spread for the local context, data gathered is only representative of the opinions and experiences of our participants and may not necessarily represent other organisations or locales.

Lack of Direct Observations: While interviews are valuable, we believe this study could have benefited from observations to help understand how a team makes the changes they choose to make and why. Interviews can shed some light on this but are limited by what the interviewee can recall at the time.

5 Related Work

5.1 "Agile Fluency Model", Larsen and Shore

The Agile Fluency Model [2] proposes how teams should look at the process of developing their agile practices. Citing the broad range of ideas on "how agile is supposed to be done" they examined agile methods in theory and practice. The model is comprised of five steps describing different levels of fluency; pre-agile, focusing, delivering, optimising, and strengthening.

One of the core elements of the Agile Fluency Model [2] is the idea that different levels of the model will suit some teams well and others may be a better fit for other teams. While different teams we studied had achieved differing levels of agility, they had all found value in their adopted practices.

Several teams (including P2, P8, P12 and P13) working within existing processes looking to employ iterations, stand-ups and retrospectives benefited from increased communication between team members and improved understanding of progress, which aligns well with the Focusing step.

More thoroughly agile teams (such as P1, P6, P16 and P18) found increased fluidity to their work, with autonomous team practices improving flow. Prioritisation of work based on delivering the most immediate value became the main focus, embodying the Delivering step.

Mature teams (like P9, P10 and P11) identified that at agile practices had become second nature they were able to rapidly adapt to changes while continuously improving their practices. These teams were often either part of an overall transformation or leading it, which fits Optimising.

The ideas that agile frameworks are not one-size-fits-all and agile is not a silver bullet for any issue would agree with the Agile Fluency Model. That said, to fit our observed teams into the model's defined steps would be somewhat inaccurate. We feel the teams we looked at better fit a spectrum from new to fluent teams. Moving from one level to another in the Agile Fluency Model does not appear to be a generational leap but a series of small steps and occasional missteps intended to develop the team's practices over time.

5.2 "Agile Transitions in Practice", Hoda and Noble

"Becoming agile: a grounded theory of agile transitions in practice" [14] studied many organisations that have undertaken, or are undertaking adoption of an agile framework, and found that the teams do so in differing ways with varying levels of success. The authors acknowledge that the process of adopting agile is daunting and fraught with challenges surrounding existing organisational culture, people, processes and tools. As we have, Hoda and Noble identify a gap between existing guidance on adopting agile and useful advice for teams undertaking such a fundamental change to their way of working. Through a Grounded Theory (GT) study with 31 participants across 18 organisations in five countries, the authors developed a theory of agile adoption as a transition much like our model's idea of gradual adoption. Rather than a simple series of steps, this paper posits that transitioning to agile involves a complex network of concurrent changes in five dimensions; software development, team, management approach, reflective and cultural practices. In our research we found the latter four to be most prevalent as our interviewees generally focused on team-oriented practices over tech-oriented ones.

While Hoda's theory for agile transitions focuses on the process of adopting agile, the core concepts identified generally agree with both our findings on adoption and on continuous improvement. The paper implies that the organisations observed only employ what we have described as the gradual adoption approach and big bang adoptions were absent, even with a sample size larger than that of our study. Our observations agree that adoption is not a one-and-done affair, even among those following a big bang adoption, the initial introduction of agile ideas is not the end. Whether teams adopt processes over time or many at once, there is still a process of iteration and improvement required for team members and other staff to learn the processes involved and to grow their practices, the key difference is time scale. Our theory on continuous improvement demonstrates that the transitory approach this paper identifies does not stop once an adoption is considered complete, but instead it persists with the team regardless of their initial adoption method. To ensure long term success in the use of agile, teams must develop and continuously improve on their processes in the initial adoption phase and beyond.

5.3 Scrum and "Scrum-but"

Some participants (P1, P5, P9, P10) used the phrase "Scrum-but" to mean they use the core concepts and rituals of Scrum, but modify those which they have found to lack usefulness through experience. "Scrum-but" tends to carry negative connotations in literature, described as the "reasons why teams can't [sic] take full advantage of Scrum [26]." And typically refers to a number of anti-patterns that may crop up in Scrum [7]. Interviewees generally acknowledged that "Scrum's roles, events, artefacts, and rules are immutable and although implementing only parts of Scrum is possible, the result is not Scrum per se

[25]." Interviewees often found pure Scrum to be unsuitable for their environments and preferred to take the valuable concepts and core practices and adapt them to their needs, using the phrase to demonstrate that they recognise that what they're using isn't exactly Scrum, but rather an adaptation of the framework to the particulars of their environment. The prominence of "Scrum-but" demonstrates that though the core ideas of a framework such as Scrum are valuable, it should be treated as a framework, meant to be adapted to the purposes of a given team and that every practice may not be applicable to every team in the same way.

6 Conclusion

In this study we identified two methods for adopting agile in an organisation, the big bang and gradual adoption.

With the big bang approach, teams adopt the entirety of an agile framework such as Scrum in order to learn the rituals and their value. Participants who had more extensive experience with agile, such as P5, P9, P10, and P11 favoured this up-front style. While this practice often has an initial productivity hit, it gives teams a solid foundation to build upon from there on.

Meanwhile, through the gradual adoption approach, teams seek to introduce specific agile practices one or a few at a time, typically beginning with iterations, stand-ups and/or retrospectives. Over time, more are introduced as the team feels they need them. Those interview participants, like P2, P8, P12, P13, and P14, who were somewhat new to agile themselves preferred this approach as they felt it was more manageable to learn.

Adoption, moving from non-agile to agile methods, is not the end of the agile journey. We found that teams then embark on a process of continuous improvement where they iteratively improve upon their current set of agile practices, adding, removing, or modifying them as need be to better suit the particular needs of their work and environment. In addition to assessing their work, teams also assess *how* they work, gathering feedback on the process they employ to understand what works well and what doesn't, with a view to addressing any shortcomings or taking advantage of opportunities for learning and improvement. As team members gain more experience with their practices, they become more receptive to further changes and more capable of contributing to and driving those changes.

More experienced teams typically favour autonomy in their work, flexibility in their methods, and a need to assess and update them over time. They seek to ensure their practices are a good fit for their work, often picking up other ideas or making incremental improvements, rather than trying to force their work to adhere to their established practices. Teams appreciate that an established and well-honed set of practices helps align team members towards the same goals and keep everyone on track.

Future research could explore how the style of adoption (big bang vs gradual transition) impact how team capabilities develop and how quickly, or take a closer look at how exactly teams go about assessing their needs, defining their goals and then adapting their practices to suit their work.

References

1. Adolph, S., Hall, W., Kruchten, P.: Using grounded theory to study the experience of software development. Empir. Softw. Eng. **16**(4), 487–513 (2011)
2. Agile Fluency Project LLC: The Agile Fluency Model (2018). https://www.agilefluency.org/model.php. Accessed 18 Oct 2018
3. Charmaz, K.: Constructing Grounded Theory. Sage, Thousand Oaks (2014)
4. Cockburn, A.: Agile Software Development. Addison-Wesley Longman Publishing Co., Inc., Boston (2002)
5. Coram, M., Bohner, S.: The impact of agile methods on software project management. In: 12th IEEE International Conference and Workshops on the Engineering of Computer-Based Systems, ECBS 2005, pp. 363–370. IEEE (2005)
6. Dreesen, T., Schmid, T.: Do as you want or do as you are told? Control vs. autonomy in agile software development teams. In: Proceedings of the 51st Hawaii International Conference on System Sciences (2018)
7. Eloranta, V.P., Koskimies, K., Mikkonen, T.: Exploring ScrumBut: an empirical study of Scrum anti-patterns. Inf. Softw. Technol. **74**, 194–203 (2016)
8. Glaser, B.: Theoretical Sensitivity: Advances in the Methodology of Grounded Theory (1978)
9. Glaser, B.G.: The constant comparative method of qualitative analysis. Soc. Probl. **12**(4), 436–445 (1965)
10. Glaser, B.G., Strauss, A.L.: Awareness of Dying. Routledge, Abingdon (2017)
11. Glaser, B.G., Strauss, A.L.: Discovery of Grounded Theory: Strategies for Qualitative Research. Routledge, Abingdon (2017)
12. Gregory, P., Barroca, L., Sharp, H., Deshpande, A., Taylor, K.: The challenges that challenge: engaging with agile practitioners' concerns. Inf. Softw. Technol. **77**, 92–104 (2016)
13. Harrison, N.: Beyond agility: organizational patterns of successful software teams. In: Agile Vancouver Conference, pp. 15–16, November 2006
14. Hoda, R., Noble, J.: Becoming agile: a grounded theory of agile transitions in practice. In: Proceedings of the 39th International Conference on Software Engineering, pp. 141–151. IEEE (2017)
15. Hoda, R., Noble, J., Marshall, S.: Agile undercover: when customers don't collaborate. In: Sillitti, A., Martin, A., Wang, X., Whitworth, E. (eds.) XP 2010. LNBIP, vol. 48, pp. 73–87. Springer, Heidelberg (2010). https://doi.org/10.1007/978-3-642-13054-0_6
16. Hoda, R., Noble, J., Marshall, S.: Grounded theory for geeks. In: Proceedings of the 18th Conference on Pattern Languages of Programs, p. 24. ACM (2011)
17. Hoda, R., Noble, J., Marshall, S.: Developing a grounded theory to explain the practices of self-organizing agile teams. Empir. Softw. Eng. **17**(6), 609–639 (2012)
18. Holton, J.A.: The coding process and its challenges. The Sage Handbook of Grounded Theory (Part III), pp. 265–89 (2007)
19. Holton, J.A.: Grounded theory as a general research methodology. Grounded Theory Rev. **7**(2), 67–93 (2008)
20. Ladas, C.: Scrumban: Essays on Kanban Systems for Lean Software Development. Modus Cooperandi Press, Seattle (2009)

21. Leffingwell, D.: SAFe® 4.0 Reference Guide: Scaled Agile Framework® for Lean Software and Systems Engineering. Addison-Wesley Professional, Boston (2016)
22. Mencke, R.: A product manager's guide to surviving the big bang approach to agile transitions. In: 2008 Agile Conference, AGILE 2008, pp. 407–412. IEEE (2008)
23. Pikkarainen, M., Haikara, J., Salo, O., Abrahamsson, P., Still, J.: The impact of agile practices on communication in software development. Empir. Softw. Eng. **13**(3), 303–337 (2008)
24. Schwaber, K., Beedle, M.: Agile Software Development with Scrum, 1st edn. Prentice Hall PTR, Upper Saddle River (2001)
25. Schwaber, K., Sutherland, J.: The Scrum Guide, vol. 12. Scrum Alliance, Westminster (2011)
26. Scrum.org: What is scrumbut? (2018). https://www.scrum.org/resources/what-scrumbut. Accessed 20 Oct 2018
27. Sugimori, Y., Kusunoki, K., Cho, F., Uchikawa, S.: Toyota production system and Kanban system materialization of just-in-time and respect-for-human system. Int. J. Prod. Res. **15**(6), 553–564 (1977)
28. Sutherland, J., Viktorov, A., Blount, J., Puntikov, N.: Distributed Scrum: agile project management with outsourced development teams. In: 2007 40th Annual Hawaii International Conference on System Sciences, HICSS 2007, p. 274a. IEEE (2007)
29. U.S. Department of Health & Human Services: Card Sorting (2018). https://www.usability.gov/how-to-and-tools/methods/card-sorting.html. Accessed 20 Oct 2018
30. Zieris, F., Salinger, S.: Doing Scrum rather than being agile: a case study on actual nearshoring practices. In: 2013 IEEE 8th International Conference on Global Software Engineering, ICGSE 2013, pp. 144–153. IEEE (2013)

Agile Methods Knowledge Representation for Systematic Practices Adoption

Soreangsey Kiv[1(✉)], Samedi Heng[2], Manuel Kolp[1], and Yves Wautelet[3]

[1] LouRIM-CEMIS, UCLouvain, Louvain-La-Neuve, Belgium
{soreangsey.kiv,manuel.kolp}@uclouvain.be
[2] HEC Liège, Université de Liège, Liège, Belgium
samedi.heng@uliege.be
[3] KU Leuven, Leuven, Belgium
yves.wautelet@kuleuven.be

Abstract. The popularity of agile methods is constantly increasing. Information and feedback on how these frameworks were adopted can easily be found in academia and industrial knowledge bases. Such a collective experience allowed the development of many approaches in the aim of simplifying the adoption process and maximizing the chances of success. These approaches provide practitioners with guidelines to help them find the practice that suits their team best. Nonetheless, these approaches are not systematic and practitioners need to go through a long process. For instance, they need to identify the important situational factors that can have a positive/negative effect on the agile practice adoption. Available experiences thus require lots of effort to be discovered. This research proposes an agile methods knowledge representation using an ontology so that the knowledge and experience on agile adoption reported in literature may be reusable and systematic. Based on this model, added knowledge and inference rules, practitioners will systematically be able to decide which practice to select and adopt, i.e, for a given goal, practitioners can retrieve which practices to achieve; from a situation, teams can tell what can be harmful and what can be useful for adopting a practice or what problems they may encounter; etc.

Keywords: Agile methods · Agile practices · Ontology · Knowledge representation · Real case study

1 Introduction

Agile methods have been increasingly adopted by the software development industry (and others) due to their flexible features that allow to better handle the changes in requirements, to improve team's productivity and align to the business needs. As no method can be a one-size-fits-all, software development teams adopt agile methods differently, i.e., depending on their specific problems, resources, goals or expectations [4]. Many empirical studies of agile methods

P. Kruchten et al. (Eds.): XP 2019, LNBIP 355, pp. 19–34, 2019.
https://doi.org/10.1007/978-3-030-19034-7_2

adoption have been published every year. The result from the Systematic Literature Review (SLR) in [5] points out that, in the methodological aspects used on agile methods tailoring research, 66.1% of their selected papers were empirical research. A simple search, also, in SpringerLink for "Daily Meeting" to this day, allows finding 1186 articles with 173 in the software engineering sub discipline. Some research papers describe their proper experience in deploying agile in their own organization, while some others discuss it based on empirical evidences collected from multiple cases. Those papers aim to share knowledge such as problems encountered, lessons learned, solutions found, etc., so that others can learn how to choose the right practices and avoid failures.

These experiences are extremely important and useful, yet time-consuming to collect and classify. Let us imagine that a development team aims to achieve a particular goal. How would they know which practices would help them to? In addition to "goal" to achieve, several variables have to be considered such as situation, project, budget, etc. which can also constrain the selection of a practice. Since the development process is complex and requires lots of effort, many teams decide recklessly to adopt specific agile methods or practices which are popular without considering any context-specific factors resulting in numerous agile adoption failures in the end [10].

To make the knowledge and experiences of the previous empirical studies easily accessible, [8] introduces a structured repository of Agile Method Fragments (AMF). This knowledge repository has been gathered through a systematic review of empirical studies on agile methods. For each AMF, the repository entry states the objectives the AMF aims to contribute to, and a set of requisites needed for its success. On top of that repository, the same authors also proposed a framework for evaluating the suitability of candidate method fragments prior to their adoption in software projects [9]. By linking (with contribution links such as help/harm) the situational factors to the requisite, practitioners can find out whether or not they have the chance to succeed with that practice adoption. Even though the repository and the framework can help practitioners to save much effort in understanding agile practices and their suitability, it is yet inefficient and not systematic enough. In order to use this framework, practitioners are expected to know what the situational factors affect the adoption. In addition, they have to figure out by themselves what parts are considered as helpful or harmful to the requisites and practices.

We argue that a better and efficient solution would be a system which can list out goals achieved by a practice, problems that may be encountered from a given situation and what the team needs to do to solve/avoid problems etc. The answers given by the system to these questions must be generated from the previous experiences of agile practitioners. This paper proposes using an "Ontology" to represent and store all these knowledge items of agile methods or practices adoption, reported in literature. Our goal is to make the existing experience reusable in a systematic manner.

This paper is organized as follows. Section 2 presents the research protocol we applied to achieve our research objective. Section 3 provides the detail of our ontology creation as well as the final ontology model in the form of a UML class diagram. Next, Sect. 4 provides the inference rules we have created for our ontology. The procedure of collecting case studies is described in Sect. 5. Section 6 provides an illustrative example of how to use our ontology when adopting an agile practice in a systematic manner. Finally, we conclude, discuss the limitations of and elaborate on future research directions of the paper in Sect. 7.

2 Research Methodology

Figure 1 depicts the research protocol we applied. We started by building the ontology which basically follows the methodology proposed in [17]. It consists of seven steps: *(1) Determining the domain and scope of the ontology*, *(2) Considering reusing existing ontologies*, *(3) Enumerating important terms in the ontology*, *(4) Defining the classes and the class hierarchy*, *(5) Defining the properties of classes slots*, *(6) Defining the facets of the slots*, and *(7) Creating instances*. The description of each step can be found in [17]. Due to limited space here, we merged step 4, 5 and 6 in Fig. 1. We, however, followed those three steps to create our ontology.

Since we need data from real case studies to build an evidence-based ontology for agile methods adoption, the process for *collecting real case studies* is also included into our research protocol. These case studies allow us to enumerate extra concepts and relationships and it also serves as data input for knowledge creation. The process of building our ontology is iterative and incremental [17]. It means that each case study from data collection was fed into the model for revising and refining the model. We repeated steps 3 to 7 until obtaining a consistent model which fits well with a representative amount of selected case studies (see Sect. 3). Two additional steps follow: *Building Inference Rules* (see Sect. 4) and *Validation Scenario* (see Sect. 6). The former aims at systematically discovering more relationships and the latter aims at providing a feasibility study, as a validation case of our approach.

3 Building the Agile Methods Ontology Model

This section describes how our ontology was built. As mentioned earlier, we started with determining the domain and scope of our ontology. We then discuss about existing ontologies, followed by how we enumerated terms to build our model. Next, we present our ontology model in the form of a UML class diagram. Finally, we describe how to insert the knowledge into the model.

3.1 Determining the Domain and Scope of the Ontology

The scope of the ontology presented here is limited to concepts, relationships and knowledge extracted from experience reported in research papers about adopting agile methods or practice for software development project. We aim at demonstrating the advantages of using the ontology for helping agile practitioners in

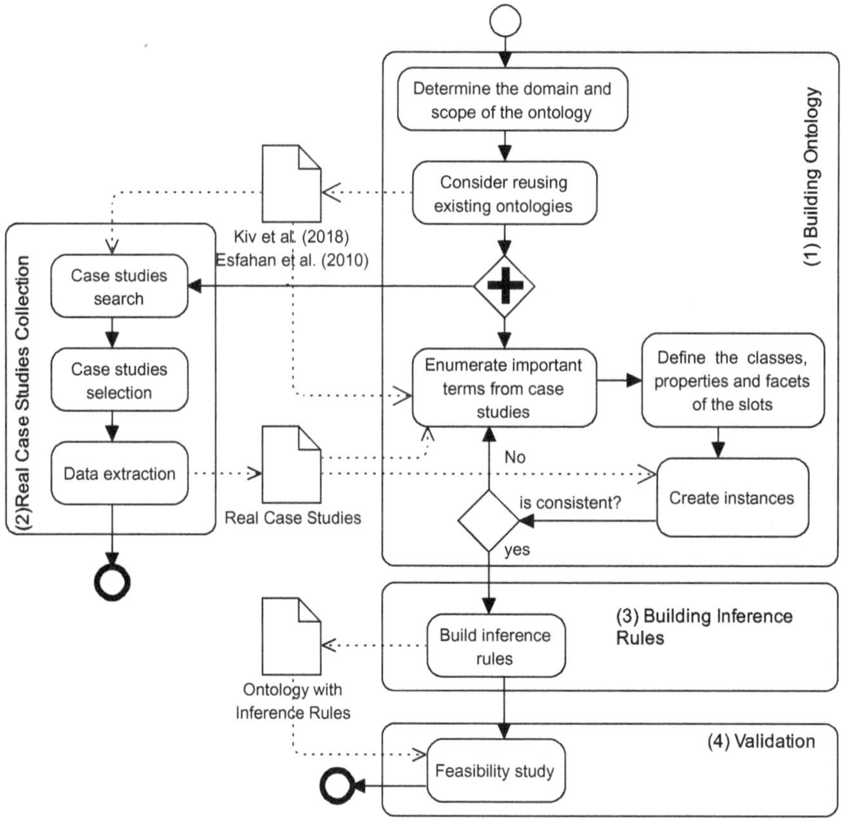

Fig. 1. Research protocol.

selecting and adopting agile practices in a systematic manner. Our preliminary study focuses on using the ontology to represent the knowledge and answer the following questions:

- *Q1: What objectives/goals can be achieved by an agile practice?*
- *Q2: What agile values and principles can be achieved by adopting a practice?*
- *Q3: What activities are part of a practice and need to be performed by the team?*
- *Q4: What are the requisites to successfully adopt a practice?*
- *Q5: What can be harmful when adopting a practice?*
- *Q6: What can be useful when adopting a practice?*
- *Q7: What kind of problems may a team encounter?*
- *Q8: What can be the solutions to a problem?*
- *Q9: What roles or responsibility distribution are needed for each practice?*
- *Q10: What are the artifacts required for a practice?*

Before building the ontology, we also considered reusing existing ones which can be found in specific libraries such as COLORE [6], DAML [2] and Protégé [3]. However, as mentioned, none of them is related to agile practices selection or adoption. We thus needed to build the model from scratch.

3.2 Enumeration of Important Terms

Three main resources help us to enumerate important terms in the ontology: (1) the repository proposed in [8], (2) the influence of the agile manifesto over agile practice selection studied in [13], and (3) the real case studies collected in research community (see Sect. 5).

We must admit that the repository proposed by [8] has inspired us in creating this ontology model. In their repository, each agile method fragment is linked to the objectives/goals it aims to contribute to and a set of requisites needed for its success. Then, the suitability of each fragment is linked to the situation of the team. For example, based on their repository, the goal of conducting "Daily Meeting" is to improve "Quality of Communication" and to conduct "Daily Meeting" successfully, it requires an "effective meeting". An "effective meeting" is suitable for the team that has a "highly available Scrum Master". Even though [8] does not give any clear definition of the concept "agile method fragment", based on our understanding from data in their repository, the authors refer this concept to "agile practice". Therefore, we use the term "practice" in our research. From these, we gathered some terms, which will then become classes, including: **practice**, **goal**, **requisite** and **situation**.

In [13] shows the importance of agile manifesto, i.e., agile values and principles, in adopting agile methods, and in [12] explains its relationship with practices. Understanding the agile manifesto allows us to know why we want to adopt an agile practice. In other words, adopting a practice can achieve the goals of adopting agile methods defined in the agile manifesto. For instance, to achieve the principle "The most efficient and effective method of conveying information to and within a development team is face-to-face conversation", "Daily Meeting" is a suitable practice. In addition, by knowing what agile value and principle a team can achieve, they can measure their level of agility. Thus, we added **value**, and **principle** to the model.

Practice, **goal**, **requisite**, **situation**, **value**, and **principle** are the starting terms of our ontology creation. Then, to be able to answer to the questions in Sect. 3.1, we refined our model based on the result from the case studies. **Activity**, **problem**, **solution**, **role** and **artifact** are thus the extra classes we added to store the extracted information. To differentiate each case study, we added another class **Team** and linked to **goal**, **practice**, **situation**, **problem**, **activity** and **solution**.

3.3 Class and Relationship

After enumerating all the terms and incremental refinement, we built the ontology model with Protégé[1]. The final model is illustrated as a UML class diagram in Fig. 2. We describe the main concepts and relationships as follows:

– **Value:** refers to the agile values as defined in the agile manifesto. Based on [12], agile value is *contributed by* the principle;

[1] https://protege.stanford.edu/.

- **Principle:** refers to the agile principle as defined in the agile manifesto and it *contributes to* agile value;
- **Goal:** is the objective that *belongs to* a team in adopting agile methods. A goal can be *achieved by* conducting agile practices and achieving this goal can *contribute to* the agile principle or another goal;
- **Practice:** refers to an agile practice. It is *adopted by* the team, is *composed of* activities and allows the team to *achieve* the goal. Conducting a practice may *require* a requisite and it can also *encounter* a problem;
- **Team:** refers to a software project team that *has* a specific situation and goal. They *adopt* agile practice and *perform* activities as part of a practice. While conducting an agile practice, a team may *encounter* a problem and, as a result, may *propose* a solution;
- **Situation:** is the state that *belongs to* a team which can affect practice adoption as it can *help* or *harm* the requisite of a practice. In our case, only the situations listed in [5] are taken into account. They are *Project type*, *business goals*, *complexity*, *team size*, *technology knowledge*, *user availability*, *requirements stability*, *organization size*, *culture*, *team distribution*, *management support*, *degree of innovation*, *previous projects*, *maturity level*, *domain knowledge*, *project budget*, *communication* and *type of contract*;
- **Activity:** is *performed by* a team as *part of* the practice. For instance, "15 min meeting every morning" is a part of the "Daily Meeting". Performing an activity can *cause* a problem, *help* or *harm* a requisite and it may also *require* a role or artifact;
- **Requisite:** is the condition which is particularly *required by* a practice in order to successfully adopt it. For instance, conducting a "Daily Meeting" requires "ease of communication" and "everyone's participation". The requisite can be *helped* or *harmed by* team situation or activity. It can also *require* a role, artifact or other requisites;
- **Problem:** is the problem *faced by* team and practice while adopting a practice. For instance, one of the problems faced by a team described in [20] when adopting "Daily Meeting" was "starting promptness as the meetings did not start on time". Problem can be *caused by* a situation, activity or other problem. Some problems can be *solved by* the solution;
- **Solution:** is the solution *proposed by* team in order to *solve* the problem. It may *require* a role or artifact;
- **Role:** is the role *required by or responsible for* an activity, solution or requisite;
- **Artifact:** it is the artifact *required by* an activity, solution or requisite.

The relationships described above are only those made between classes which were manually built. In the ontology, we can discover more of them from reasoning using inference rules. They are listed in Table 2 (Sect. 4).

Class Hierarchy: One of the decisions to make during modeling is when to introduce a new class or when to represent the distinction through different property values [17]. For instance, there are seventeen different types of **Situation**; in line with [17], since each type has a different effect to the **Requisite**,

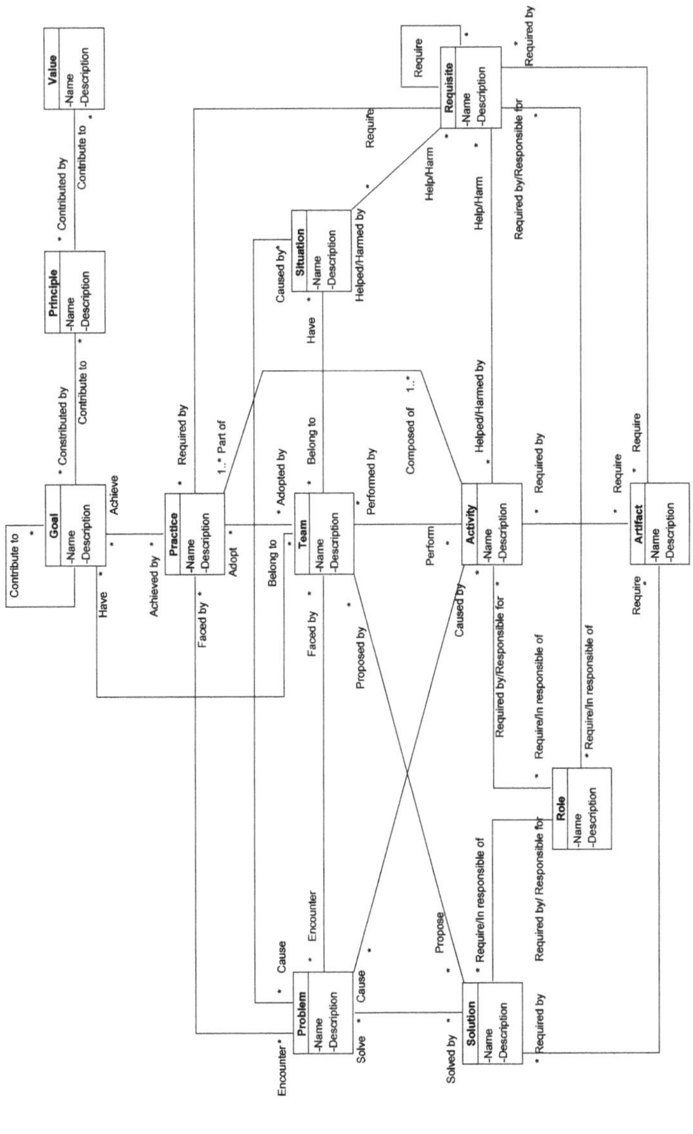

Fig. 2. An evidence-based ontology for agile methods adoption.

we thus create a subclass for each of them in our ontology model. To simplify the representation, we excluded these 17 sub-classes from Fig. 2.

Property: There are two types of property: data property and object property. Data property links individuals–i.e., instances and data values. Object property links individuals and individuals. Both links are built in the form of "Domain - data/object property - Range". For instance, the link "Practice - Name - String" means that, data property Name has Practice as domain and String as range. Another example, "Practice - Achieve - Goal" has Practice as the domain and Goal as the range of object property Achieve.

Every class in our model has only two data properties–i.e., Name and Description. They are the only common things to describe each class by agile practitioners. Their type is String. The domain and range of each object Property were built based on their relationships as in Fig. 2.

3.4 Instances Creation

In this section, we explain how data extracted from real case studies were inserted into our ontology. For illustration, we take a partial data extracted from a selected paper ([20] in the references at the end of the paper). The paper is about a case study of a software development project having three distributed teams – two are located in Norway and the other one is located in Asia. All teams have used Scrum with all the recommended practices for more than two years. Based on their experience, having distributed team causes some problems while conducting "Daily Meeting", such as starting promptness and information distribution.

To insert knowledge into the ontology we need to (1) analyze the description to know what should be created as individuals and in which class, (2) create individuals, and after that (3) connect the individuals by adding the data and object property to each individual. Table 1 shows the individuals and links we created for this case.

Table 1. An instance creation based on a case study.

Class name: individual	Object property	Class name: individual
Team:team1	Have	Situation:Distributed_team
Team:team1	Have	Situation:2_years_agile_experience
Team:team1	Adopt	Practice:Daily_meeting
Team:team1	Encounter	Problem:Starting_promptness
Team:team1	Encounter	Problem:Information_distribution
Practice:Daily_meeting	Encounter	Problem:Starting_promptness
Practice:Daily_meeting	Encounter	Problem:Information_distribution
Situation:Distributed_team	Cause	Problem:Starting_promptness
Situation:Distributed_team	Cause	Problem:Information_distribution

4 Building Inference Rules

Inference is one of the techniques to improve the quality of data integration by discovering new relationships, automatically analyzing the content of the data, or managing knowledge [1]. A simple example of the inference can be: If a taxi driver must be an adult; so if someone is a taxi driver then she/he must be an adult. Another simple example related to agile practice can be: if a team adopts a practice and that practice achieves a goal, we can infer that the team achieves that goal.

It is possible to build any relationship directly in the ontology but this will only weight down and complicate the model. Also, without the inference rule, we cannot discover any relationship between instances more than what we manually insert. That is not the efficient way of using knowledge. Therefore, if a relationship can be discovered by reasoning, we use the inference rule. Table 2 lists all the inference rules we have built in our ontology to discover more relationships in order to answer the questions in Sect. 3.1.

Similarly to ontology creation, there are different ways in writing inference rule. For instance, "If a problem is caused by an activity and that activity is part of a practice → that practice encounters that problem" can be written as "If a practice is composed of an activity and that activity causes a problem → that practice encounters that problem". However no repetitive inference rule should allow answering the same question.

5 Case Studies Data Collection

Following the procedure of ontology creation, we need to repetitively create the model and feed the data to see whether or not it can represent the knowledge we want to use in the future. Actually, there is no way to validate the model because new case studies keep coming in and the model can always be improved over time. The best we can do in this paper is to feed a good amount of case studies and try to answer our predefined questions.

We decided to take ten different case studies. For diversity, we took two cases for each of the five most commonly used agile practices based on the 12th VersionOne agile survey. They are *Daily stand-up*, *Sprint/iteration planning*, *Retrospectives*, *Sprint/iteration review*, and *Short iterations and release planning*.

To collect the documents that report about applying a specific agile practice in real projects, we basically followed the steps for conducting SLR described in [13]. We briefly describe those steps hereafter:

- **Keyword:** Even though we only took two cases for each practice, we tried to retrieve all the papers related to each practice adoption to check and select the best two. Keywords are thus the name of each practice, which are "daily standup", "sprint planning OR iteration planning", "retrospectives", "sprint review OR iteration review", "short iterations" and "release planning".

Table 2. Inference rules for answering questions in Sect. 3.1.

Question	Inference rules
Q1	***R1***: *If a practice is composed of an activity and that activity achieves a goal → that practice achieves that goal.*
Q2	***R2***: *If a practice achieves a goal and that goal contributes to a principle → that practice achieves that principle.*
	R3: *If a practice achieves a principle and that principle contributes to a value → that practice achieves that value.*
Q2	*Can be discovered with direct relationship.*
Q4	***R4***: *If a practice requires a requisite and that requisite is helped by another requisite/situation/activity → that practice requires all of that requisite/situation/activity.*
Q5	***R5***: *If a situation/activity harms a requisite and that requisite is required by a practice → that situation/activity harms that practice.*
	R6: *If a team has a situation and that situation harms the requisite → that team harms that requisite.*
	R7: *If a team performs an activity and that activity harms the requisite → that team harms that requisite.*
Q6	***R8***: *If a situation/activity helps a requisite and that requisite is required by a practice → that situation/activity helps that practice.*
	R9: *If a team has a situation and that situation helps the requisite → that team helps that requisite.*
	R10: *If a team performs an activity and that activity helps a requisite → that team helps that requisite.*
Q7	***R11***: *If a practice is composed of an activity and that activity causes a problem → that practice encounters that problem.*
	R12: *If a team performs an activity and that activity causes a problem → that team encounters that problem.*
	R13: *If a team has a situation and that situation causes a problem → that team encounters that problem.*
	R14: *If a team encounters a problem_1 that causes another problem_2 → that team encounters the problem_2.*
Q8	*Can be discovered with direct relationship.*
Q9	***R15***: *If a person is responsible for an activity → that person is required for that activity.*
Q9& Q10	***R16***: *If a practice is composed of an activity and that activity requires a role → that practice requires that role.*
	R17: *If a team performs an activity and that activity requires a role/artifact → that team requires that role/artifact.*

- **Search Engines:** We took the formal data from well-known digital libraries in the field of software engineering: IEEEXplore, ScienceDirect, ACM Digital library and SpringerLink. We set the publication years to between 2000 and

2018, the field to Software Engineering, and the search terms matching title of the paper, keywords or abstract.
- **Selection Criteria:** With a big list of papers related to each practice, we did an abstract screening then a full-text screening with the following criteria:
  - Empirical study or research study with case study validation related to agile methods or agile practices usage or adoption;
  - Paper that has a significant discussion related to the keyword practice. As the result, it must describe the usage experience and/or the lesson learned and/or the problem and/or the challenge and/or the solution to the problem;
  - Paper with a good description of team situations and goal.
- **Data Extraction:** We extracted data based on the questions defined in Sect. 3.1. Basically, we tried as much as we could to extract the following information from each paper: **goal**, **activity**, **requisite**, **situation**, **problem**, **solution**, **role** and **artifact**.

While many of them meet the criteria, we decided to choose the two most descriptive cases, the ones which can answer best the questions in Sect. 3.1. They are Stray, et al. [20] and Moe and Aurum [15] for **Daily meeting**, Berteig, M. (2008) and Ochodek, M. & Kopczyńska (2018) for **Short iteration**, Gregorio [11] and Moe, et al. [16] for **Sprint planning**, Maham [14] and Paasivaara and Lassenius [18] for **Sprint retrospective**, and Santos [19] and Eloranta [7] for **Sprint review**.

6 Feasibility Study

Once the ontology model was built, and knowledge and inference rules added, the model is ready to be used. In this section, we provide an illustrative example of how to use our ontology when adopting an agile practice in a systematic manner.

As an illustrative scenario, consider an agile software development team which is assigned to develop a mobile application. The team has the following situation: (1) Some of team members are new and others have an extensive experience with mobile application development. (2) The team is working in two locations and only one team has direct access to their clients. (3) All of them are neophytes to distributed development. (4) Some of them are new to agile methods and others have been developing some projects with Scrum for a few years. The team decides to use Scrum. The Scrum Master understands that bad communication can cause some problems in adopting "Daily Meeting". Therefore, his goal is to make communication effective. He is wondering if there are reports or documents discussing about the problems related to communication encountered by a distributed team when adopting "Daily Meeting". What are their solutions for addressing these problems? Such information is very useful for the Scrum Master and may inspire him to adopt "Daily Meeting" successfully.

With the same Protégé Tool only requires four simple steps in order to get the answers. (1) Creating a new individual to represent development team, (2)

Table 3. Relationship in ontology format for feasibility scenario.

Class name: individual	Object property	Class name: individual
Team:TestTeam	Have	Situation:Distributed_team
Team:TestTeam	Have	Situation:2_years_agile_experience
Team:TestTeam	Have	Situation:No_agile_experience
Team:TestTeam	Have	Situation:User_hardly_available
Team:TestTeam	Have	Situation:No_domain_knowledge
Team:TestTeam	Have	Situation:Experience_in_technology_knowledge
Team:TestTeam	Have	Situation:Virtual_communication
Team:TestTeam	Have	Goal:Quality_of_Communication
Team:TestTeam	Adopt	Practice:Daily_meeting

connecting their team individual with the existing individuals which match the team's situation and goal, (3) executing the reasoning to get all the individuals linked to the team, (4) using query to get more answers to the question described in Sect. 3.1.

With the above scenario, we created individual "Team:TestTeam" to represent the development team. Then, we linked TestTeam to different individuals based on the team's situation and goal as in Table 3.

Next, we started the reasoner to discover more individuals linked to the TestTeam. At once, all the inference rules in Table 2 were executed. Among

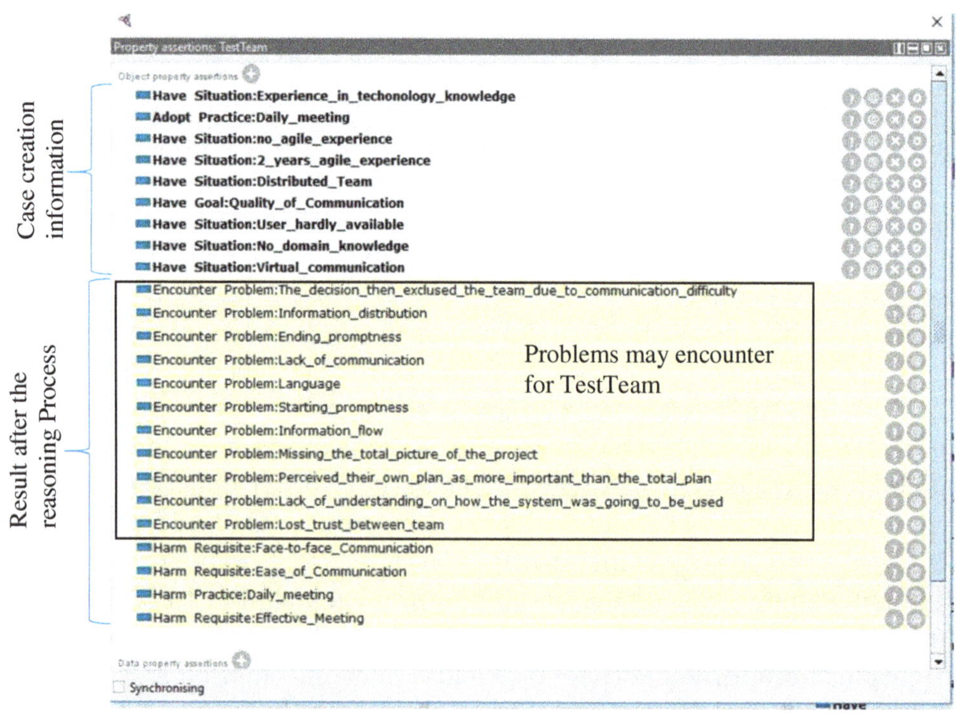

Fig. 3. Case result: problems encountered by team.

these 17 rules, R6, R7, R9, R10, R12, R13, R17 are related to the Team. That is why, from the individual TestTeam, the Scrum Master can have the answers related to problems that his team may encounter and to the situation of the team that helps and harms the requisite of the "Daily Meeting". Figure 3 exposes the result from the reasoning. As expected, the TestTeam may encounter multiple problems since its situations are harmful for the requisite as well as the "Daily Meeting".

Since **Solution** is not linked to the **Team**, in order to get answers, it requires to run a query. In our case, we used SPARSQL. The query and result shown in Fig. 4 are the solutions to the problem that the TestTeam may encounter. As an example, two solutions may address the problem "Information distribution". They are "Rotate scrum master role among the team members" and "Pass a token". More answers for the ten predefined questions in Sect. 3.1 can be found at https://goo.gl/sSBAZo.

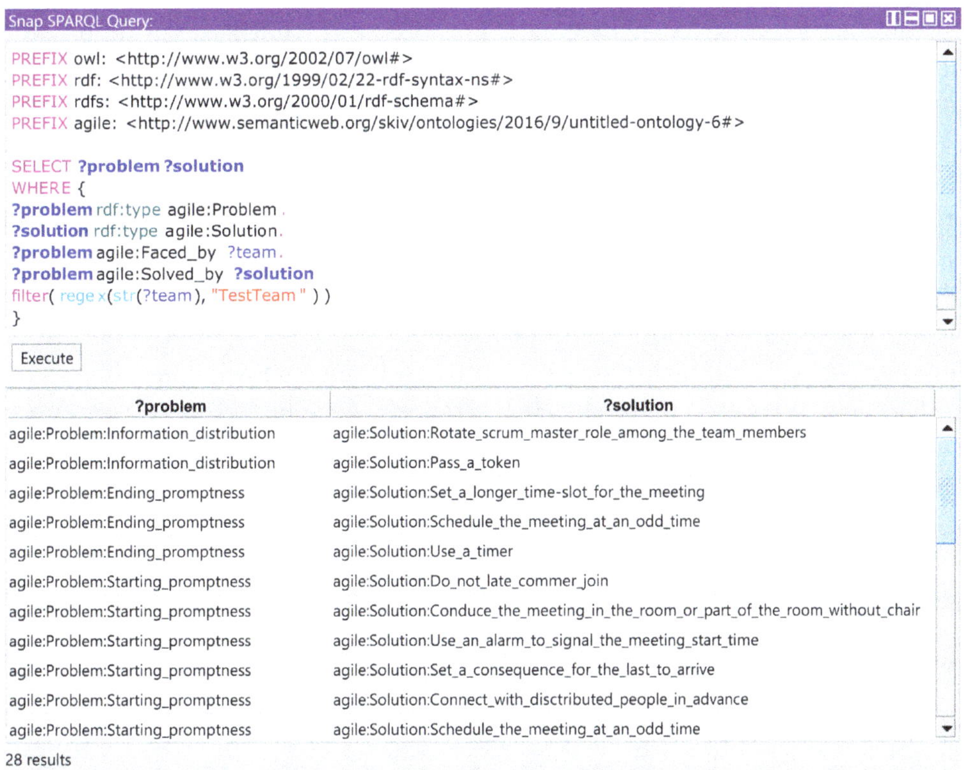

Fig. 4. Case result: proposed solution.

7 Conclusion and Future Work

In this paper, we presented the creation and uses of an ontology to support knowledge representation aiming at recycling agile adoption experience. It has been built on the basis of knowledge extracted from empirical evidence reported in existing literature. Seventeen inference rules have been added to systematically discover more relationships among concepts in our ontology.

Through knowledge representation, practitioners using it dispose of a tool to systematically and effectively support their own agile adoption. By using Protégé, in just four simple steps, they can systematically answer common questions related to the selection and adoption of a particular agile practice. Examples include determining what goal can be achieved by adopting a practice; what can be harmful and what can be useful for adopting a practice into a particular situation; what problem may be encountered and what does the team need to do to solve/avoid that problem, etc. To get answers, agile practitioners simply need to select the existing situations in the model that match their own. In addition, as the answers are generated from previous experiences, they would be very helpful and pragmatic.

The main limitation at this stage of this research concerns the handling of conflict situations. For instance, the feasibility scenario allows team members to be neophyte or expert in agile methods. In this case, our model cannot make a conclusion for such a mixed situation. It can only tell what is helpful and what is harmful about each situation independently. Another limitation concerns the fact that some of the answers cannot be generated by the reasoning – i.e, the model cannot provide what situations are considered as harmful if agile practitioners choose to adopt a specific practice. It will list all the problems caused by the situation regardless of the practice adopted by the agile practitioners. Getting such answer requires using a query too complex for agile practitioners in learning. Finally, the included knowledge is still limited; with only ten case studies, there are situations which the model cannot answer.

For addressing the limitation, we plan to add more knowledge into our ontology in the near future. Within the SLR process, we selected in total more than 100 case studies for the five most commonly used practices. We hope to improve our model by adding not only these knowledge but also additional inference rules. Moreover, we also plan to build a user friendly Computer-Aided Software Engineering (CASE) Tool available for agile practitioners for using and encoding knowledge themselves so that the knowledge base would be increased. Finally, a real experimentation with agile software development teams will be conducted to get their feedback on the usefulness of our approach.

References

1. Inference. https://www.w3.org/standards/semanticweb/inference
2. DAML ontology library (2004). http://www.daml.org/ontologies
3. Protege ontology library (2018). https://protegewiki.stanford.edu/wiki/Protege_Ontology_Library
4. Abbas, N., Gravell, A.M., Wills, G.B.: Using factor analysis to generate clusters of agile practices (a guide for agile process improvement). In: 2010 AGILE Conference, pp. 11–20. IEEE (2010)
5. Campanelli, A.S., Parreiras, F.S.: Agile methods tailoring-a systematic literature review. J. Syst. Softw. **110**, 85–100 (2015)

6. COLORE: Semantic technologies library. http://stl.mie.utoronto.ca/colore
7. Eloranta, V.P., Koskimies, K., Mikkonen, T.: Exploring ScrumBut—an empirical study of scrum anti-patterns. Inf. Softw. Technol. **74**, 194–203 (2016)
8. Esfahani, H.C., Yu, E.: A repository of agile method fragments. In: Münch, J., Yang, Y., Schäfer, W. (eds.) ICSP 2010. LNCS, vol. 6195, pp. 163–174. Springer, Heidelberg (2010). https://doi.org/10.1007/978-3-642-14347-2_15
9. Esfahani, H.C., Yu, E., Cabot, J.: Situational evaluation of method fragments: an evidence-based goal-oriented approach. In: Pernici, B. (ed.) CAiSE 2010. LNCS, vol. 6051, pp. 424–438. Springer, Heidelberg (2010). https://doi.org/10.1007/978-3-642-13094-6_33
10. Fitzgerald, B., Russo, N., O'Kane, T.: An empirical study of system development method tailoring in practice. In: ECIS 2000 Proceedings, p. 4 (2000)
11. Gregorio, D.D.: How the business analyst supports and encourages collaboration on agile projects. In: 2012 IEEE International Systems Conference (SysCon), pp. 1–4. IEEE (2012)
12. Kiv, S., Heng, S., Kolp, M., Wautelet, Y.: An intentional perspective on partial agile adoption. In: Proceedings of the 12th International Conference on Software Technologies - Volume 1, ICSOFT, pp. 116–127. INSTICC, SciTePress (2017)
13. Kiv, S., Heng, S., Kolp, M., Wautelet, Y.: Agile manifesto and practices selection for tailoring software development: a systematic literature review. In: Kuhrmann, M., et al. (eds.) PROFES 2018. LNCS, vol. 11271, pp. 12–30. Springer, Cham (2018). https://doi.org/10.1007/978-3-030-03673-7_2
14. Maham, M.: Planning and facilitating release retrospectives. In: Agile 2008 Conference, pp. 176–180. IEEE (2008)
15. Moe, N.B., Aurum, A.: Understanding decision-making in agile software development: a case-study. In: 34th Euromicro Conference on 2008 Software Engineering and Advanced Applications, SEAA 2008, pp. 216–223. IEEE (2008)
16. Moe, N.B., Aurum, A., Dybå, T.: Challenges of shared decision-making: a multiple case study of agile software development. Inf. Softw. Technol. **54**(8), 853–865 (2012)
17. Noy, N.F., McGuinness, D.L.: Ontology development 101: a guide to creating your first ontology (2001)
18. Paasivaara, M., Lassenius, C.: Scaling scrum in a large globally distributed organization: a case study. In: 2016 IEEE 11th International Conference on Global Software Engineering (ICGSE), pp. 74–83. IEEE (2016)
19. Santos, R., Flentge, F., Begin, M.-E., Navarro, V.: Agile technical management of industrial contracts: scrum development of ground segment software at the European Space Agency. In: Sillitti, A., Hazzan, O., Bache, E., Albaladejo, X. (eds.) XP 2011. LNBIP, vol. 77, pp. 290–305. Springer, Heidelberg (2011). https://doi.org/10.1007/978-3-642-20677-1_21
20. Stray, V.G., Lindsjorn, Y., Sjoberg, D.I.: Obstacles to efficient daily meetings in agile development projects: a case study. In: 2013 ACM/IEEE International Symposium on Empirical Software Engineering and Measurement, pp. 95–102. IEEE (2013)

Agile Practices

Leadership Gap in Agile Teams: How Teams and Scrum Masters Mature

Simone V. Spiegler[1,2(✉)], Christoph Heinecke[2], and Stefan Wagner[1]

[1] Institute of Software Technology, University of Stuttgart, Stuttgart, Germany
{simone.spiegler,stefan.wagner}@iste.uni-stuttgart.de

[2] Robert Bosch Automotive Steering GmbH, Schwäbisch Gmünd, Germany
Christoph.Heinecke@bosch.com

Abstract. *Motivation:* How immature teams can become agile is a question that puzzles practitioners and researchers alike. Scrum is one method that supports agile working. Empirical research on the Scrum Master role remains scarce and reveals contradicting results. While the Scrum Master role is often centred on one person in rather immature teams, the role is expected to be shared among multiple members in mature teams.
Objective: Therefore, we aim to understand how the Scrum Master role changes while the team matures.
Method: We applied Grounded Theory and conducted qualitative interviews with 53 practitioners of 29 software and non-software project teams from Robert Bosch GmbH.
Results: We discovered that Scrum Masters initially play nine leadership roles: Method Champion, Disciplinizer on Equal Terms, Coach, Change Agent, Helicopter, Moderator, Networker, Knowledge Enabler and Protector. They transfer some of those roles to the team while it matures. The Scrum Master provides a leadership gap, which allows team members to take on a leadership role.
Conclusion: The Scrum Master role changes while the team matures. Trust and freedom to take over a leadership role in teams are essential enablers. Our results support practitioners in implementing agile teams in established companies.

Keywords: Agile teams · Scrum Master role · Maturity

1 Introduction

Recently, more and more organisations implement agile teams. Yet, it is not entirely clear how to become agile. At present, a very popular agile approach is *Scrum* [21]. Scrum proposes the role of the Scrum Master who takes on a team leadership role [18]. The Scrum Master is considered to be a facilitator of the Scrum process and enables a team to work in a self-organised and cross-functional way. Furthermore, the Scrum Master protects the team from external disruptions [21].

P. Kruchten et al. (Eds.): XP 2019, LNBIP 355, pp. 37–52, 2019.
https://doi.org/10.1007/978-3-030-19034-7_3

Yet, empirical research on Scrum teams found that the Scrum Master sometimes acts as a barrier to teams becoming agile in early stages. The reason is that Scrum Masters tend to stick to a command-and-control mode [18]. In contrast, teams applying agile methods for three years on average appear not to struggle with the Scrum Master and are even supposed to share the leadership role [20].

These diverging results could be explained by changes in the maturity of agile teams. A team learns how to be agile while undergoing different maturity stages [12]. Hence, agility of a team is a process that unfolds over time [24]. Yet, to the best of our knowledge, there is no empirical analysis of the changing leadership role of the Scrum Master during the agile journey.

To be able to support organisations in the agile transformation, our research objective is to explore the Scrum Master role and how the role changes while the team matures. We believe investigating the changing leadership role of the Scrum Master will provide valuable insights into how teams can become agile.

We collected data in 11 business divisions of the conglomerate Robert Bosch GmbH, primarily operating in the automotive industry. We applied Grounded Theory [10] and conduced qualitative semi-structured interviews with 53 Scrum practitioners from 29 different software and non-software project teams that had applied Scrum over a period of three months up to three years.

We help practitioners in understanding how the Scrum Master can enable a team to become agile in an established company by providing empirical insights on the agile transformation at Robert Bosch GmbH. Applying Role Theory [1,14], the 53 interviews revealed that Scrum Masters incorporate *nine different roles* which they *transfer to the team while it matures*. We further introduce the concept of a *leadership gap* into research on agile teams which enables team members to take on a leadership role themselves. Hence, we conclude that the Scrum Master role changes while the team matures.

2 Related Work

Several authors describe agile teams as being empowered to work in a self-organised and cross-functional manner and that those teams continuously learn and adapt to changing conditions [5,23]. Cross-functionality implies to understand each other's roles and domains within one team and to be able to work with each other due to a shared understanding [14]. Self-organisation indicates that teams enjoy a high level of freedom considering how to do their work [4]. It is no longer the supervisor who assigns tasks to individuals but the team members themselves assign tasks to themselves [4]. If Scrum teams are led by command-and-control, e.g. members cannot chose their tasks, agility will not materialise [7,14].

Empirical research on the concept of a Scrum Master shows conflicting results regarding the Scrum Master behaviour. Moe et al. [18] find that team members rarely take over responsibility, while Srivastava and Jain [20] arrive at the conclusion that all team members should be able to take on the Scrum Master role. Moe et al. [18] observed the implementation of agile methods within one

Scrum team over a period of 9 months. They found that the Product Owner and the Scrum Master tend to take over a leadership role most of the time. They describe how a Scrum Master posed a barrier to self-organisation: The person started to control team members which made them stop revealing their impediments and, as a consequence, resulted in weak team leadership and lack of trust. The authors also describe, however, that team leadership improved over time in such a way that more and more team members took over responsibility. Srivastava and Jain [20], who investigated teams that had been working in an agile way for three years on average, outline that the aim of an agile team is to lead themselves. However, they refer to Carson et al. [2] and acknowledge that taking over responsibility in a Scrum team is a process that unfolds over time due to a shared purpose, social support and voice.

How to evolve from an immature team to a mature one and which role the Scrum Master plays in this journey is yet not clear. We have not found any empirical study on the Scrum Master that specifically examines how the Scrum Master role changes while the team matures.

Cockburn [3] refers to the Japanese philosophy of Shu-Ha-Ri and describes Scrum as a maturity model for agile adaption. Likewise, Gren et al. [12] state that depending on the maturity level of a team, team members practice agile work differently. In the introduction of his doctoral research, Gren [11] suggests that leadership should adapt to different maturity stages of agile teams. He refers to Situational Leadership Theory [13,17] and claims that leaders of agile teams need to demonstrate more monitoring at an early stage but can delegate tasks at a later stage of team development. Hoda et al. [16] examine both mature and immature teams and discover six different self-organising roles. They claim that roles can be transferred from formal role keepers in rather immature teams to any team member with the right set of skills in more mature teams.

Since the Scrum Master role has been shown to either display command-and-control behaviour of one formal role keeper in an immature team [18] or has been suggested to be played by multiple group members in mature teams [20], we believe that the Scrum Master role can be transferred from one individual to distinct team members while the team matures. Yet, this transfer has not been empirically investigated.

3 Study Design

3.1 Research Question

Our research objective is to understand the changing leadership role of the Scrum Master in an agile team over time.
RQ1: Which roles does the Scrum Master play in an agile team?
RQ2: In which way do team members take on the Scrum Master role over time?
RQ3: How are roles transferred from the Scrum Master to the team members?

3.2 Context and Subject Selection

We chose Grounded Theory because this method is applied in research fields with scarce knowledge and it aims at generating new theory on social interaction between actors [10]. Furthermore, this method increasingly gains popularity among researchers to investigate human aspects of agile working [15]. Since it is an interpretative approach the research question should be embedded in the specific context under study [10].

We conducted this study at Robert Bosch GmbH. The Robert Bosch GmbH employs more than 410,000 people in 60 different countries worldwide. The company history dates back to 1886 and can therefore be classified as an established company. The conglomerate is active in four different business areas: mobility solutions, industrial technology, consumer goods as well as energy and building technology. Each business area consists of various subsidiaries and business divisions. Therefore, market conditions and subcultures vary wildly.

While the agile transformation used to be a central project, now each division is responsible for its own agile transformation. Even though there exist a role description for a Scrum Master behaviour, there is neither an obligatory training nor a general rule regarding the Scrum Master. Each team can decide on its own how to train the team and Scrum Masters in the agile way of working. For example, they could book a training internally or externally of the company or not book a training at all.

Two authors have direct access to the field. We collected data on the topic between June 2017 and November 2018. We identified Scrum practitioners either via our personal network or via intranet and first contacted them by email. We conducted interviews according to availability and willingness to take part.

We collected data from 11 business divisions which have slightly different subcultures. Most divisions were active in the automotive industry, while others produced domestic appliances and gardening tools. Interviewed teams stated that they apply the method Scrum mostly in modified form, e.g. w.r.t. the regularity of Scrum meetings. All Scrum Masters were without disciplinary power, responsible for the Scrum process and in charge of team development. Most practitioners of the company call the Scrum Master role *Agile Master*, indicating that this role should adapt to the specific team, rather than sticking to the Scrum approach by the book. Thus, we consider the sample fitting to examine maturity and the changing Scrum Master role.

In total, our data includes 22 Scrum Masters, 8 Product Owners and 23 team members from 14 software development and 15 non-software project teams. The size of teams ranged from 5 to 12 members and often included diverse nationalities. Since the age of teams stretched from three months up to three years, we expected the maturity of teams to vary. To respect participants' confidentiality, we cite them by SM (Scrum Master), TM (team member) and PO (Product Owner).

3.3 Data Collection and Analysis Procedure

The research problem should be allowed to emerge during the study while collecting data at the research field [10]. We observed Scrum events, such as the daily stand-up, review, planning and retro, of various agile teams and conducted three rounds of qualitative interviews. To identify a focus topic, the authors first conducted unstructured interviews with practitioners to discover which focus topic related to leadership in agile teams would be interesting to be explored. The interviews revealed that Scrum Masters struggled with empowering the team for self-organisation, while some practitioners also reported that self-organisation of agile teams improved over time.

In a follow-up study we conducted semi-structured face-to-face interviews of 45 min on average. Interviewees were asked about their personal experiences on agile projects with a focus on the Scrum Master role and what they had learned since they had started to apply the Scrum method. The guiding questions are available online [19].

Interviews were audio-taped and transcribed. We coded the collected data by applying Glaser's Grounded Theory [10]. We openly coded transcripts sentence-by-sentence and aligned codes that appeared to be alike to one concept. We constantly reflected those concepts critically. We aligned concepts if they appeared to be alike to build categories [10].

We identified multiple activities (concepts) the Scrum Masters claimed to do to support the Scrum teams and further aligned the different activities to nine roles (categories).

One bundle of concepts described one category. For example the category *change agent* contained the concepts *serving as a role model*, *changing habits*, and *convincing project teams of the agile way of working.*

Grounded Theory follows an iterative approach in which each step determines the next step to be taken during the research [10]. Previous interviews had revealed that the Scrum Master role had changed over time and that team members started to take over more responsibility. Drawing on theoretical sampling [10], we conducted a third round of interviews where we approached the Scrum Master role additionally from the team's perspective and addressed teams as a whole. This showed that team members of rather mature teams also had learned to play some of the Scrum Master roles.

Additionally, Scrum Masters explained that they gradually lead the team less and also that sometimes they would empower the team by doing nothing at all, which we labelled *leadership gap.* Through constant comparison [10] of various interviews and observations we identified nine different Scrum Master roles and developed a substantive theory [10] which we labelled the *role transfer process.*

3.4 Validity Procedure

At the beginning of each interview, participants were informed about the purpose of this study and assured of confidentiality, so as to receive open and honest responses.

The majority of participants spoke openly, also about their personal concerns what was not working well in their organisation or in their agile team. There were three people from three different teams whose overly positive statements did not match with the comments on the same topic from other interviewees of the very same team. Since the authors could not be sure whether social response bias applied or the interviewees were really overly positive people, those three participants were excluded from the sample.

4 Results

Our first two research questions aimed at understanding *which roles the Scrum Master plays in an agile team* (RQ1) and *in which way team members take on the Scrum Master role over time* (RQ2).

We identified a set of **nine different roles** that Scrum Masters played. While some teams reported that the leadership roles were rather centred on the Scrum Master, other teams revealed that the Scrum Master role had changed over time. In the latter cases, **team members started to take over some of the roles** themselves and the Scrum Masters reduced the extent to which they played those roles. In the following Sect. 4.1 we will describe the nine Scrum Master roles. Each role description is divided into three parts:

1. Description of the role in general (RQ1)
2. How the Scrum Master played that role (RQ1)
3. How team members took over that role after some time (RQ2).

4.1 Nine Scrum Master Roles

Role 1: Method Champion. Organises meetings and get-togethers, teaches the method, supports formulating tasks and setting goals, visualises information, and discusses how to adapt the method during the retrospective.

Scrum Master: A large majority of Scrum Masters mentioned the method to be their main task when working with agile teams. Many emphasised that they continuously helped the team to adapt the method to their specific context.

Team: In newly established agile teams, members rather waited until the Daily Stand-Up to speak about issues with each other. Over time, teams started to speak with each other right away when an issue occurred. Some teams stated that the Scrum Master had initially organised team events but after some time the team members organised such events themselves. Also, two teams explicitly stated that their team visualised information on a board on their own initiative and that this was the way they learned and exchanged knowledge.

Role 2: Disciplinizer on Equal Terms. Supports the team to keep to the rules, ensures that the team focuses on relevant topics and makes sure that team members attend the meetings. Discipline is accomplished via communication on a par. Interaction on equal terms creates non-hierarchical spaces which are important to speak openly with each other.

Scrum Master: Initially, some team members were reluctant to follow the Scrum process. When the Scrum Master insisted on discipline, however, such as only talking for a certain amount of time during the daily or to follow up on measurements they had agreed on during the retrospective, the team members started to see the benefit. It is important to note that discipline was described to focus on the Scrum process, not on direct control of team members. If individuals were controlled directly, they reported to loose sense of responsibility.

Team: Over time, team members learned to focus and prioritise their own work. For example, team members reported to only do one thing at a time and not everything at the same time as they used to do in the past, or they stopped their peers from endless discussions.

Role 3: Coach. Observes team members and uncovers which kind of behaviour is missing in a team to improve teamwork, provides feedback, and helps teams to find out what they wish to change and how to do so.

Scrum Master: Scrum Masters reported to initiate team-building activities, brought developing conflicts to the surface and helped the team to solve them. Coaching was considered important to foster teamwork and self-organisation.

Team: Several interviewees described how the Scrum Master built trust among team members, e.g. during the retrospective. After some time they established psychological safety [9] and started to open up and to provide feedback to each other. It was no longer merely the Scrum Master who provided feedback to the team.

> *The retrospectives [...] push us to actually stand up for some opinion, to say what is wrong or to open up, and then he [the Scrum Master] unleashed the monster. I have always been very critical about lots of stuff, but now I see that everyone is critical sometimes, now I see that they [the other team members] actually care to say "look, I am not happy about this" and speaking openly had never happened before.* (TM)

Role 4: Change Agent. Serves as a role model, changes habits, and convinces newly established project teams of the agile way of working.

Scrum Master: While a large majority helped team members get used to the method step by step, others wanted to help people develop a certain mindset, such as not being afraid of failure or openness towards results. Either way, their overall aim was to convince individuals why the agile way of working made sense.

> *At the beginning, it was a bit tough to convince some team members of the agile approach. But now I think our team does not want to work in a different style anymore. There is a drive in our team that some team members even would like to go further. They have been infected with the agile virus and they want more and more.* (SM)

Team: We did not come across a team members who started to act as a Change Agent pro-actively, such as convincing others of the method. However, several agile teams started to serve as role models for other teams by being agile. The Change Agent role might be important at the beginning of a newly established team. But while the team matures, this role might become obsolete.

> *Back then when I started with agile development, it was rather amusing. Because we felt like animals in a circus. At first, there was astonishment, then amusement, later interest and, finally, they asked whether they [our partner team] couldn't do it the same way. But this was not a process of a few days. It rather took several months.* (PO)

Role 5: Helicopter. Possesses the ability to see the bigger picture, to know who possess the right skill for a certain task, to include relevant stakeholders and to structure work.

They identified cross-boundary links between individuals and tasks from different technical expertise or domains towards a common goal.

> *In our team, I don't feel like I am the boss or anything of that kind. I am just the one in my team who is best at keeping track of things and to give them a general direction.* (SM)

Team: Due to regular communication and visualisation, team members developed a shared understanding [14,18] while they matured, so that they were aware of who had certain knowledge or skills. Developing a Helicopter perspective helped team members to think in networks, to serve as sparring partners for each other and to be fast in handing over the work to another professional of another expertise.

> *In the beginning, I think you don't know who has more experience in a certain area or expertise in another area. But slowly I get to know everyone and can judge who can support me in which difficulty in the quickest possible way. [...] But in the end I know, okay, I have a problem here and who can support me.* (TM)

Role 6: Moderator. Moderates all kind of meetings and builds a bridge between perspectives and domains. This role is considered to be important to develop the necessary cross-functional understanding for agile teamwork.

Scrum Master: They mediated between individuals from different domains and helped the team to build a shared understanding and to tolerate each other.

Team member: No interviewee elaborated on a situation in which a member played the Moderator successfully. One team reported that they had tried letting team members lead the retrospective but it had ended up in a planning instead. Two teams felt that the Scrum Master should be the Moderator since they considered it to be difficult to remain neutral during a discussion when being part of the team.

Role 7: Networker. Connects the team with relevant stakeholders, e.g. managers and experts, from within and outside the organisation.

Scrum Master: The way in which Scrum Masters used their network depended on the current need of the team. Scrum Masters reported that they included formal leaders to gain the support for the agile approach. Another Scrum Master reported how he had invited an expert for a certain method to train the team. Yet another Scrum Master stated that he knew colleagues from facility management whom he could call whenever the team needed organisational support.

> *You don't have to be better at designing than a design engineer. But you have to somehow show him ways to solve his problems. And if it is only by referring him to another design engineer.* (SM)

Team: The Scrum Master provided contacts and empowered the team members to build their own network over time. This increased their scope of action and enabled them to quickly react to challenges.

> *For example, that one has an information for someone, that he normally would not have access to as a planning guy. [...] Actually, I bring in my network from production and the developer his network and the TEF person yet another. During the open discussion at the Daily Stand-Up, I can say that I have a problem. Someone knows someone who can help me with it.* (TM)

Role 8: Knowledge Enabler. Realises which kind of knowledge the team needs, e.g. expert information or methodological skills, and supports team members to acquire that knowledge, e.g. sends them to training or conferences, and schedules knowledge exchange meetings. Furthermore, this role promotes iterative learning, e.g. learning from mistakes, and fosters learning-by-doing.

Scrum Master: Some Scrum Masters urged teams to take time for learning. A few of them convinced managers that agile teams must sit close to each other to approach each other easily, learn from each other and build a shared understanding.

> *They just do not know the whole approach and how to access it. They know classic learning like you go to a training or you study a book, but in this field, you have so many user groups, meet-ups [...]. And we also try to just propose a nice event. They can meet other people there and discuss with them. For example, we all went to a conference together.* (SM)

Team: While some team members expected the Scrum Master to have the technical expertise to provide feedback, other interviewees had learned to receive feedback from their peers. They shared their progress and served as a sparring partner to each other. They also reported to just walk over to colleagues and ask for information, sit together when they had questions or collaborate on tasks.

> *Today it is all very easy going. I just go over to my colleague's desk, sit down for, like, 45 min and work with him on a topic. Nobody says anything against that. It is very informal, but it also happens that I personally have to answer some questions.* (TM)

Role 9: Protector. Shelters teams from inappropriate requests from the Product Owner, managers, disciplinary leaders and other departments.

Scrum Master: Scrum Masters reported protecting the team from re-prioritisation or too high workload by the Product Owner. Furthermore, they sheltered the team from management intervening in daily business or overruling decisions the team had come up with.

> *But then, I also pushed some things through in certain teams, [...] in which managers had taken decisions again. I had to go to the management and tell them "that is not OK, you make a mistake". Then they had to compromise and later they were really glad that they had reacted that way. Because the team gave the right hints after all. That is a situation in which one has to fight a battle on behalf of the team.* (SM)

Team: One team implemented a role called "Batman" that was responsible for the protection from external requests that were unrelated to the respective sprint goal. The role keeper changed depending on day and time. Two teams reported that they struggled because the Scrum Master currently had no time to stick with the team regularly. One team stated that it had happened twice that management removed members temporarily during the absence of the Product Owner. The Product Owner wished that there was a Scrum Master on a regular basis to defend the team. Likewise, a Product Owner of another team said that he struggled with not intervening in operational work and tended to tell people what to do. He wished that there was a Scrum Master regularly to stop him from disturbing. Thus, we suggest that it might be difficult for teams to protect each other from management in an established company.

Investigating which role the Scrum Master plays (RQ1) and in which way it changes over time (RQ2), we found that **the Scrum Master played nine different roles which he transferred to the team while it matured.** In addition, we found that some roles were more suitable for a transfer to the team members than others. In the following, we will elaborate on how roles were transferred from the Scrum Master to the team members.

4.2 The Role Transfer Process

Our third research question was: *How are roles transferred from the Scrum Master to the team members?* We found that roles were transferred via **three steps** we labelled the **role transfer process** (shown in Fig. 1). Before we elaborate on the role transfer process in depth, we exemplify the concept by referring to the following story:

When asked how he had learned to take over responsibility, one team member said that he had faced a major challenge in an area in which he had no previous experience. He had encountered a lack of leadership since no expert was there to support him. He said that, initially, he was afraid of taking over the responsibility necessary to tackle the challenge. Yet, he was left alone and had to solve the challenge himself. He had felt a sense of personal responsibility. Consequently, he had decided to take over a leading role. He felt a high level of self-efficacy after he had solved the challenge successfully and became a very proactive team member afterwards. He stated that in his current project, he missed such a lack of leadership and that he had observed that team members were reluctant to self-assign tasks. We name this lack of leadership which provides the opportunity for a team to take on a leadership role the **leadership gap**.

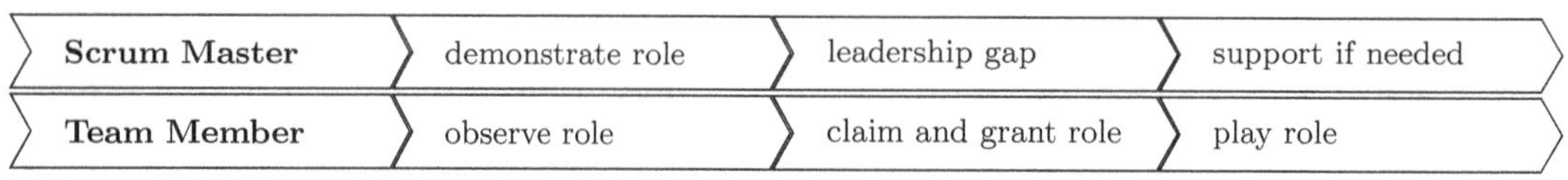

Fig. 1. The three steps of the role transfer process.

We found that the role transfer process consists of three steps: **The first step** describes how the Scrum Master serves as a role model by performing all nine roles. The Scrum Master demonstrates how to perform the activities of the roles, while team members observe and communicate regularly on the meaning of the roles, e.g. with the help of visualisation. They build a **shared understanding** concerning the Scrum Master role which leads to role clarity.

> *If you want to do Scrum, you have to make sure that people understand the different roles.* (SM)

The second step describes that Scrum Masters stop playing certain roles themselves after some time and simultaneously prevent management and Product Owners from taking on the respective role. While some teams stated that management allowed them to actually decide, others experienced that management, Scrum Masters or Product Owners were reluctant to hand over power and, consequently, team members did not take over leadership roles. Contrarily, team members who face a leadership gap in which no one plays the specific role get the opportunity to take on the roles themselves. If a team member claims the leadership role for him- or herself, other team members allow the respective team member to take over that role and accept the new role keeper.

> *As a Scrum Master I can provide strong support at the beginning to get started. But then I have to retreat gradually so that the team gets into the mode of self-organisation. Because if you do not create some free space or a vacuum, nobody will jump in.* (SM)

> *I try to help colleagues to find their way into the roles. It is always tricky to keep the balance between what the team should do by themselves and what should be done by the PO or SM. That is one thing that one has to reflect upon and to level out. [...] The most exciting thing is to bear the silence until someone says something and to wait until someone else gets active. [...] Also we have to give them some free space to experiment and try out themselves.* (SM)

Scrum Masters stated that they either provided a leadership gap on purpose by not playing certain roles but waiting that team members would take on the opportunity and play the role, or they were not playing the role because they were absent which gave the team the chance to perform the role.

> *I did not have sufficient capacity to do everything myself. Therefore, some team members took over tasks, e.g. one guy arranged a timer, another one took care of the whiteboard. They were quite proactive as a team. [..] They did not tell me: "You are in the Scrum Master role, you have to make things better for us."* (SM)

The third step describes that team members play most of the roles while the Scrum Master only continues to perform a role when still needed. The Moderator and Protector roles were found to be difficult to be transferred to the team, e.g. because the role keeper should remain unbiased. This indicates that the Scrum Master role does not become obsolete but is played to a lesser extent by a formally appointed person over time. Therefore, we suggest that some roles should always be played by the Scrum Master, which is a similar result as the findings by Hoda et al. [16] who discovered that in the absence of specific formal role keepers some aspects of agile working lost the team's attention, such as the retrospective.

> *It takes a lot of energy but is quite nice to experience when the team gradually walks by itself. At the same time, the time effort by the Scrum Master can be reduced.* (AM)

Answering our third (RQ3) we found that a **leadership gap enabled roles to be transferred from the Scrum Master to team members during the role transfer process.**

5 Discussion and Relation to Existing Evidence

Our research objective was to explore how the Scrum Master role changes while the team matures. We discovered that the Scrum Master comprises nine leadership roles. While the team matures, more and more roles are transferred from the Scrum Master to the team. At the heart of the role transfer process lies the leadership gap: a lack of leadership which provides the opportunity for team members to step up and take on leadership roles which were previously filled by the Scrum Master.

Several authors found that interference from Scrum Masters, Product Owners or management decreased self-organisation of teams [7,14,18], while communication among team members improved when the Scrum Master was absent [18]. We believe that our finding of providing a leadership gap that allows teams to take over leadership roles fits well with those earlier observations.

Furthermore, the Scrum process, e.g. retrospectives, stimulates psychologocial safety [6,9,14] which empowers team members to take on leadership roles. In line with other researchers our research provides empirical evidence that human interaction and the method go hand in hand [6]. Based on our results, we argue that the Scrum method combined with a certain behaviour, such as communication on equal terms, fosters a supportive team environment, such as mutual understanding and trust [18]. This empowers teams to take on leadership roles while they mature.

6 Practical Implications

Many practitioners on the management level have set the agile transformation of their organisations as one of their top priorities. This is often associated with the common misconception that when implementing agile projects their teams are instantly "doing twice the work in half the time" as the famous title of the book on the Scrum method promises [22]. Few have understood and accepted the time required for the team development process.

When agile teams are implemented in established companies, individuals have to learn a new way of leadership in teams, which will lead to slower delivery of work products at the beginning. Management should grant sufficient time to teams to allow them to regularly reflect upon the leadership roles during the retrospective, learn their meaning and content, build a mutual understanding and figure out how and to what extent to take on leadership roles. Teams need time to try the roles and learn them, possibly by failure. Just like any newbie in a formal leadership position needs time and is given time to learn the role, agile teams need time to learn the leadership roles of Scrum.

Furthermore, even though management expects employees to change and take on more responsibility, some managers are reluctant to grant leadership roles to the teams. External pressure, top-down changed targets and shifted priorities as well as frequent changes of the team setup destroy the sheltered space within which agile teams can grow. In established companies, it is easy to re-staff project teams because authorities have the legitimate power to do so, but it is a supreme discipline to protect the team and create hierarchy-free space for team development by the Scrum Master demonstrating lateral leadership.

Therefore, management must provide a Scrum Master to protect the team and shelter it while it matures. The Scrum Master has to be granted sufficient managerial power to protect the team and to preserve the leadership gap as a major enabler for the team's transformation. Simultaneously, the Scrum Master must be patient and wait until team members take on responsibility when they face a lack of leadership. Likewise, team members have to learn how to practice new ways of interacting with their team and managers, and to develop the courage to bridge the leadership gap when provided, even though it might feel inconvenient at the beginning.

7 Limitations and Future Work

To assure the quality of our research, we critically discuss construct validity, external validity and reliability:

To increase **construct validity**, we used multiple sources of evidence by capturing the Scrum Master role from three different angles involving Scrum Masters, Product Owners and team members. The researchers discussed the extracted results and built concepts and theories. Additionally, emerging results were frequently reflected critically with various agile practitioners from the company. Furthermore, the main author observed multiple agile teams at the company site over a period of 1.5 years. The final results were supported by the observations and fruitful discussions with practitioners.

All participants work at the same conglomerate, mostly in the automotive industry. To increase **external validity**, we tried to ask an equal number of project teams at each division. Despite their slightly similar overall working culture, the 11 business divisions embrace different subcultures. Still, we do not claim our results to be universally applicable and they might be limited to the specific context. Further studies should compare our findings on the changing Scrum Master role with the results emerging from other conglomerates.

Reliability: Since we used an open-ended semi-structured questionnaire that guided us through the interviews, the different interviews followed a similar structure. Yet, we asked participants about past events and what they had learned over time. Memories of individuals tend to change in retrospective. Therefore, these interviews are difficult to replicate. A cross-sectional follow-up survey on a nominal scale containing the nine roles with the respective activities we have identified would increase the reliability of this study.

So far we have only investigated how the Scrum Master role changed over time using an exploratory approach based on retrospective narratives of interviewees. We have not yet quantitatively aligned group maturity stages to the changing Scrum Master role. In a future research project, we aim to map research on maturity of agile teams [12] to the different Scrum Master roles we have identified to provide valuable insights on maturity and the changing Scrum Master role in each team development stage.

Furthermore, we have not yet captured the perspective of the management who may experience providing the leadership gap differently. Taking this aspect into account, we would like to extend this study in the near future and dig deeper into strategies on how the Scrum Master protects the leadership gap from management and Product Owner by referring to the boundary-spanning role of team leadership literature [8].

References

1. Belbin, R.M.: Team Roles at Work. Routledge, Abingdon (2012)
2. Carson, J.B., Tesluk, P.E., Marrone, J.A.: Shared leadership in teams: an investigation of antecedent conditions and performance. Acad. Manage. J. **50**(5), 1217–1234 (2007)
3. Cockburn, A.: Agile Software Development, vol. 177. Addison-Wesley Boston, Boston (2002)
4. Cockburn, A., Highsmith, J.: Agile software development, the people factor. Computer **34**(11), 131–133 (2001)
5. Conboy, K.: Agility from first principles: reconstructing the concept of agility in information systems development. Inf. Syst. Res. **20**(3), 329–354 (2009)
6. Dingsøyr, T., Fægri, T.E., Dybå, T., Haugset, B., Lindsjørn, Y.: Team performance in software development: research results versus agile principles. IEEE Softw. **33**(4), 106–110 (2016)
7. Drury, M., Conboy, K., Power, K.: Obstacles to decision making in agile software development teams. J. Syst. Softw. **85**(6), 1239–1254 (2012)
8. Druskat, V.U., Wheeler, J.V.: Managing from the boundary: the effective leadership of self-managing work teams. Acad. Manage. J. **46**(4), 435–457 (2003)
9. Edmondson, A.: Psychological safety and learning behavior in work teams. Adm. Sci. Q. **44**(2), 350–383 (1999)
10. Glaser, B.G., Strauss, A.L.: Discovery of Grounded Theory: Strategies for Qualitative Research. Routledge, Abingdon (2017)
11. Gren, L.: Psychological group processes when building agile software development teams. Ph.D. thesis, University of Gothenburgh (2017)
12. Gren, L., Torkar, R., Feldt, R.: Group development and group maturity when building agile teams: a qualitative and quantitative investigation at eight large companies. J. Syst. Softw. **124**, 104–119 (2017)
13. Hersey, P., Blanchard, K.H., Natemeyer, W.E.: Situational leadership, perception, and the impact of power. Group Organ. Stud. **4**(4), 418–428 (1979)
14. Hoda, R.: Self-organizing agile teams: a grounded theory. Ph.D. thesis, Victoria University of Wellington (2011)
15. Hoda, R., Noble, J., Marshall, S.: Developing a grounded theory to explain the practices of self-organizing agile teams. Empir. Softw. Eng. **17**(6), 609–639 (2012)
16. Hoda, R., Noble, J., Marshall, S.: Self-organizing roles on agile software development teams. IEEE Trans. Softw. Eng. **39**(3), 422–444 (2013)
17. Kozlowski, S.W.J., Watola, D.J., Jensen, J.M., Kim, B.H., Botero, I.C.: Developing adaptive teams: a theory of dynamic team leadership. Team effectiveness in complex organizations: cross-disciplinary perspectives and approaches, pp. 113–155 (2009)
18. Moe, N.B., Dingsøyr, T., Dybå, T.: A teamwork model for understanding an agile team: a case study of a scrum project. Inf. Softw. Technol. **52**(5), 480–491 (2010)
19. Spiegler, S. V., Heinecke, C., Wagner, S.: Interview guidelines for "leadership gap in agile teams: how teams and scrum masters mature" (2018). https://doi.org/10.5281/zenodo.2243113
20. Srivastava, P., Jain, S.: A leadership framework for distributed self-organized scrum teams. Team Perform. Manage.: Int. J. **23**(5/6), 293–314 (2017)
21. Sutherland, J., Schwaber, K.: The scrum guide: the definitive guide to scrum: the rules of the game (2017). http://scrumguides.org/

22. Sutherland, J., Sutherland, J.J.: Scrum: the art of doing twice the work in half the time. Currency (2014)
23. Takeuchi, H., Nonaka, I.: The new new product development game. Harv. Bus. Rev. **64**(1), 137–146 (1986)
24. Werder, K., Maedche, A.: Explaining the emergence of team agility: a complex adaptive systems perspective. Inf. Technol. People **31**(3), 819–844 (2018)

BAM - Backlog Assessment Method

Richard Berntsson Svensson[1(✉)], Tony Gorschek[2], Per-Olof Bengtsson[2], and Jonas Widerberg[3]

[1] Department of Computer Science and Engineering, Chalmers | University of Gothenburg, Gothenburg, Sweden
richard.berntsson.svensson@gu.se
[2] Software Engineering Department, Blekinge Institute of Technology, Karlskrona, Sweden
[3] Telenor Sweden, Campus Grasvik 12, Karlskrona, Sweden

Abstract. The necessity of software as stand-alone products, and as central parts of non-traditional software products have changed how software products are developed. It started with the introduction of the agile manifesto and has resulted in a change of how software process improvements (SPI) are conducted. Although there are agile SPI methods and several agile practices for evaluating and improving current processes and ways-of-working, no method or practices for evaluating the backlog exists. To address this gap, the Backlog Assessment Method (BAM) was developed and applied in collaboration with Telenor Sweden. BAM enables agile organizations to assess backlogs, and assure that the backlog items are good-enough for their needs and well aligned with the decision process. The results from the validation show that BAM is feasible and relevant in an industrial environment, and it indicates that BAM is useful as a tool to perform analysis of items in a specific backlog.

Keywords: Backlog Assessment Method · Agile · Software process improvement · Software process assessment · Case study

1 Introduction

The pervasive and necessary presence of software as stand-alone products, but also as central parts of the offering of traditionally non-software products (e.g. raging from cars to washing machines) has changed the way we have to do software intensive product development [1]. Continuous delivery, flexible engineering methods and ways of working has been one answer to the increased pace and level of software intensive product development. It started off with the agile manifesto in 2001 [2], but speeding up into a myriads of interpretations of "agility" and its realization through the introduction of many agile software development methods (ASD), e.g. Scrum [3].

However, regardless of which development method, software process improvement (SPI) [4] is still important for improving the capabilities of the software

P. Kruchten et al. (Eds.): XP 2019, LNBIP 355, pp. 53–68, 2019.
https://doi.org/10.1007/978-3-030-19034-7_4

development teams and organizations [5]. Instead of focusing on optimizations as in traditional development, SPI in ASDs has focused on high flexibility and responsiveness that can be standardized both within and across organizations [6]. Hence, the agile perspective changes how to conduct SPI, and requires new SPI mechanisms [5]. Also, improvement and learning is to some extent "built in" to ASDs, e.g., Scrum has the retrospective phase [7].

As a part of our industry collaboration with Telenor Sweden we noticed that one of the main concepts and structures of their agile implementation, namely the Backlog(s), had some challenges. The backlog is among the most, if not the most used agile practice, described as "the heart of Scrum" [8]. Backlogs are the engines for business, planning, and development. However, how do agile teams know if the backlog is good enough and well managed, or if the content of the backlog is appropriate and aligned in relation to the competences working with it and the decision process utilized?

There are guidelines, e.g. INVEST [8] and DEEP [3], of how backlog items should be written and managed. In industry, the backlog items vary greatly, and this is especially true for backlogs that are used for collecting items from multiple sources continuously, and there are seldom any formal checkpoints for ensuring conformity or quality as in traditional software development methods. With great variation of backlog items in the backlog, there is a challenge to align the decision process (people and method for decisions) to be able to handle the varying contents of the backlog. Often items are deferred or delayed as detail is low or abstraction too high, and/or decisions are made based on assumptions as a way to fill the gaps of incomplete information. Therefore, to enable agile organizations to assess backlogs, and assure that the backlog items are good-enough for their needs, and well aligned with the decision process, we developed and evaluated the Backlog Assessment Method (BAM) in close cooperation with Telenor Sweden. BAM was designed to be light-weight, simple to apply, as well as adaptable to the organizations needs and preference - consistent with a method to be used during a retrospective phase for example.

The remainder of this paper is organized as follows. In Sect. 2, background and related work are presented. Section 3 describes the motivation of the development of BAM, while Sect. 4 presents BAM. Section 5 presents lessons learned from using BAM in practice, and Sect. 6 presents the conclusions.

2 Background and Related Work

Agile software development methods (ASD) require new SPI methods to fit the context and principles of ASD. One reason for this is that the "traditional" SPI methods have heavy bureaucracy [5], while the agile SPI methods need to be flexible and responsive to local needs, and encourage self-organizing teams [9]. Thus, new challenges for conducting SPI in ASD have emerged [5].

Complying with the agile principles, agile SPI methods have been proposed and evaluated in the literature. In a systematic literature review, Santana et al. [10] investigated which SPI approaches are used for agile SPI. Santana et al. [10] concluded that there are three main approaches to agile SPI, (1) top-down approaches where the goal is to "fit" agile practices into predefined models, e.g. the agile maturity model [11] and agile-CMMI SPI method [12], (2) agile SPI methods that are based on improving team members' behavior, which is proposed in the agile manifesto [2], and (3) agile SPI methods that are based on improving practices in order to deliver better software. Moreover, Salo and Abrahamsson [5] proposed an iterative improvement process for conducting SPI within individual agile project teams to improve the development process based on the teams' experiences and context knowledge, while Ringstad et al. [13] suggest to use diagnosis and action planning to improve teamwork in agile software development. In addition to the agile SPI efforts, there exist many practices in agile methodologies to evaluate and improve current processes. For example, Crystal includes a reflection workshop [14] and Scrum has sprint retrospective [7]. Moreover, Value Stream Map [15] and retrospectives [16] are practices that can be used to evaluate and improve current processes.

Although there are agile SPI and several agile practices for evaluating and improving current processes and ways of working, there are no similar methods or practices for evaluating the most used agile practice, namely the backlog. A well-managed backlog that is well aligned with the decision process can greatly reduce the time for planning meetings and time-to-market. However, if the backlog is ill-managed, used as a dumping ground, and not aligned with the decision process, it may have severe impacts on product development. In particular, since the backlog should provide a centralized and shared understanding of what to build, and in which order to build it [3]. Despite the importance of the backlog in ASD, there are no methods/frameworks for assessing the backlog other than pre-emptive ones. Instead, the literature suggests following guidelines when writing the backlog items (i.e., requirements as user stories) to make sure that the backlog items, once they have been written, follow a certain guideline. One suggested guideline for writing the items is INVEST [8] where the backlog items should be Independent, Negotiable, Valuable, Estimatable, Sized appropriately, and Testable. Once the items have been written and placed in a backlog, it is important to manage, organize, and administrate the backlog items, which is called *grooming* [3,8]. Grooming includes creating and refining details about an item, and to estimate and prioritize them. An example of a guideline that can be followed when Grooming a backlog is DEEP [8].

However, from the process assessment at Telenor Sweden (see Sect. 3.2 for details) we observed that backlogs are frequently used for managing all kinds of information. Often the backlog items vary greatly, and there are seldom any formal checkpoints for ensuring conformity or quality. In addition, obsolete backlog items are common to be found in backlogs in industry [17], meaning that information in form of obsolete requirements is visible in backlogs to a large extent in practice [17]. The obsolete backlog items may lead to, e.g. higher estimates of the items and thus affect the decision-making [18].

3 Research Context: Case Description and Motivation

The development of BAM was prompted by challenges/improvement issues identified at Telenor Sweden. Telenor Sweden's pragmatic use of their backlog to collect items from multiple sources continuously identified challenges for the organization to handle and process all items in the backlog in an effective and efficient manner, as described in Sect. 3.2.

3.1 Case Company Description

Telenor is one of the world's major mobile operators with 208 million mobile subscribers. Telenor provides tele, data, and media services in the Nordic, Central, and Eastern Europe and Asia, and have operations in 13 markets, and additionally 14 markets through the ownership of VimpelCom Ltd. Telenor has more than 36,000 employees worldwide, and 1,900 at Telenor Sweden. Telenor Sweden has worked with agile and backlogs for about 10 years.

As a developer of software and services, adopting an agile approach makes sense to avoid rigid front-heavy development. The core scenario is that in the Telenor Sweden case, backlogs are used in multiple stages, which is a common practice in agile software development [8] from an initial backlog where items of large variety are collected, then the items are "sorted" into product backlogs, and finally in a spring backlog, as illustrated in Fig. 1.

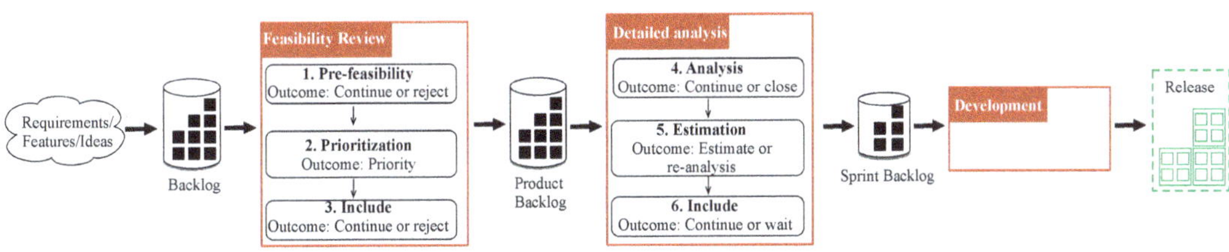

Fig. 1. A simplified overview of the decision process for items

In each backlog containing items, the items are analyzed and refined, and sometimes broken up/merged/dismissed before progressing to the next backlog, e.g. in feasibility review and detailed analysis phases (as illustrated in Fig. 1) through several decision-points. This way of working joins business analyst/product management level and product planning with subsequent product realization (sprint backlog) levels. This is one of the main goals of becoming a complete agile organization. It is also in line with the general levels of decision-making in agile software development [19]. In agile software development, decisions about products and release plans are made at a *strategic level* (similar to the feasibility review in Fig. 1, while decisions related to project management with the aim to determine the best way to implement the strategic decisions are made at *tactical level* (detailed analysis phase in Fig. 1. Finally, decisions about the implementation are made at the *operational level* (development phase in Fig. 1.

Telenor Sweden's agile process supports product planning and development and they have good ideas of using their backlogs at different levels which enables other roles, teams, and parts of the organization to work "agile". However, this creates several challenges, which are detailed below.

3.2 Motivation

The case study presented in this paper was carried out at Telenor Sweden in Karlskrona for one of their major product lines (due to confidentiality reasons, no information about the project can be revealed). The overall aim was to identify improvement potential in their development process. Therefore, the first step was to perform a process assessment of their current development process.

Research Design. First, brainstorming sessions, meetings to plan the assessment, and selection of which projects and roles to involve in the assessment were conducted. The selection of interview subjects was conducted in close cooperation with a "gate-keeper" at Telenor Sweden. Five interview subjects representing different roles were chosen, 1 process developer, 1 business analysts, 1 product manager, 1 project manager, and 1 operational manager. Data was collected using semi-structured interviews [20] and documents, i.e. archival data collection [21]. The interviews were carried out by one interviewer and one interviewee. For all interviews, we took records in form of written extensive notes. The study of documents was a substantial part of the overall assessment. The analyzed documents included backlogs, formal process descriptions, decision and meeting protocols. All of the extensive notes from the interviews, and the relevant documents were analyzed using content analysis [20].

Undesired Consequences. From the process assessment results, it was possible to identify three undesired consequences (UDC) that may stem from incomplete information about backlog items, too abstract backlog items, or having the wrong scope for a particular backlog and point in time. The three UDC are illustrated in Fig. 2, and described in more detail below.

UDC1: Postponed Backlog Items. Postponed backlog items refer to items that are not good enough for analysis/decision-making due to incomplete information (see UDC1 in Fig. 2). That is, backlog items with incomplete information are not aligned with the decision process (i.e. decisions at a certain point in time require certain information), and thus the process and the team members involved in a certain decision point cannot do their jobs. This may lead to that backlog items are excluded throughout the entire development process, from feasibility review to development. Postponed backlog items, which are often kept in the backlog, risk becoming obsolete items [17], and can even clog up the backlog. New items are continuously added to the backlog thus inflow is often higher than removal and completion. This may lead to a backlog that is not only cluttered, but also has too much information (items). The mere fact that the postponed items are visible to the decision teams have an impact on the accuracy of the

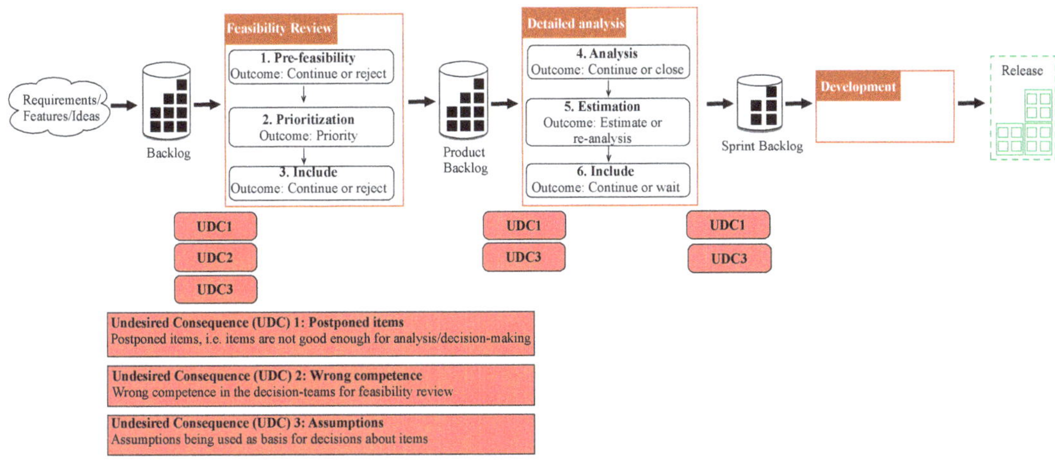

Fig. 2. Three undesired consequences

decisions, estimates, priorities, and analysis [22], where the estimates can be twice as high as the actual effort [18].

UDC2: Wrong Competence in the Decision-Teams. If several of the backlog items during the pre-feasibility review (Step 1, Fig. 2) are technically oriented, e.g. related to software architecture, and no architects are present, the feasibility review and its decisions are made without the required competence, or get postponed as more information is requested. This may lead to several problems downstream, not least that assumptions about realization and inaccurate estimates as well as architectural impact can lead to degradation and increased technical debt [23]. If technical expertise is called in to join the decision team the UDC is handled by changing the process and/or team composition. However, the continuous nature of item processing in backlogs would demand that completely dynamic teams with people representing all competences be "on-call" continuously. This may not always be practical, especially not in situations where items range in thousands, many decision meetings process items continuously, and several products are handled by teams distributed over locations.

UDC3: Assumptions Being Used as Basis for Decisions. If items are under or over-specified for a particular development phase there is an increased risk of false assumptions (UDC3, Fig. 2) being made, and the rest of the analysis/development phase "downstream" can inherit the issues. The later in the development process this is discovered the costlier to correct, not to mention the analysis effort wasted on the incorrect analysis track. Both in the feasibility review and in the detailed analysis (Steps 3 and 6, Fig. 2), if a backlog item that is under-specified is treated as an item with the right specification level, then the inclusion decision may be wrong. Hence, items with high business value may be excluded from the product/release planning as a consequence of competition of features for resources. During the effort estimation (Step 5, Fig. 2), if the under-specified backlog item is treated as an item with the right specification level, the estimates will be based on inadequate information. Thus, the items are potentially underestimated, which invalidates projected lead-times and potentially causes missed opportunities such as being first on the market with a new feature, gaining market shares, loss of sales, and lower revenue.

4 Backlog Assessment Method

This section gives an overview of BAM and the guidelines of how it can be used to plan, execute, and analyze the results of the backlog assessment.

BAM offers a visual analysis and grading of backlog items. The visualization serves as a focal point for the stakeholders to collectively discuss if the backlog items have appropriate detail, size, maturity, and most importantly, if the decision-making process within the development organization can handle the variation of the items in the backlog. Thus it is important to realize that BAM does not suggest a level, rather allows the span to be estimated based on the real items in the backlog, then compared to the capacity of the organization and how the items are intended to be used. BAM has the benefit of using concrete artifacts (actual backlog items) as a base for the assessment, rating items on a scale based on four main perspectives that were identified in collaboration with practitioners at Telenor. The four main perspectives, which are descried in detail in Sect. 4.4, are: Scope, Abstraction/Level, Maturity, and Detail.

The decision of which backlog to assess, selection of a representative sample of items from the backlog, team members to involve - as well as the details of the actual assessment are detailed in Fig. 3. The following sub-sections describes each step of BAM in more detail.

4.1 Step 1: Identify Relevant Backlog

An organization may have several products, thus several product backlogs, or different type of backlogs for the same product, as seen in Step 1, Fig. 3. Having multiple backlogs at several different levels is not an uncommon way to organize the work and requirements in industry. In particular for large organizations where the work requires decisions on multiple levels to select what to realize in the next phase/sprint. The case company Telenor has, in essence, three types of backlogs for a product, one backlog before the feasibility review, one product backlog, and one sprint backlog as illustrated in Fig. 1. In the first backlog all incoming requirements/ideas/features (called items from hereon in) are initially gathered before a feasibility review takes place. An item is then, either dismissed or it progresses to the product backlog, and then to the sprint backlogs. Each of these backlogs contains items that are inherently specified in different ways. That is, the scope in the initial backlog is wider with less details, and in the later backlogs the information is refined and detailed. This is not unlike any engineering process where requirements (items) are refined and evolve as they progress through the organization, from potential idea to on-queue for development. Weather or not there are one or several types of backlogs, Step 1 in BAM is to select a backlog to assess. A general tip here is, not to see the selection as finite as you could study several backlogs over time.

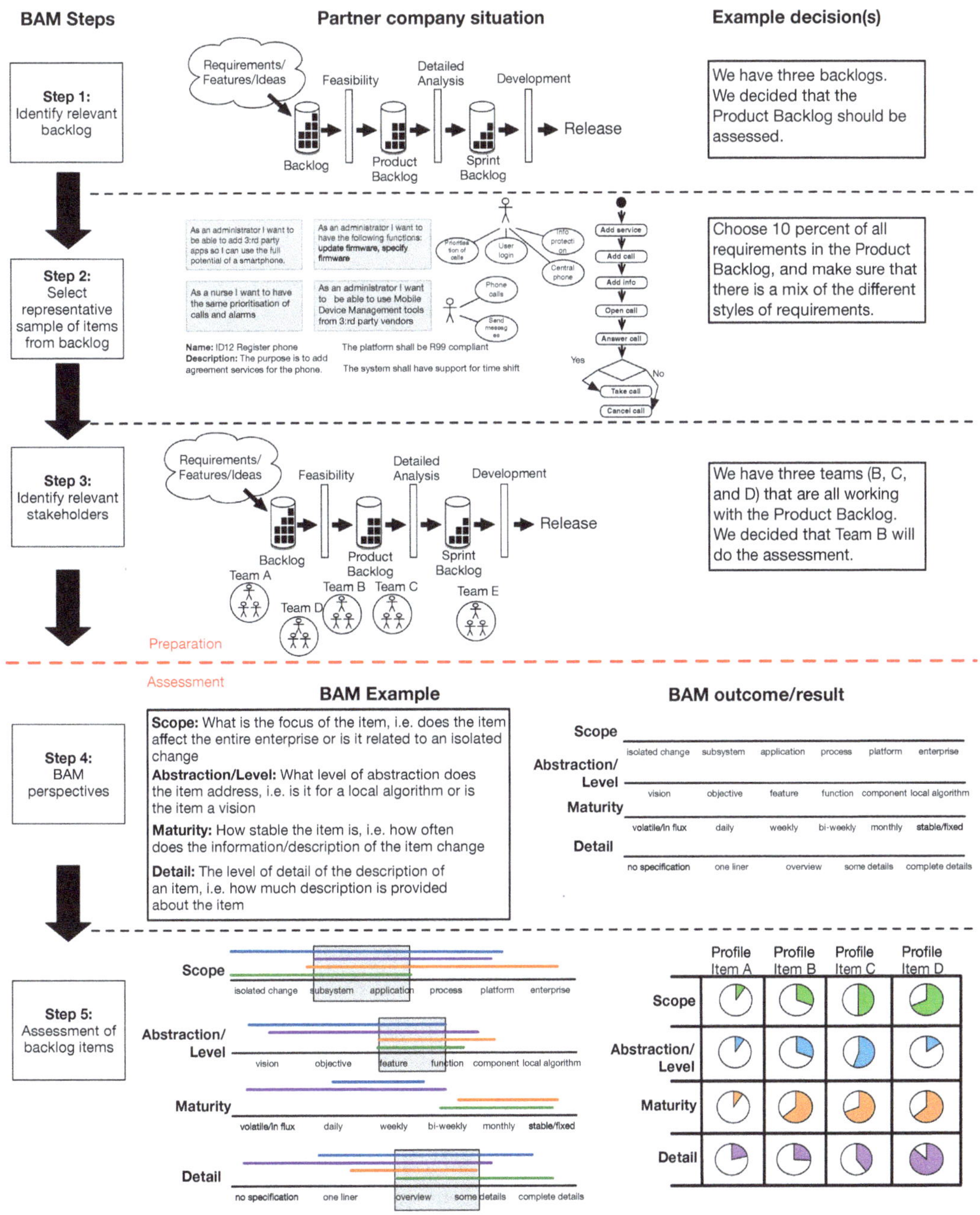

Fig. 3. The five main steps in the backlog assessment method (BAM) (Color figure online)

4.2 Step 2: Select Representative Sample of Items from the Backlog

A backlog consists of items that should be included in the product or action taken in relation to it [3]. Regardless of what items that are present in a backlog, they should be written as user stories [8]. However, in practice, not all items that should be included in the product are included in the backlog, and not all items are written as user stories. Instead, it is common to write items using natural language [24,25]. Telenor Sweden uses several different styles of writing/specifying requirements/backlog items, including use-case diagrams, use-case scenarios, and natural language, as seen in Step 2, Fig. 3. This is not surprising as different specification styles are appropriate at different levels in the decision chain as the abstraction levels differ, and the items are used for different purposes [26].

To have a representative assessment of a backlog, it is important to include items written in all of the existing specification styles that are present in the backlog. Also, it is important to have a good and manageable sample size of items to be able to perform a simple and easy assessment of a backlog - it is better to perform several small assessments than one big one. Whether or not there are items written in one or several specification styles, Step 2 in BAM is to select a representative sample of items from the backlog. To select a representative sample, 10% of all the items, which in the case company was about 100 items, was considered appropriate. However, if the backlog contains thousands of items, then 10% may be too many items. In this case, it is better to select between 50 and 100 items as this size is manageable from an effort perspective (taking one day). In this case representativeness of the selection comes second to the scalability of the assessment.

4.3 Step 3: Identify Relevant Stakeholders

The next step is to identify the relevant stakeholders, which may include the team(s) working with the backlog, and/or any other role(s) that use the items in the backlog for, e.g. decision-making, planning future products/sprints, estimations, coordination with other teams/products, or prioritization. The identification of stakeholders could be a simple one-to-one mapping, one backlog and one team working with the backlog, or there could be multiple teams working with the same backlog, (Step 3, Fig. 3). At Telenor there is usually one team with various roles from different departments/areas working with the backlog in the feasibility phase, while other teams work with the product and sprint backlogs. That is, it is not the same team/roles that work with the items from potential ideas to on-queue for development. This is an important characteristic of the case in hand, but also for several organizations that try to use backlogs as a coordination mechanism outside development projects. Multiple roles, multiple teams, representing one or several parts of the organization and/or several products might be relevant to involve in the assessment. Regardless of how many teams/roles that are working with the selected backlog, Step 3 in BAM is to identify the relevant stakeholders for the assessment of the backlog. During the assessment of a backlog at Telenor Sweden, four stakeholders were selected to perform the assessment. It is a good start to start with 4–6 stakeholders to get a first quick overview of the backlog. It should be observed that in our case some stakeholders had multiple roles and thus were involved in several decision points.

4.4 Step 4: BAM Scales

At the core, BAM consists of four *BAM perspectives*, as seen in Step 4, Fig. 3. These are used to grade individual items in the backlog. The four *BAM perspectives* are described in below.

Scope. Does the item focus on an isolated change, or is the scope the entire enterprise? The scope of items in the initial backlog is generally wider, e.g. having the scope of the entire enterprise; while in the later backlogs (e.g. product or sprint) the scope often narrows - a natural consequence of refinement and break down. From a scope perspective, it is important that the stakeholders working with a backlog item can conceptualize the item in relation to the length of the sprint. Otherwise, they may have difficulties to break down the item [27]. The scope is different as breakdown of all items directly would result in wasted resources as many items put in the initial backlog that are compared and then passed on refined, or also often dismissed as other items are relatively more important to realize.

Abstraction/Level. Does the item address a local algorithm, a feature, or a vision? The *Abstraction/Level* of an item can differ even if the *Scope* is the same. For example, if an item has the *Scope* of a sub-system, the item can address a local algorithm for the sub-system, or it can address the future vision of the same sub-system.

Maturity. How often does an item change? One of the "tools" used in agile to embrace change is actually the backlog itself, which should accommodate easy change to items. Albeit change is to be embraced - maturity is connected to change. In an initial backlog (pre-project, where items are collected for e.g. a feasibility review) item may change on a daily basis. However, stability should increase in later backlogs - even if change is still a reality and has to be embraced.

Detail. What is the level of specification of an item. Items in a backlog should have different levels of detail depending on what backlog they are specified in. However, the closer to realization (sprint backlog) an item comes, generally the more detail is present to reflect the analysis and choices made for its realization. Greater detail in later backlogs allow team members to know what they are committing to [27]. However, even in the early backlog it is important to have adequate details about the items (good-enough for decisions and prioritization) otherwise it may result in wrongly dismissed or selected items. Too much detail is also undesirable as it would constitute waste. BAM does not suggest a "correct" level, rather it offers a visual evaluation of current state of items in a backlog, and gives practitioners the ability to judge if the level is appropriate, or not, given their needs in relation to a specific decision point and backlog.

4.5 Step 5: Assessment of the Backlog

In the fifth and final step of BAM, the identified stakeholders perform the assessment. Each stakeholder individually estimates items by grading them using each of the four perspectives from Step 4. The assessment is performed using predefined templates as seen in Step 4, Fig. 3. The template can be used in two ways, (1) using one template for each item, or (2) adding several items to the same template. The case company used one template for several items (see Fig. 4, Items A - D) by placing the item's ID on the scale (to preserve confidentiality, the two examples of detail for Items A and C are anonymized in terms of feature detail). For example, Item A has the *Scope* of an isolated change, the *Abstraction/Level* is graded as vision, the *Maturity* of the information for Item A is in-flux, and the *Detail* of Item A is specified as a one-liner.

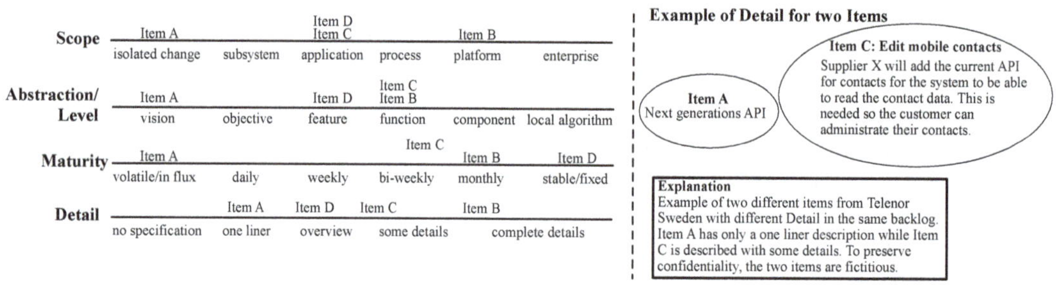

Fig. 4. Example of an assessment of two backlog items

The reason for adding the item's ID in the template is to be able to perform a sanity check of the assessment. At Telenor, the sanity check was used for two main reasons. First, to have concrete examples of items when presenting the overall assessment makes it easier to understand and discuss the assessment. Second, the items were used as input if one or more stakeholders had completely different assessments of the same item. Thus, the provided item was used to calibrate the overall assessment. A notable observation is that the actual estimation itself served as a learning experience and coordination effort between different roles and competences, in essence building a shared understanding of not only the perspectives themselves, but more importantly of the needs of fellow co-workers. Thus details in an item that was considered as unnecessary by one stakeholder was important for another. This allowed for an understanding to be built, as well as the realization that one person's "waste" could be another person's critical information.

When all stakeholders have completed their assessment, an overview of the results is constructed (Step 5, Fig. 3). The constructed overview comes in two parts. First, the overview shows the total estimated span of items in the backlog for each of the four perspectives combined with the overlap of all stakeholders. At Telenor Sweden, the four stakeholders had different opinions about the span of items in their backlog (see Step 5, Fig. 3). Each of the colored lines represents one stakeholder. For example, one stakeholder believed that the *Scope* of the items span from an isolated change to the platform (blue line), while another stakeholder believed that the *Scope* spans from an isolated change to the application (green line). The grey boxes represent the shared view among the stakeholders for each scale. Second, the assessment results can also be used to create "typical profiles" of items that exist in the same backlog, as seen in Step 5, Fig. 3. Four typical item profiles were identified in one backlog at Telenor. For example, one typical profile (profile Item A, Step 5 in Fig. 3) was items with a narrow *Scope*, wide *Abstraction/Level*, with constantly changing information (*Maturity*) that was specified with little *Detail*. In the same backlog, other items (profile Item D) had a wider *Scope*, more *Mature* information that was specified in greater *Detail*.

5 BAM Case Study Evaluation

As BAM was completed, it was set to be evaluated in an industrial environment in a real development project. The idea was to use BAM for an actual backlog and backlog items in order to evaluate its steps and components (e.g. the four BAM perspectives), and to check if BAM could help in assessing backlogs as a process assessment activity in order to help agile teams to continuously reflect on how to become more effective, efficient and coordinated.

Research Design. The selection of backlog and practitioners for participating in the evaluation was conducted in cooperation with the case company. Seven practitioners representing different roles were selected. The roles chosen were: 1 Process developer, 2 Business analysts, 2 Product managers, 1 Project manager, and 1 Operational manager. The selected practitioners identified 100 backlog items that were used as a representative sample of items from the backlog (Step 2 in BAM, Fig. 3). Then the practitioners used the template for BAM perspectives (Step 4 in BAM, Fig. 3) to perform the assessment of the backlog items (Step 5 in BAM, Fig. 3). After the practitioners had used BAM, data - in terms of BAM's usability and usefulness - was collected. Semi-structured interviews [20] were used to ask questions about how BAM was perceived by the practitioners. The interviews were carried out by one interviewer and one interviewee. For all interviews, we took records in form of written extensive notes. The extensive notes were analyzed using content analysis [20].

5.1 Lessons Learned

Through the evaluation of BAM with Telenor Sweden, we observed experiences summarized below as lessons learned.

Ease of Use. In general, the practitioners at Telenor found that BAM is easy to understand, and that the five steps of BAM make sense for assessing a backlog. The practitioners explained that the steps of BAM are helpful and easy to follow, and in particular the provided examples for each step (Fig. 3). In addition, BAM does not seem to take too much time to use in practice. An assessment of about 100 items for one backlog with 4–5 practitioners did not take more than a day, and if the number of items is decreased to 30–40 items, then the time spent on the assessment is only 3–4 h, which could be done on a regular basis by individual teams without formalizing it and getting "permission" or a budget.

Identification of Gaps. Using BAM as a tool to perform analysis of items in a specific backlog, and the decision process associated with decision points tied to the backlog, enabled us to identify gaps. This in turn gave input to either put some criteria as to good-enough item analysis and specification, and/or changes to the decision process. Often slight modifications of both are needed as per observations at Telenor Sweden. This gave potential to remove the likelihood of undesired consequences (as explained in Figure 2), but also speed up processing and decrease the clutter in the backlog of lingering items. BAM does not introduce the "correct" levels, rather, allows an estimation of span of the items in a backlog according to the four perspectives - which in turn can be compared to the decision making process and the capabilities of a team responsible for a specific backlog. Just as extensive technical detail might not be necessary for a quick feasibility analysis, abstract business goals are too abstract for a technical development team. BAM thus supports:

1. How items should be specified (good-enough) for a specific backlog,
2. what level of information and investment into analysis is needed for a team,
3. how the decision-making process should look like to be aligned with the backlog items to enable reduced time for planning and analysis until an item can be dismissed or selected for evolution into a subsequent backlog.

BAM will not in-itself solve undesired consequences (e.g. UDC1 - UDC3). However, by assessing the backlog items it is possible to get an overview of the level of information in the backlog, and get the ability to see the typical item profiles and level of span of said items. This can then be used to identify potential issues with the alignment between the backlog and the decision-making process. If the decision-making process is not aligned with the backlog, there is a risk that the teams either spend more time and resources in analyzing the backlog items to make sure that all of them have a similar level of information, or that the team may want to change the decision-making process and criteria to handle all kinds of item profiles by, e.g. changing team member profiles or adding more team members. BAM can also successfully be complemented with a Value Stream Mapping [15] activity to gauge the delays and times of items in play, and the changes as backlog item details and decision processes are tweaked.

5.2 Limitations

Selection bias (*construct validity*) [21], in terms of selecting participants to interview in relation to the process assessment and the evaluation of BAM, is a threat to this study. Selection bias is always a threat to all studies where the participants are not fully randomly sampled. The threat is that only participants with a negative attitude of the current processes and ways-of-working, and/or having a positive attitude towards BAM were selected. To minimize this threat, the participants were selected based on their experiences and roles by a "gate-keeper" at Telenor Sweden. That is, the researchers did not influence the selection of the participants for the interviews, nor did the researchers influence the selection of which participants/teams that applied BAM in practice. Incorrect data (*internal validity*) [21] is a validity threat to all empirical studies. To minimize this threat, the researchers had the opportunity to validate, both during the interviews and after the interviews by contacting the participants about the answers and interpretations of the answers, which minimizes the risk of misunderstandings (i.e. collecting wrong (incorrect) data). *External validity* [21] is related to the ability to generalize the results from this study beyond the case company. Although Telenor Sweden is a large company developing software and services, it is not representative for all large software developing organizations. However, the aim of qualitative studies is not to generalize beyond the studied setting, instead, qualitative studies aim to explain and understand the phenomenon that is studied [20]. However, some of the issues introduced as motivation behind BAM (see Sect. 3.2) may be generalized for organizations that are using or introducing ASD methods. Moreover, from the concepts, practical application, and evaluation of BAM (as described in Sects. 4 and 5) may give an overview of the specific situation of Telenor Sweden, thus allowing other organizations to judge similarity and potential for BAM being relevant for them.

6 Conclusions

The Backlog Assessment Method was developed and evaluated in close cooperation with Telenor Sweden. BAM is based on the identified needs in industry and the observations that existing agile practices and agile SPI methods only provides guidelines of how backlog items should be written, and guidelines of how to keep the backlog groomed. However, there are no methods or practices for assessing the current backlog and the backlog items. BAM addresses this issue, aiming to enrich the overall picture of the information in the backlog.

As part of BAM's development, evolvement, and refinement, the complete version of BAM was evaluated at Telenor Sweden with seven industry practitioners using a real backlog and actual backlog items from a product. The evaluation was performed to assure BAM's applicability in industry, and that the model is useful as part of agile SPI improvements for individual teams. During the evaluation at Telenor Sweden, the results show that BAM is feasible and relevant in an industrial environment, and the evaluation results indicate that BAM is useful as a tool to perform analysis as to items in a specific backlog, and the decision process associated with the backlog. The main benefit of using BAM is the use of concrete artifacts as the base for the assessment to give visual indications as to how the backlogs are used. The value is in getting results from an evaluation as discussion and decision support material to the practitioners working with the backlogs, thus BAM does not prescribe any correct level or processes.

The next phase that will be undertaken in the validation and evolvement of BAM, as described in this paper, is further evaluations in industry in different domains where the long-term effects, in terms of benefits and challenges of using BAM, need to be investigated to fully validate its feasibility and scalability.

Acknowledgements. The work and results presented in this paper were performed and produced in close cooperation between industry and academia. The authors would like to thank everyone involved in the development and evaluation of BAM at Telenor Sweden.

References

1. Petersen, K., Wohlin, C.: A comparison of issues and advantages in agile and incremental development between state of the art and an industrial case. J. Syst. Softw. **82**, 1479–1490 (2009)
2. Agile Alliance: Manifesto for agile software development (2001). https://www.agilealliance.org/agile101/the-agile-manifesto/. Accessed 5 Jan 2019
3. Cohn, M.: Succeeding with Agile: Software Development Using Scrum. Addison-Wesley, Boston (2009)
4. Aaen, I., Arent, J., Mathiassen, L., Ngwenyama, O.: A conceptual MAP of software process improvement. Scand. J. Inf. Syst. **13**, 81–101 (2001)
5. Salo, O., Abrahamsson, P.: An iterative improvement process for agile software development. Softw. Process. Improv. Pract. **12**(1), 81–100 (2007)
6. Nerur, S., Balijepally, V.: Theoretical reflections on agile development methodologies. Commun. ACM **50**, 79–83 (2007)
7. Schwaber, K.: Agile Project Management with Scrum. Microsoft Press, Washington DC (2004)
8. Rubin, K.S.: A Practical Guide to the Most Popular Agile Process. Addison-Wesley, Boston (2013)
9. Allison, I.: Towards an agile approach to software process improvement: addressing the changing needs of software products. Commun. IIMA **5**(1), 67–76 (2005)
10. Santana, C., Queiroz, F., Vasconcelos, A., Gusmao, C.: Software process improvement in agile software development: a systematic literature review. In: 41st Euromicro Conference on Software Engineering and Advanced Applications, pp. 325–332 (2015)
11. Patel, C., Rumachandran, M.: Agile maturity model (AMM): a software process improvement framework for agile software development practices. Int. J. Softw. Eng. **2**(1), 3–28 (2009)
12. McCaffery, F., Pikkarainen, M., Richardson, I.: AHAA - agile, hybrid assessment method for automotive safety critical SMEs. In: 30th International Conference on Software Engineering, pp. 551–560 (2008)
13. Ringstad, M.A., Dingsøyr, T., Brede Moe, N.: Agile process improvement: diagnosis and planning to improve teamwork. In: O'Connor, R.V., Pries-Heje, J., Messnarz, R. (eds.) EuroSPI 2011. CCIS, vol. 172, pp. 167–178. Springer, Heidelberg (2011). https://doi.org/10.1007/978-3-642-22206-1_15
14. Cockburn, A.: Crystal Clear: A Human-powered Methodology for Small Teams. Wesley, Stoughton (2005)
15. Khurum, M., Petersen, K., Gorschek, T.: Extending value stream mapping through waste definition beyond customer perspective. J. Softw.: Eval. Process. **26**(12), 1074–1105 (2014)
16. Derby, E., Larsen, D.: Agile Retrospectives: Making Good Teams Great!. Pragmatic Bookshelf (2006)
17. Wnuk, K., Gorschek, T., Zahda, S.: Obsolete software requirements. Inf. Softw. Technol. **55**(6), 921–940 (2013)

18. Gren, L., Berntsson Svensson, R., Unterkalmsteiner, M.: Is it possible to disregard obsolete requirements? - An initial experiment on a potentially new bias in software effort estimation. In: 10th International Workshop on Cooperative and Human Aspects of Software Engineering, pp. 56–61 (2017)
19. Aurum, A., Wohlin, C., Porter, A.: Aligning software project decisions: a case study. Int. J. Softw. Eng. Knowl. Eng. **16**(6), 795–818 (2006)
20. Robson, C.: Real World Research. Blackwell (2002)
21. Runeson, P., Höst, M., Rainer, A., Regnell, B.: Case Study Research in Software Engineering: Guidelines and Examples. Wiley, Hoboken (2012)
22. Eppler, M.J., Menigs, J.: The concept of information overload: a review of literature from organization science, accounting, marketing, MIS, and related disciplines. Inf. Soc. **20**(5), 325–344 (2004)
23. Tom, E., Aurum, A., Vidgen, R.: An exploration of technical debt. J. Syst. Softw. **86**(6), 1498–1516 (2013)
24. Savolainen, J., Kuusela, J., Vilavaara, A.: Transition to agile development - rediscovery of important requirements engineering practices. In: 18th IEEE Requirements Engineering Conference, pp. 289–294 (2010)
25. Berntsson Svensson, R., Olsson, T., Regnell, B.: An investigation of how quality requirements are specified in industrial practice. Inf. Softw. Technol. **55**(7), 1224–1236 (2013)
26. Lauesen, S.: Software Requirements: Styles and Techniques. Addison-Wesley, Boston (2002)
27. Berczuk, S.: Back to basics: the role of agile principles in success with a distributed scrum team. In: Agile Conference, pp. 13–17 (2007)

The Unfulfilled Potential of Data-Driven Decision Making in Agile Software Development

Richard Berntsson Svensson(✉), Robert Feldt, and Richard Torkar

Department of Computer Science and Engineering,
Chalmers|University of Gothenburg, Gothenburg, Sweden
richard.berntsson.svensson@gu.se, robert.feldt@chalmers.se,
richard.torkar@cse.gu.se

Abstract. With the general trend towards data-driven decision making (DDDM), organizations are looking for ways to use DDDM to improve their decisions. However, few studies have looked into the practitioners view of DDDM, in particular for agile organizations. In this paper we investigated the experiences of using DDDM, and how data can improve decision making. An emailed questionnaire was sent out to 124 industry practitioners in agile software developing companies, of which 84 answered. The results show that few practitioners indicated a widespread use of DDDM in their current decision making practices. The practitioners were more positive to its future use for higher-level and more general decision making, fairly positive to its use for requirements elicitation and prioritization decisions, while being less positive to its future use at the team level. The practitioners do see a lot of potential for DDDM in an agile context; however, currently unfulfilled.

Keywords: Data-Driven Decision Making · Agile · Survey

1 Introduction

When developing software-intensive products, agile methods have become the *de facto* way to develop software across almost every industry. The introduction of agile methodologies has changed the way software is developed [1], how Requirements Engineering (RE) is conducted [2], and how decisions are made [3]. In transitioning to Agile Software Development (ASD), learning about the customers, collecting customer/user feedback, and involving a customer representative in development, requirements engineering, and decision making, are important [4]. In addition, ASD teams, due to delivering working software in short iterations, are frequently involved in short-term decisions and need to adopt to a fast decision making process [5].

With digital networks connecting an increasing number of people, devices, and products, a vast amount of diverse data is available. Industries gather data

P. Kruchten et al. (Eds.): XP 2019, LNBIP 355, pp. 69–85, 2019.
https://doi.org/10.1007/978-3-030-19034-7_5

and knowledge from their customers, suppliers, alliance partners, and competitors. For example, mobile phones, cars, transportation vehicles, and automation systems, are developed to generate data about their customers and usage of their activities. This diverse data is not only generated internally within software-intensive companies, but also from public, proprietary, and purchased sources [6]. Software developing companies need to focus on exploiting the available data to gain competitive advantages [6], which will transform how business are generated, how RE is performed, and how decisions are made [7]. In particular, the recent resurgence of interest in artificial intelligence (AI) and machine learning (ML) accelerates these trends due to their promise of more automated and powerful data analysis.

However, despite the vast amount of data that is available for decision making, the decisions and selection of what to include in the next product release cycle, are commonly based on the product managements and/or stakeholders' previous experiences, opinions, intuitions, various criteria, arguments, or a combination of one or several of these information sources [4,7]. These decisions are typically subjective, frequently inconsistent, and often lack explanations as well as links to which data and evidence they were based on. Moreover, when stakeholders make decisions based on, e.g., opinions, intuitions, and arguments, the decisions are more likely to be influenced by politics and individual agendas [8–10] rather than, e.g., business opportunities or customer value. In addition, even when data is more clearly being taken into account in decisions, too much data and information may distract the decision maker rather then inform them. According to Wnuk et al. [12], irrelevant information is visible in practitioner backlogs to a large extent today, and recent research shows that it can negatively impact decisions [13].

In order to benefit from data-driven decision making (DDDM), not only is the quality of the processing techniques and tools directly related to the quality of the decisions [17], but also the quality of the visualizations used to support decision makers [17]. While visualization of software engineering data has shown promise in supporting practitioners' decisions, the focus has often been on specific phases or problems, e.g., testing and quality assurance [11], rather than throughout development processes and in agile settings. In the literature, most of the attention in DDDM has focused on the development of new techniques, technologies, and tools for data processing [14], while few (if any) have investigated DDDM from the practitioners' perspectives and the specific and important context of agile development has not been in focus.

This paper presents the results of an empirical study that includes data collected through an emailed questionnaire with 84 respondents from 28 agile software developing companies from 9 domains. The study investigate how common the use of data for decision making is in industry today, how often data is used, the respondents opinions about the usage of data in the future, and how data can improve decision making.

The remainder of this paper is organized as follows. In Sect. 2, we outline the background to data-driven decision making. Section 3 describes the research methodology, while Sect. 4 presents an overall statistical analysis of the data. Section 5 presents and discuss the results, and finally Sect. 6 presents the conclusions.

2 Background

Data-driven decision making (DDDM) has become a critical ability for organizational success. Several studies have demonstrated the benefits of DDDM, e.g., Brynjolfsson et al. [16] showed that DDDM is strongly related to higher productivity, higher return on assets, return on equity, and market value.

In the literature, there are several defined steps in DDDM, starting with data capturing and resulting in decision making. For example, Chen and Zhang [14] identify five steps; data recording, data cleaning/integration/representation, data analysis, data visualization/interpretation, and decision making. Although steps are identified, most of the attention in the literature has focused on the development of new techniques, technologies, and tools. Techniques for DDDM involve a number of disciplines with a number of specific techniques and tools in each discipline. For example, fundamental mathematics, statistics, and optimization tools are used as input to data analysis techniques such as data mining, machine learning, neural networks, signal processing, and visualization methods [14]. Current DDDM tools can be divided into three categories: batch processing tools, stream processing tools, and interactive analysis tools [14]. For more details about different techniques, technologies, and tools, we refer to [14]. We also see an increased interest in applying AI and machine learning in a software engineering context [15] and supporting decisions during development is one of the key application types.

The quality of the decisions when using DDDM may improve or degrade based on the quality of the data and the processing techniques and tools [17]. However, the quality of the decisions are not only based on pre-processing techniques, processing techniques and tools, it is also related to the quality of the visualizations of the data to the decision makers, the decision makers' understanding and knowledge about the data sources, the decision makers' ability to interpret data processed data, and the decision makers' knowledge about the relationships of the data [17]. As one example, Feldt et al. [11] showed how visualisation of testing-related data, without any advanced modeling, could foster understanding and support decisions around software quality in an iterative development context. Thus, in order to benefit from DDDM, it is important to focus also on other aspects than just the pre-processing and processing techniques, technologies, and tools.

3 Research Method

The objective of this study was to investigate how common the use of data for decision making is in industry today, how often data is used, and the respondents' opinions about the usage of data in the future, with a special focus on the agile context in which modern-day software is developed. Given the objective, and that the research questions are geared towards the opinions of the respondents, we chose to use a survey as the research method and emailed a questionnaire for data collection. Surveys are an appropriate strategy for getting empirical descriptions about trends, attitude and/or opinions of the studied population [18,19]. In addition, surveys are useful for analyzing large populations, given an adequate response rate [20,21]. The motivation for using an emailed questionnaire was to maximize coverage and participation. The following research questions provided the focus for the empirical investigation:

- **RQ1:** How do software practitioners view data as part of decision making in agile software developing companies?
- **RQ2:** To what extent is data used for decision making and requirements engineering in agile software developing companies?
- **RQ3:** How can data be used to improve future decisions in agile software developing companies?

3.1 Survey Study

The survey was executed through the creation of an emailed questionnaire that was designed based on the research questions using a mix of open-ended and closed questions [19]. In order to test the reliability and validity of the survey instrument, a pilot study was conducted with one industry practitioner. Based on the feedback from the pilot study, the survey instrument was (lightly) revised. The instrument (see Table 1) had three parts. The first part gathered demographic information about the respondents. The second part mainly addressed how, and how often data is used in decision making today, while the third part focused mainly on how data can be used for decision making in the future. Part 1 only contained free-text questions. All of the questions in Parts 2 and 3 contained Likert-type scale and free-text questions. The free-text area was added to allow the respondents to expand and/or explain their answer.

Data Collection. Subjects were sampled primarily through personal contacts and previous collaborators in industry and we encouraged them to also spread the survey within their organisations. Hence, the sample can be described as convenience sampling [19]. We provided the contacts with the questionnaire (emailed questionnaires) and information about the goals of the survey, and asked them to answer the questions and to spread the questionnaire to their colleagues. Each contact person reported back how many people they had forwarded the questionnaire to. A total of 124 subjects received the questionnaire, and 84 completed the mandatory questions and returned the questionnaire to the researchers. That is, we obtained a response rate of 67.7%. Without going through personal contacts in industry we likely would not have been able to get this high a response rate.

Data Analysis. The data was analyzed using descriptive statistics with diverging stacked bar charts for the graphical visualization. In addition, we built a linear

Table 1. Survey instrument

ID	Question
Q0	What company do you work for?, How many employees does your company have?, What role do you generally have in your work?, What software development process do you use?
Q1	Data is important for decision-making
Q2	Data is highly valued for decision-making
Q3	Data is treated as an asset
Q4	Data is used to identify new business opportunities
Q5	Data is used to predict future trends and behavior
Q6	Decision makers use data for decision-making
Q7	Teams use data for decision-making
Q8	Data is used as part of requirements elicitation/identification
Q9	Data is used for prioritization of requirements/features
Q10	Data should be important for decision-making
Q11	Data should be highly valued for decision-making
Q12	Data should be treated as an asset
Q13	Data should be used to identify new business opportunities
Q14	Data should be used to predict future trends and behavior
Q15	Decision makers should use data for decision-making
Q16	Teams should use data for decision-making
Q17	Data should be used as part of requirements elicitation/identification
Q18	Data should be used for prioritization of requirements/features

model (ordered logit) using a Bayesian approach [22,23] to statistically analyse the data. The analysis is described in more detail in Sect. 4.

3.2 Validity Threats

To avoid evaluation apprehension (*construct validity*) [24], we guaranteed the respondents complete anonymity. Another threat is 'hypothesis guessing' [24], which was minimized by clearly expressing the need for honesty in the instructions to the respondents; however, it is not possible to completely dismiss this threat. In addition, the background of the subjects, e.g., experience, may influence the results; however, since the respondents have different competences and roles we believe that this risk is limited. It is not possible to exclude the possibility that the respondents misunderstood the questions (*conclusion validity*) [24]. To minimize this threat, we conducted a pilot study with an industry practitioner, which also minimized the threat of instrumentation (*internal validity*) [24]. One threat that cannot be ignored is the interest of the respondents in the topic, which may influence the representativeness. This is difficult to counter since the willingness to participate and the interest in the topic may be linked. There are also threats to validity based on selection bias and the convenience sampling; even though we sent to most of our contacts in agile software organisations and approached them in a standardised way, the final sample might not be representative for a global population of developers. For example, they were all from organisations in Sweden.

4 Analysis

To plot and assess visually the difference between distributions of responses in Likert scale data is hard. As an example, if we examine Fig. 1, we see that there is a difference between the distribution of answers on two questions (Q16, on top in the figure, and Q17, on bottom) but it is not clear how to judge how large the difference is. Also, if we only use descriptive statistics, which is the default analysis technique for survey data in software engineering, it is difficult to assess the uncertainty of our conclusions. In contrast, a Bayesian statistical analysis does not have the same problem. Thus, in line with recent arguments for use of Bayesian methods in empirical software engineering we thus, first, start with such an analysis [25,26].

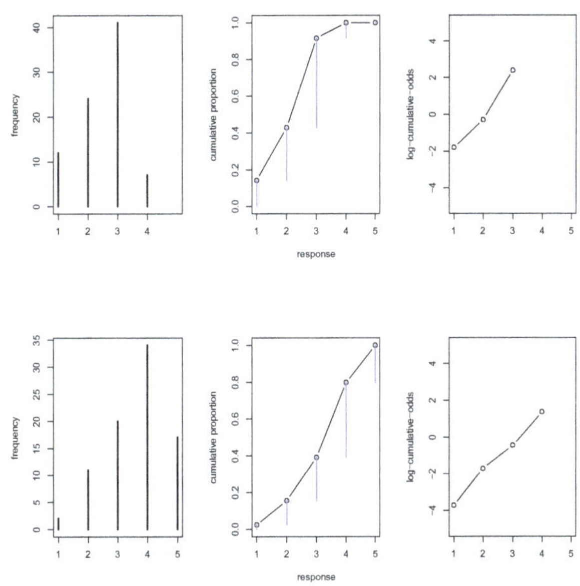

Fig. 1. Plots of Q16 (top) and Q17 (bottom). Left: Histogram of discrete response in the sample. Middle: Cumulative proportion of each response. Right: Logarithm of cumulative odds of each response. Note that the log-cumulative-odds of Level 5 is infinity if there are responses among all five levels $[1, \ldots, 5]$, as in Q17 (for Q16 there were no responses on Level 5).

In order to assess differences in Likert scale data one could assume normality and use a t-test, or make use of some of the non-parametric tests such as Mann-Whitney U or χ^2.

However, Likert scale data is not only categorical, it is also of an ordered nature but where we cannot assume that the 'distance' between consecutive pairs of answers is the same. Thus it is not clear that we can assume the data is normally distributed or that the distribution of scores for different answers has the same shape (distribution family) [27]. Given these problems, in our view, the most conservative approach to analyze Likert scale data is to build a simple linear model using a Bayesian approach but keeping data categorical [22,23]. This way we will get a posterior distribution with which we can assess uncertainty. To this end we build two overall models to study the general trends in our data:

$$\begin{aligned} R_i &\sim \text{Ordered}(p_i) \\ \text{logit}(p_i) &= \beta_T * \text{temporal}_i \\ \beta_T &\sim \mathcal{N}(0, 10) \end{aligned} \tag{1}$$

$$\begin{aligned} R_i &\sim \text{Ordered}(p_i) \\ \text{logit}(p_i) &= \beta_Q * \text{req}_i \\ \beta_Q &\sim \mathcal{N}(0, 10) \end{aligned} \tag{2}$$

where R_i is the ith response with an ordered categorical outcome, and Model 1 (Eq. 1) compares the answers for questions about the present (Questions 1–9, see Fig. 4) versus future (Questions 10–18, see Fig. 4) use while Model 2 (Eq. 2) compares the non-RE (Questions 13–16, see Fig. 5) versus the RE-specific (Questions 17–18, see Fig. 5) questions. We use the logit link function to translate the linear model's real numbers to probability mass (and hence constrain it to lie between zero and one). The linear model (in Eq. 1) then is simply a parameter β_T that we will estimate given the data at hand (temporal). The data is coded as 0/1, representing 'present' (today) and 'future', respectively. Finally, we assign a prior to β_T, $\mathcal{N}(0, 10)$, with a mean of 0 and a large variance of 10. This is a (very) weakly informative prior that only gives a pressure towards realistic parameter values. We also verified that the analysis was not sensitive to the prior selection (i.e., a sensitivity analysis was conducted).

For the other model (Eq. 2) we simply change the parameter. Instead of estimating β_T using 'temporal' data, we estimate β_Q for our variable 'question', which is coded 0/1, representing question with a 'non-RE' (Q13–16) and 'RE' focus (Q17–18), respectively.[1]

Figure 2 visualizes the results from running the first model and drawing 250 samples from the posterior distribution. It is obvious that low Likert scale values are much more common for the 'present' compared to the 'future' category. For example, we see that the number of answers of option 1 ('Strongly disagree') is roughly around 70% for questions about the present (today) state but decreases down to only 5% for the future state. We can also see that the uncertainty is not large with variations only in the range of 1–7% for all the answer alternatives.

[1] The models overall sampled well with mixed chains, $\hat{R} \ll 1.1$, and an effective sample size of $n_{\text{eff}} \gg 0.2$.

When comparing non-RE and RE questions using Model 2 in Fig. 3, we can also see some trends even if they are less clear and the uncertainty is higher as visualized by the, relatively speaking, broader bands of posterior predictions. However, the model clearly shows that we see a difference between non-RE and RE related questions with the average of the β_Q, being $\mu = -0.53$ $\text{HPDI}_{95\%}[-0.87, -0.19]$, i.e., the 95% highest posterior density estimate (HPDI) does not cross 0. This indicates that answers to the RE questions are generally lower (i.e. towards more disagreement with the statement in the question) than for the non-RE ones and that this difference is clear.

After this detailed, statistical analysis of the general trends in the responses the following Section will discuss the results in more detail.

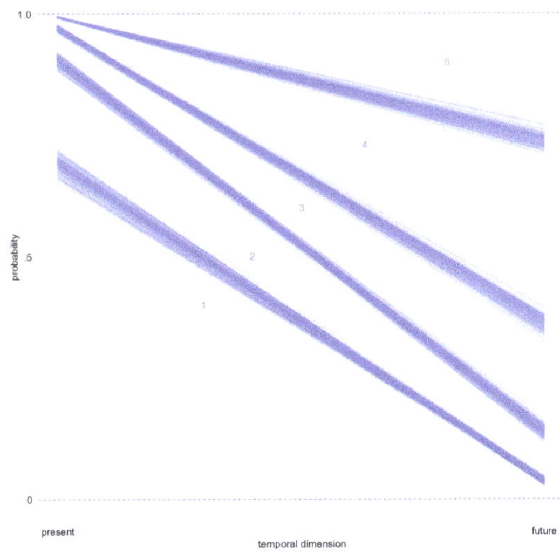

Fig. 2. Posterior predictions (250 draws) of the ordered categorical model (present vs. future perspective). As is clearly evident, the probability for lower Likert scale values, e.g., 1 or 2, is much higher when the perspective is 'present', compared to 'future', i.e., everything is shifted upwards. This indicates less agreement at present and more agreement for the future, i.e. there is unfulfilled potential since the present state has a higher percentage of low disagreement answers.

5 Results and Discussion

This section presents the results of the survey, organized according to the research questions in Sect. 3.

5.1 Survey Respondent Demographics

A total of 84 industry practitioners completed the questions of the survey. The respondents come from 28 agile software developing companies varying in size and domain. In total, the respondents came from nine different domains, with the top three being Telecommunication (27%), Consulting (18%), and Transportation (13%), see Table 2. The size of the companies where the respondents

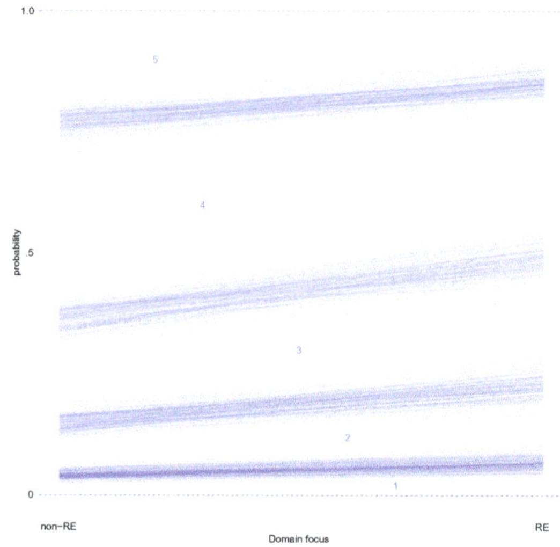

Fig. 3. Posterior predictions (250 draws) of the ordered categorical model (non-RE vs. RE perspective). We see some trends, i.e., respondents are more positive in non-RE focused questions, but there is quite much uncertainty visualized here by the broader clusters of lines. However, the parameter β_Q, which represents the domain focus, indicates that the trend is non-negligible ($\mu = -0.53$ $\text{HPDI}_{95\%}[-0.87, -0.19]$).

work, in terms of number of employees, ranges from 25 up to 5,000. With respect to the respondents' roles, see Table 3, the top three are developers (17%), scrum masters (15%), and product owners (14%) with a fairly even distribution of other, common roles also represented. For the development processes used at the companies see Table 4 where Scrum (43%) is the most used, followed by (the general option) Agile (29%), Kanban (15%), and then DevOps (12%). Note that the Agile category means that a respondent did not specify which agile methodology they used. Overall, we consider these respondents representative for a broad set of domains, roles and sizes of companies, even if they are all active in a Swedish context. The one role that is less clearly represented is Requirements Engineer although several of the respondents also partly do work with requirements in one form or another, as is common in agile development.

5.2 View of Data in Decision Making (RQ1)

In analyzing Research Question 1 (RQ1), this section examines the respondents' view of data as part of decision making in ASD companies. In Fig. 4, we can see the respondents' answers to each question. Each row shows the distribution of answers for that question aligned horizontally so that positive responses are to the right of the mid (zero) line while negative responses are to the left.[2] This makes it possible to compare the answers between different questions.

In general, looking at Fig. 4, we can see that it follows the general trend identified in the statistical analysis above, i.e., respondents disagreed with the

[2] Note that the neutral, mid answer option (on the 5-category Likert scale) is split in half, with half of them shown in a lighter (gray) color to the left and the other half in darker (gray) color to the right of the mid (zero) line.

Table 2. Distribution of respondents based on domains

Domain	Respondents
Telecommunication	27%
Consulting	18%
Transportation	13%
Consumer electronics	11%
Surveillance	10%
Control systems	8%
Retail	5%
Camera	5%
Banking	4%

Table 3. Distribution of respondents based on roles

Roles	Respondents
Developer	17%
Scrum master	15%
Product owner	14%
Project manager	11%
Tester	11%
Senior software engineer	11%
Product manager	10%
Architect	6%
Requirements engineer	6%

Table 4. Distribution of respondents based on development process

Development process	Respondents
Scrum	43%
Agile	29%
Kanban	15%
DevOps	12%
XP	1%

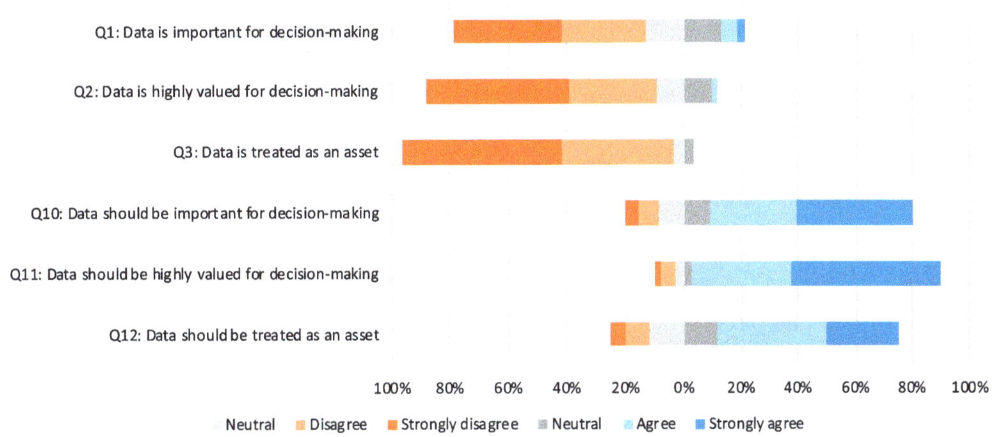

Fig. 4. Respondents' view of data as part of decision making. Present (Q1–Q3) and future (Q10–Q12).

statements more in questions about the current state while agreeing more in questions about the future. For example, we see that a majority of the respondents disagreed or strongly disagreed that data is important (66% for Q1) and highly valued (79% for Q2) in today's decision making. However, a majority of the respondents agreed or strongly agreed that data should play an important role (71% for Q10) and be highly valued (87% for Q11), when making decisions in the future. Examining if data is treated as an asset today (Q3), 93% of the respondents disagreed or strongly disagreed, while 63% of the respondents agreed or strongly agreed that data should be treated as an asset in the future (Q12). Although the respondents have a positive view of how data should ideally be viewed for decision making, their answers indicate this is not how it is being viewed at present in their organisations.

5.3 Use of Data in Decision Making (RQ2)

In analyzing Research Question 2 (RQ2), this section examines to what extent data is used (present) and should be used (future) in decision making and requirements engineering in ASD companies, as illustrated in Fig. 5. Figure 5 is constructed in the same way as Fig. 4, with the exception that the zero line, i.e., the neutral answer, is set to the answer 'About half of the time'. In general, Fig. 5 shows that data is seldom (never or sometimes) used in today's decision making or in Requirements Engineering (RE) (Q4–Q9 in Fig. 5). However, a vast majority of the respondents believe that data should be used most of the time or always in future decision making and RE (Q13–Q18 in Fig. 5).

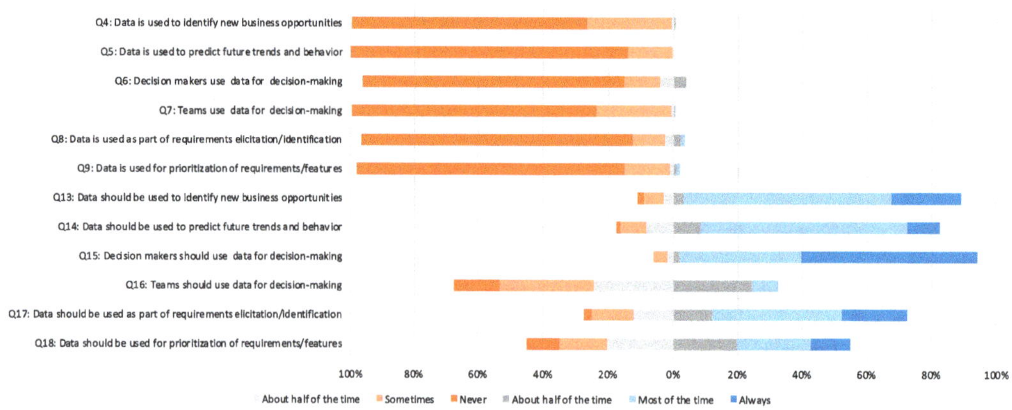

Fig. 5. Use of data as part of decision making. Present (Q4–Q9) and future (Q13–Q18)

Looking closely into what extent data is used in today's decision making, for all questions (Q4–Q9), more than 90% of the respondents stated that they never or only sometimes use data in decision making and RE, where more than 73% of the respondents stated that they never use data today. No respondent stated that they always use data. Only 1% of the respondents stated that they use data most of the times for requirements elicitation/identification (Q8) and requirements prioritization (Q9). Instead of using data, the respondents explained in the free-text answer that decisions are mainly based on 'gut-feeling', the decision-makers' experiences, or the value for customers.

That is, the decisions may be subjective [7], politically influenced [8], and/or biases could be involved [13]. Instead of using data when prioritizing requirements, respondents detailed that requirements are prioritized using various criteria (e.g., cost, cost/benefit, customer value, business value), numerical assignment, experiences, 'gut-feeling', or a combination of these. This is inline with other studies on how requirements are prioritized in ASD companies today [28].

When asking the respondents to what extent data should be used in decision making in the future, 93% of the respondents believe that decision makers should always, or most of the time use data for decision making (Q15), 85% believe that data should always, or most of the time be used to identify new business opportunities (Q13), and almost 75% believe that data should always, or most of the time be used to predict future trends and behaviours (Q14). Only 8% of the respondents believe that (agile) teams should always, or most of the time use data for decision making (Q16), while almost half of the respondents (43%) believe the (agile) teams should never, or only sometimes use data when making decisions. No explanation was provided by the respondents in the free-text answers for these questions.

One possible explanation may be that the respondents believe that DDDM is only useful and beneficial for high-level decisions. This is supported by the high confidence in using DDDM for identifying business opportunities (Q13) and to predict future trends and behaviours (Q14). When such high-level decisions are made, including creating product strategies, road-maps, and release plans, the respondents may believe that teams do not need DDDM when, e.g., breaking down high-level requirements to low-level ones. Another explanation may be related to today's development processes and short sprints, which may not be well suited for DDDM at the team level.

To create and rapidly release software-intensive products in the future, it is crucial that the products are based on data and real-time feedback from the customers [7]. Thus, when moving from a subjective decision-making process, mainly based on experiences, to a DDDM process, changes in infrastructure and methodologies are needed in the development processes [7].

For RE, 60% of the respondents believe data should always, or most of the times be used when eliciting/identifying requirements in the future (Q17), while 15% believe data should never, or only sometimes be used for requirements elicitation/identification. Only 35% of the respondents believe data should always, or most of the time be used when prioritizing requirements, 25% believe it should never, or only sometimes be used, while as many as 40% answered that data should be used about half of the times when prioritizing requirements (Q18).

When we analyzed the data by building a simple linear model (Eq. 1) using a Bayesian approach, the results show a difference between today ('present' in Fig. 2) and the future. In Fig. 2, we see that the lower Likert scale values (e.g., answers 'never' and 'sometimes') are more common for Present, while the higher Likert scale values (e.g., answers 'always' and 'most of the time') are more common for the Future. That is, the respondents, with a high certainty, are positive to use DDDM in the future. When comparing RE related questions (Q17 and

Q18) with non-RE related questions (Q13–Q16), the Bayesian model (Eq. 2) shows a difference, as shown in Fig. 3. That is, although the respondents are positive to use DDDM in the future in general (as shown in Fig. 2), the respondents are more positive to use DDDM in non-RE related decisions compared to RE-related decisions.

Reasons for Using (not Using) Data. We asked the respondents what the reasons for using data in today's decision making is. According to the respondents, the main reason is that DDDM improves the decisions. One respondent explained that when data has been used as input to decision makers, the decisions have been more informed and more transparent. Another reason mentioned by the respondents was, if data is available, then we use it.

A few respondents also gave reasons for partial data use: although the data is there and can improve decisions, it requires a lot of work to filter the data and to present the data in a way that is useful for the decision makers; thus it is only used sometimes for critical/important products/strategies.

Looking at Table 5, we see that *data is not available to us at the company* is the most common reason (82% of the respondents). Most of the respondents who stated that data is not available, also mentioned several other reasons for not using DDDM, including *too much data is available out there* (79% of the respondents), *do not know how to use the data* (73% of the respondents), and *do not know how to make the data relevant to us* (70% of the respondents). Several of the most mentioned reasons for not using DDDM are related to the decision makers' understanding of the data (including the visualization), and how to make use of it. This confirms the findings in [17]. In order to fully benefit from DDDM, the quality of the data is important as it is directly related to the quality of the decisions [17]. Therefore, it is surprising that only 6% of the respondents mentioned that data is not used in today's decision making due to the quality of the data. Either, decision making in agile is different or respondents are less aware of these important considerations.

5.4 How Can Data Improve Decision Making (RQ3)

We asked the respondents if they believe data could help them in making better decisions (Q19 in Table 6). Eleven percent of the respondents believe data will improve their decisions (answered 'yes'), while a majority (58%) believe that data, in combination with other aspects (described below), will lead to better decisions. Close to a third (29%) of the respondents believe data may help in making better decisions but they weren't sure (i.e., they answered 'maybe'). Their stated reasons were: (1) have not used data hence do not know if it will lead to better decisions, (2) it depends on which data, the quality of the data, and who makes decisions, (3) and what kind of decisions and when the decisions are made. Only 2% of the respondents do not believe data will help in making better decision. One respondent explained this by stating *"data can never replace my own experiences and gut-feeling"*.

Table 5. Reasons for not using data in decision making

Reason	Respondents
Data is not available to us at the company	82%
Too much data is available out there	79%
Do not know how to use the data	73%
Do not know how to make the data relevant for us	70%
Do not know how to link/use data in relation to decisions	52%
Do not have appropriate tools	31%
Which data should be used?	23%
Cannot trust the data	11%
Do not know how to access the data	7%
Not sure about the quality of the data	6%
Too many systems/tools that store the data	4%

Table 6. Respondents' views if data improves decision making

Q19: Do you believe that you could have made better decisions if data was used as input to decision making?	Respondents
Yes	11%
Yes, if combined with...	58%
Maybe	29%
No	2%

The respondents identified five aspects that needs to be combined with DDDM in order to make better decisions. The five aspects are: (1) own experience, (2) business value, (3) customer value, (4) input from key stakeholders, and (5) experiences from others.

In order to be able to use the full potential of DDDM and thus truly change how decisions are made in ASD, new approaches to provide and visualise constructive and understandable data (information) to the decision makers are needed. By combining understandable visualizations of data and human expertise, the future of DDDM in ASD looks promising.

6 Conclusions

There is a general trend towards data-driven decision making (DDDM), i.e., basing and driving decision making on and with data. However, there has been a lack of studies on how software practitioners view and use this and, in particular, in an agile context. In this study we thus performed a survey and collected questionnaire responses from 84 software practitioners working with agile software development.

Our main result is that the practitioners see a lot of potential for DDDM but that this potential is currently unfulfilled. While very few respondents indicated more wide-spread data-driven decision making in their current practice, a clear majority saw it as important and highly valued in the future. They were more positive to its future use for higher-level and more general decision making, fairly positive to its use for requirements elicitation and prioritization decisions, while being less positive to its future use at the team level. Multiple reasons were given for data not being used today, in particular it may not be available, be available in too large quantities, or it may not be clear how to use it, make it relevant and link it to decisions. Notably, respondents seemed less concerned about quality and trust issues around data.

Our results show that there is an unfulfilled potential for data-driven decision making in agile software development contexts. Future research should investigate this in more detail and also develop new automated data collection, analysis and visualisations techniques and methodologies that augments existing, agile decision processes by linking relevant data to specific decision contexts.

References

1. Petersen, K., Wohlin, C.: A comparison of issues and advantages in agile and incremental development between state of the art and an industrial case. J. Syst. Softw. **82**, 1479–1490 (2009)
2. Schön, E-M., Winter, D., Escalona, M.J., Thomaschewski, J.: Key challenges in agile requirements engineering. In: Agile Processes in Software Engineering and Extreme Programming, XP, pp. 37–51 (2017)
3. Moe, N.B., Aurum, A., Dybå, T.: Challenges of shared decision-making: a multiple case study of agile software development. Inf. Softw. Technol. **54**, 853–865 (2012)
4. Olsson, H.H., Bosch, J.: From opinions to data-driven software R&D: a multi-case study on how to close the 'Open Loop' problem. In: 40th Euromicro Conference on Software Engineering and Advanced Applications, pp. 9–16 (2014)
5. Cockburn, A., Highsmith, J.: Agile software development: the people factor. Computer **34**(11), 131–133 (2001)
6. Provost, F., Fawcett, T.: Data science and its relationship to big data and data-driven decision making. Big Data **1**(1), 51–59 (2013)
7. Maalej, W., Nayebi, M., Johann, T., Ruhe, G.: Toward data-driven requirements engineering. IEEE Softw. **33**(1), 48–54 (2016)
8. Milne, A., Maiden, N.: Power and politics in requirements engineering: embracing the dark side? Requir. Eng. J. **17**(2), 83–98 (2012)
9. Magazinius, A., Börjesson, S., Feldt, R.: Investigating intentional distortions in software cost estimation-an exploratory study. J. Syst. Softw. **85**(8), 1770–1781 (2012)
10. Magazinius, A., Feldt, R.: Confirming distortional behaviors in software cost estimation practice. In: 37th EUROMICRO Conference on Software Engineering and Advanced Applications, pp. 411–418 (2011)
11. Feldt, R., Staron, M., Hult, E., Liljegren, T.: Supporting software decision meetings: heatmaps for visualising test and code measurements. In: 39th EUROMICRO Conference on Software Engineering and Advanced Applications, pp. 62–69 (2013)

12. Wnuk, K., Gorschek, T., Zahda, S.: Obsolete software requirements. Inf. Softw. Technol. **55**(6), 921–940 (2013)
13. Gren, L., Svensson, R.B., Unterkalmsteiner, M.: Is it possible to disregard obsolete requirements? - an initial experiment on a potentially new bias in software effort estimation. In: 10th International Workshop on Cooperative and Human Aspects of Software Engineering, pp. 56–61 (2017)
14. Chen, C.L.P., Zhang, C.-Y.: Data-intensive applications, challenges, techniques and technologies: a survey on big data. Inf. Sci. **275**, 314–347 (2014)
15. Feldt, R., Neto, F.G., Torkar, R.: Ways of applying artificial intelligence in software engineering. In: 6th International Workshop on Realizing Artificial Intelligence Synergies in Software Engineering, pp. 35–41 (2018)
16. Brynjolfsson, E.: Strength in numbers: how does data-driven decision making affect firm performance? SSRN (2011). https://ssrn.com/abstract=1819486
17. Janssen, M., van der Voort, H., Wahyudi, A.: Factors influencing big data decision-making quality. J. Bus. Res. **70**, 338–345 (2017)
18. Punter, T., Ciolkowski, M., Freimut, B., John, I.; Conducting on-line surveys in software engineering. In: International Symposium on Empirical Software Engineering, pp. 80–88 (2003)
19. Robson, C.: Real World Research. Blackwell, Oxford (2002)
20. Creswell, J.W.: Educational Research: Planning, Conducting, and Evaluating Quantitative and Qualitative Research. Pearson, London (2011)
21. Gliner, J.A., Morgan, G.A.: Methods in Applied Settings: An Integrated Approach to Design and Analysis. Lawrence Erlbaum Associates, Mahwah (2000)
22. Gelman, A., Carlin, J.B., Stern, H.S., Dunson, D.B., Vehtari, A., Rubin, D.B.: Bayesian Data Analysis. Chapman & Hall/CRC Texts in Statistical Science. Taylor & Francis, Abingdon (2013)
23. Carpenter, B., et al.: Stan: a probabilistic programming language. J. Stat. Softw. **76**(1), 1–32 (2017)
24. Wohlin, C., Runeson, P., Höst, M., Ohlsson, M.C., Regnell, B., Wessén, A.: Experimental Software Engineering - An Introduction. Kluwer Academic Publisher, Dordrecht (2000)
25. Furia, C.A., Feldt, R., Torkar, R.: Bayesian data analysis in empirical software engineering research. arXiv preprint arXiv:1811.05422 (2018)
26. Torkar, R., Feldt, R., Furia, C.A.: Arguing practical significance in software engineering using Bayesian data analysis. arXiv preprint arXiv:1809.09849 (2018)
27. Bürkner, P-C., Charpentier, E.: monotonic effects: a principled approach for including ordinal predictors in regression models. PsyArXiv: psyarxiv.com/9qkhj (2018)
28. Daneva, M., et al.: Agile requirements prioritization in large-scale outsourced system projects: an empirical study. J. Syst. Softw. **86**(5), 1333–1353 (2013)

Check for updates

Empowering Agile Project Members with Accessibility Testing Tools: A Case Study

Viktoria Stray[1(✉)], Aleksander Bai[2], Nikolai Sverdrup[1], and Heidi Mork[3]

[1] Department of Informatics, University of Oslo, Oslo, Norway
{stray,njsverdr}@ifi.uio.no
[2] Norwegian Computing Center, Oslo, Norway
aleksander.bai@nr.no
[3] NRK, Oslo, Norway
heidi.mork@nrk.no

Abstract. There is a growing interest in making software more accessible for everyone, which is emphasized by the numerous suggestions passed into law in many countries. However, many software organizations that use agile methods postpone or neglect accessibility testing. We aimed to understand how accessibility testing can be better integrated into the daily routine of agile projects by conducting a case study in a Norwegian software company. We investigated three accessibility testing tools: automatic checker, simulation glasses, and a dyslexia simulator. We hosted sessions at which agile project members used the tools while thinking out loud, responded to questionnaires, and were interviewed at the end. Additionally, we observed the project members for 18 workdays. Our results show that all three tools are suitable for agile projects. Especially the automatic checker and simulation glasses worked well in finding accessibility issues and were described as easy to use by the project members. Software organizations should empower their agile project members with low-cost and efficient accessibility testing tools to make their products more accessible for all. Doing this early and often in the development cycle may save the project from potential high costs at a later stage.

Keywords: Accessibility testing · Usability · Cambridge simulation glasses · SiteImprove accessibility checker · WCAG · Agile software development · Universal design

1 Introduction

Creating software that is accessible for everyone (including users with impairments) is an important consideration for an increasingly digital society. Accessibility focuses on enabling people with the widest range of capabilities to use a product or removing barriers that can interfere with the user experience [1]. However, putting accessibility into practice remains a challenge in software development [2], and agile methods are especially under scrutiny for not offering enough consideration for accessibility [3, 4].

Testing for accessibility means testing how users with impairments and disabilities (e.g., dyslexia or impaired vision) will experience the software product. Although agile

P. Kruchten et al. (Eds.): XP 2019, LNBIP 355, pp. 86–100, 2019.
https://doi.org/10.1007/978-3-030-19034-7_6

methods highlight principles such as delivering working software and regular testing, incorporating accessibility testing throughout an agile process is complicated and less common [3, 4], and it can be an expensive endeavor [5]. Accessibility testing is often postponed to the late phases of software development which breaks with the principle of delivering working software frequently [6]. Researchers argue for easier methods to make finding accessibility flaws more effective in agile software projects [6, 9, 10]. Agile projects face a growing complexity with a variety of organizational constraints such as universal design, legislation, and security, forcing the cross-functional agile team to adjust their practices and experiment with new team structures (e.g., BizDev teams) [7, 8]. Thus, now might be a good time to include practices and tools that let agile teams test for accessibility issues throughout the project.

In an agile process, which features short iterative cycles, it would be difficult to fit costly and time-consuming accessibility testing into regular testing procedures. Accordingly, there is a need to find methods that integrate well with agile approaches. Methods and tools that can be utilized often without being too resource- and time-intensive will fit well with agile principles. Our motivation for this project was thus to improve accessibility in agile software development by testing different methods that are considered fast and efficient.

The benefits of having an accessible solution are apparent. Poorly developed software with regard to accessibility is aggravating to impaired users and can make the product miss out on potential users, giving the issue both social justice and economic motivation. Research has also shown that software that accommodates accessibility and inclusion will benefit all users, including those without any impairments [11]. Also, for software to be considered working, it needs to be thoroughly tested and ready to be delivered to customers or production. If software fails to be sufficiently accessible, it cannot be considered to be working. For the goal of having working software, accessibility testing needs to be a part of every iteration that involves features which can affect the accessibility of the software. Motivated by this, we set out to investigate how accessibility testing can be integrated into agile software development, by answering the following research question:

RQ: How do agile project members experience using accessibility testing tools?

To address this question, we conducted a case study [12] where we had the participants test three different accessibility tools and respond to a questionnaire about the tools they tested. The participants were also interviewed and observed.

The remainder of this paper is organized as follows. Section 2 outlines the relevant background on accessibility testing in agile software development. Section 3 discusses different testing tools. Section 4 describes the data collection. Section 5 presents the results, and Sect. 6 discusses the results and implications for practice. Section 7 concludes and suggests future work.

2 Background

Failing to make a product accessible can be costly, as it will increase the probability of having to make late and expensive changes in the development process and further lead to prolonged development time. A product with which the user cannot achieve their goal through the usual procedure will also lead to a reduction in users and increase the need for additional support and assistance to help guide the users, such as help-desk services and on-site support [13]. Those who do include accessibility in their development process will find that the cost for testing procedures can take its fair share out of the development budget, especially since the requirements for accessibility testing often are complex [14].

Investing in accessibility testing early and throughout the development process can yield a substantial return on investment [15]. Detecting mistakes early lowers the cost of fixing the error and avoids the accumulation of big, time-consuming problems at the end of the development process. Accessibility testing, however, has the unfortunate fate of often being conducted at the very end of development [2]. Reduction in the amount of work needing to be done in the maintenance phase can also be a substantial benefit, as a significant portion of the life-cycle expenditure of a software product can congregate in this later stage.

2.1 Accessibility Testing in Agile Software Development

Dissatisfaction surrounding traditional accessibility test methods is a prevalent theme in other research. Researchers have investigated usability issues in agile development (e.g., [16–18]) but few researchers have investigated accessibility testing in agile projects. As Luján-Mora and Masri [9] argue, accessibility is difficult to achieve with traditional software development practices, due mainly to its habit of being implemented too late in the development process. They propose that agile development can significantly help to improve web accessibility due to its focus on regular testing.

Similarly, Eklund and Levingston [6] discuss how usability can benefit from agile development. They propose a set of steps one can use to incorporate usability techniques in agile development, such as conducting smaller tests and reviews to cover more of the development process as well as to rely extensively on external consultants with expert knowledge on accessibility testing. Meszaros and Aston [19] describe the introduction of early accessibility testing in an agile development process using testing methods such as paper prototypes to locate accessibility bugs, wizard of Oz testing, and usability stories. This resulted in a higher acceptance by end users. Kane [3] highlights the lack of accessibility testing in agile development and proposes techniques to integrate more accessibility testing into already established agile practices.

3 Testing Tools

Testing for accessibility entails testing for a multitude of different impairments and disabilities in various states. When ensuring a product works for users with eyesight-related issues, for example, one has to consider aspects such as different levels of visual perception, color blindness, complete blindness, tunnel vision, and so on. All of these affect the user experience in different ways and create different challenges that must be solved. Without any tools, a developer would have to retain an extensive amount of knowledge to meet the demands of accessibility testing, which would be hard to put into practice. One solution is to hire expert help from accessibility consultants or recruit people with different impairments to conduct user testing. However, this is an expensive solution and should be done when the product moves into a more stable phase.

One of the most significant challenges in testing for accessibility is that one has to account for a wide range of people. Using one super-tool that can take account of everything is not realistic due to the diversity of impairments and the different ways they affect users. When testing with accessibility in mind, there is a need to evaluate everything from content, layout, comprehensibility and technical implementation to compatibility with other accessibility tools, such as a screen reader.

There are some tools that we considered but decided not to include. For example, we considered a screen reader and WCAG (Web Content Accessibility Guidelines). However, both tools are intensive regarding the knowledge required to operate them, and this does not fit very well into an agile process with short iterative cycles. A screen reader is a software tool intended mainly for use by people suffering from mildly impaired vision to complete blindness. The biggest challenge of using a screen reader is that it required extensive training in order to operate the tool correctly. It may take years to achieve a proficient use of a screen reader, and advanced users can navigate around an obstacle that novice users cannot. WCAG is the de facto practiced method used to check for accessibility. WCAG is presented as a set of specifications categorized into four broad principles containing 61 numbered paragraphs of success criteria. Each criterion has its own detailed page, specifying the intent, examples, techniques, key terms, and related resources associated with the paragraph. The techniques and success criteria will, altogether, give a total of 379 different pages, each with a description, examples, additional resources, test procedures, and expected test results. From our earlier research, we know that developers perceive WCAG as tedious, cumbersome, and time-consuming to use in agile projects [14].

We chose the testing tools SiteImprove, Cambridge simulation glasses, and a dyslexia simulator (where we developed a Chrome browser extension), briefly presented below, based on other studies that have categorized testing tools according to barrier groups and cost-benefit [14, 20]. Since we wanted testing tools that could be easily integrated into an agile process (low cost and little prior knowledge), we found these to be the best candidates.

3.1 SiteImprove Accessibility Checker

SiteImprove is an automatic checker and browser extension that can analyze a web-page for breaches of many WCAG criteria. When activated, the extension will automatically analyze the currently opened web-page for noncompliance with the different levels of the WCAG technical standard. It distinguishes between the different categories of the WCAG standard and organizes them into groups. Each instance of error can give a direct link to the WCAG manual for a more detailed explanation of why the error exists and includes suggestions about how one can achieve compliance with WCAG. Other notable features are the ability to highlight where the error exists on the site itself and in the public source code by highlighting in the browser's developer tools.

One of the most significant drawbacks with automatic checker tools is that there are many things they cannot check, at least not until we have better artificial intelligence. For instance, an automatic checker can make sure that images have alternative HTML tags, but it cannot check if the description is accurate and meaningful.

3.2 Cambridge Simulation Glasses

A person can identify accessibility faults by wearing blurred glasses while interacting with the interface or object that is under examination. For our testing, we used the Cambridge simulation glasses. The glasses are thin enough to stack several pieces of glasses in sequential layers, enabling the tester to be in control of the degree of reduced vision. Before using the glasses, the tester performs a quick eyesight evaluation using a Snellen chart that comes with the glasses or can be printed out. The chart indicates how many glasses the tester should wear to simulate reduced vision (a 95% coverage of the general population). Most people will need two pair of glasses, but those with very good eyesight might require three glasses. While wearing the glasses, the tester interacts with whatever is to be evaluated for accessibility, and any possible shortcomings should be made readily apparent for the tester as they might struggle to use the solution.

3.3 Dyslexia Simulation

The dyslexia simulator is a small and simple browser extension that tries to simulate how a dyslectic user or someone with some other reading disorder might experience a website. Dyslexia is a common learning disability, and the condition can severely hamper a user's ability to comprehend a website. Dyslexia impedes the ability to read, and how software is presented can significantly affect the difficulty of interaction for a dyslectic user, especially in sites that feature much text or require the user to write [21]. The tool will test a website by shuffling the letters in words, making it difficult to read.

When testing a solution, the tester operates the interface as normal with the dyslexia software running; if there are areas that become difficult to perceive, the tester can use that as an indication for something that might become difficult for someone with reading difficulties to perceive. The dyslexia simulation tries to highlight issues related to a neurological impairment, which is challenging to test for. It is difficult to make software that can detect areas affected by such disabilities, and it is difficult for a tester to understand what the impaired user might experience. There are several WCAG paragraphs detailing the issues related to reading impairments and steps to help in the matter.

We used a dyslexia simulator in a pilot study that was a script the user had to rerun for each use, which was cumbersome. Therefore, for this study, we made an extension for the Google Chrome web browser (now available on the Chrome web store) that is easier to install and use.

4 Data Collection

We conducted this study in a Norwegian software company that makes digital services and solutions for banks. We observed the project members in their daily routines and during agile practices such as daily stand-up meetings [22] and retrospective meetings [23]. We documented their behavior, and conversation topics and were especially looking for matters where accessibility issues could play a part. We also interviewed four members with different roles and responsibilities. The reviews of the three testing methods were conducted by hosting sessions in which the participants tried out accessibility testing tools, answered questionnaires about the tools, and were interviewed at the end of the session, see Table 1 for an overview of the data collection.

Interview questions and testing tasks were made after determining what information was needed and how much time we could have with the participants. As recommended by [24], every tester had filled out a background survey before the session. After a pilot attempt of the testing session, it was decided to use a publicly available website not affiliated with the participants, after we found the participants' knowledge of their products to influence their ability to judge the accessibility.

All the testing sessions were originally scheduled for one hour each, where we had time to test three methods, which involved a quick briefing of the participants about the tools and instructions on how to use them. In the testing sessions, the participants were instructed to solve pre-made tasks that required them to use the tools to locate accessibility faults in a website. As the participants used the tools, they would comment on their experience and be prompted with questions by the interviewers to reflect on the experience. After completing the tasks, they filled out a questionnaire.

Having finished testing, the participants were asked a series of questions regarding their thoughts on each tried method, comparing the methods and identifying which one they preferred and which one they disliked. They were further asked about the ramifications of accessibility testing, and how they thought accessibility testing could be integrated into their routines.

Table 1. Data collection

Data	Explanation	Number
Full work days observed	We observed the project members in their daily work	18 days
Stand-up meetings	We observed teams having daily stand-up meetings	15 meetings
Team meetings	We observed meetings in the agile teams, including 2 retrospective meetings	5 meetings
Interviews outside of tests	We interviewed one team leader, one developer, one UX designer, and one architect	4 interviews
USE questionnaires	Seven of Cambridge simulation glasses, seven of SiteImprove, five of dyslexia simulator	19 answers
Testing sessions with end interviews	We tested and interviewed four developers, one software tester, and two UX designers	7 sessions

4.1 The Accessibility Testing Tools

We tested three different accessibility testing tools. Five participants tested three tools while two participants tested two tools because of less time available. The participants were encouraged to think aloud. When they forgot to talk while they were using the tools, we reminded them to do so. Below, we will describe how we tested each of the tools.

SiteImprove. Before we began, the participants were instructed to install the extension on their computers, and they were also given a quick overview of what it does at the start of the session. The SiteImprove user test was conducted without any specific tasks or scenarios in mind, as the tool does not need any extraordinary web features to be able to highlight its capabilities. The participants would explore the tool and investigate the different layers of information on a given website. When they had questions about the tool or were stuck, we guided them in the right direction. After exploring the tool on the given website, five of the participants switched to sites they were working on or were more familiar with to get a better sense of what the tool was telling them.

Simulation Glasses. After a brief introduction and determining how many glasses each tester should wear, the participants who tested the simulation glasses where given tasks to complete while wearing the glasses (Fig. 1). The tasks involved interacting with a web interface and completing two scenarios. The scenarios involved finding and booking airplane tickets online from one of the leading airlines in Scandinavia.

Fig. 1. A participant testing with simulation glasses

Dyslexia Simulation. Before we began, the participants were instructed to install the extension. We described how the tool worked and how it could help them discover accessibility vulnerabilities. Participants were asked to navigate a website with the dyslexia extension turned on and complete two scenarios. The scenarios involved finding information about prices, luggage, and legal requirements. The chosen web pages contained a lot of text to afford the extension something to work with.

4.2 USE Questionnaire for Tool Evaluation

Every participant filled out a questionnaire for each of the methods they tested. The questionnaire for evaluation of the testing methods is a post-session rating metric named the "Usefulness, Satisfaction, and Ease of use (USE) Questionnaire" [25]. The USE Questionnaire is a validated questionnaire that consists of 30 questions divided into four categories. We considered this questionnaire to be helpful in assessing whether each of the methods was suitable for agile projects, by stating general questions about satisfaction with usability and ease of use on a seven-point Likert scale.

4.3 End Interview After Test

At the end of each testing session, we asked the participants a set of prepared questions to gauge what they thought about the testing tools. They were asked to compare the tools in different ways and to talk about how they experienced using each of the tools. We also asked them whether they believed they would use the tools in the next three weeks, which tool they felt discovered most faults, and how the tools could be integrated into the daily agile workflow routines. Also, we had some general questions about how accessibility aspects affected the products they were developing.

5 Results

From the interviews, it became evident that many project members did not know much about accessibility testing before they tried the tools. One developer suggested that a reason was that they did not learn it in their software engineering education, and he also claimed it was not a common theme in work discussions. From our observations, we could confirm that there was little talking about accessibility among the project members. In none of the 20 observed meetings was there any discussion of accessibility issues. However, all interviewees were positive to learn about tools to help them test for accessibility throughout the agile project. Even though many had little experience with the tools, all participants managed to install the tools in a short amount of time.

5.1 SiteImprove Accessibility Checker

Seven participants evaluated the SiteImprove tool. As Fig. 2 shows, the method did very well, with a high score for all categories. The percentage reflects how well a category scored on the Likert scale from one to seven, where seven is 100% and one is 0%. The tool received a total score of 4.98 ($\sigma = 0.40$) with a 95% confidence interval between 4.68 and 5.28.

SiteImprove scored very high in the Usefulness category with a score of 5.43 ($\sigma = 0.42$), which is well above the average of 4.0. Ease of Learning received a score of 4.82 ($\sigma = 0.41$) since most of the operations are provided automatically by starting the extension.

The method also scored high in Ease of Use with a score of 4.87 ($\sigma = 0.42$) even if some had minor complaints and somewhat struggled: "*The tool points out that there are faults, but it is hard to spot where the faults are*". However, many stated that SiteImprove was much better to use than WCAG. One developer said, *"This is close to a developer tool (…). I like that it makes references to WCAG. I have tried to look at the WCAG documentation, but found that difficult"*.

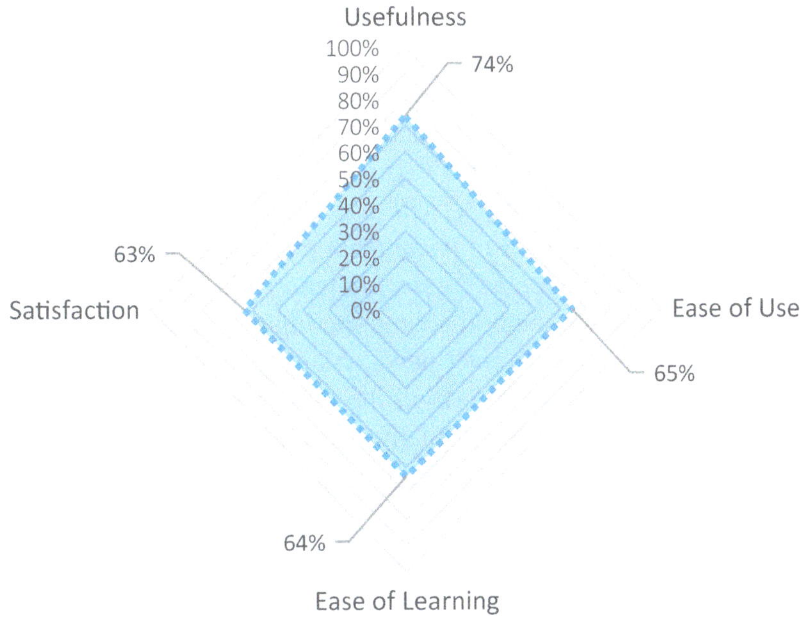

Fig. 2. SiteImprove evaluation results

5.2 Cambridge Simulation Glasses

Seven participants also evaluated this method. As Fig. 3 shows, the glasses got high scores in all categories and had the highest total score of 6.15 ($\sigma = 0.48$) among all the methods. The 95% confidence interval for the method was between 5.79 and 6.51.

Not surprisingly, since this method requires the participant only to wear glasses, this method scored very well on both Ease of learning with a score of 6.79 ($\sigma = 0.12$)

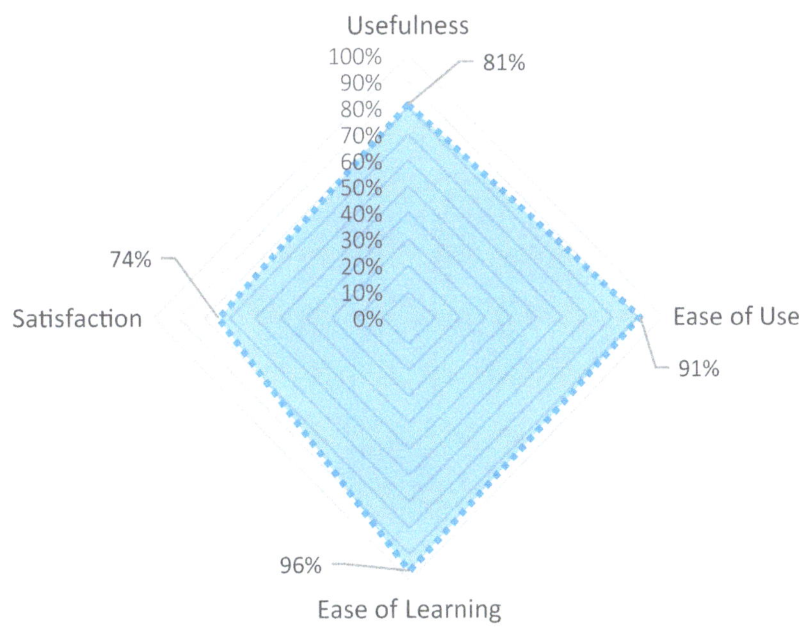

Fig. 3. Cambridge simulation glasses evaluation results

and Ease of use with a score of 6.45 (σ = 0.49), One developer said, "*The glasses gave quick results and were easy to use. I also like that they are tangible*", while another developer said, "*I want to have these glasses on my desk and use them often*".

Also for the Usefulness category, the method scored high with 5.88 (σ = 0.48), and the sub-question "Is it useful" scored 6.57 (σ = 0.73), which is well above the average for the category. A designer said, "*I will use these glasses in meetings between developers and business developers to make them aware of how the different solutions they are discussing will be perceived by people with reduced sight*".

Regarding Satisfaction, the method scored the highest of all with 5.47 (σ = 0.84), and this was also reflected in the interviews. Many participants mentioned that the method was fun to use, and many also tried the glasses on their own after the session was completed. During the interviews, many participants mentioned that the method created more awareness of the challenges associated with bad contrast and small fonts.

5.3 Dyslexia Simulation

Five participants evaluated the dyslexia simulation tool, and as Fig. 4 shows, this method was also regarded highly. The tool had the second highest evaluation in the Ease of learning category with a score of 6.35 (σ = 0.3). This is not unexpected since the method requires only the push of a button in the browser to be enabled. Both Usefulness and Ease of use also had high scores with 5.33 (σ = 0.57) and 5.62 (σ = 0.67). A designer said, "*The dyslexia simulator makes me realize how important it is to use common and simple words because those are easier to recognize when they are scrambled. I will definitely use this tool to show the management how it will be perceived by people with dyslexia if we use long text with difficult words*".

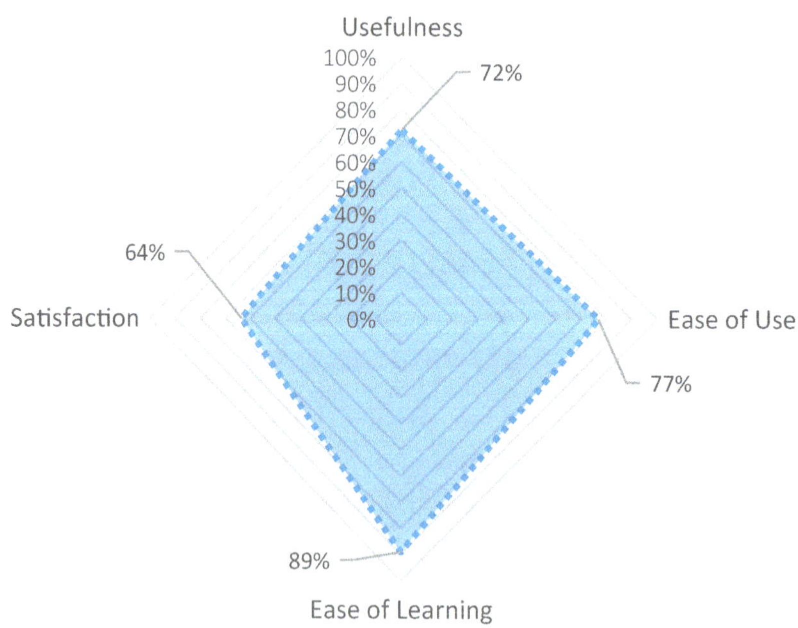

Fig. 4. Dyslexia simulation evaluation results

Overall the Dyslexia simulation method did good, in particular in the category Ease of learning, as Fig. 4 shows. The method itself scored well above neutral (4) and might have received even better scores if not for some bugs in the extension. This is also reflected in the sub-question for Ease of use where the question "I don't notice any inconsistencies as I use it" scored 4.00 ($\sigma = 0.89$), which is well below all the other sub-questions. This is also probably connected to the fact that the extension did not adapt all the text on the webpage.

The tool scored well overall with a total score of 5.53 ($\sigma = 0.53$) and a 95% confidence interval between 5.14 and 5.92. In the interviews, many participants said that the method was an eye-opener experience. Participants also liked that it was easy to visualize problems with too much text on a web page and that it emphasizes the importance of writing good and readable text: One developer said, *"I like this plugin. I now see that the way you structure the text is very important. When you have too much text close together, it is hopeless for a person with dyslexia"*. Contrarily, some noted that it could be difficult to understand how good the method was at finding issues.

6 Discussion

Good accessibility is difficult to achieve, mainly due to its complex nature and the wide range of people who must be considered. It does not help that accessibility testing is conducted late in the development process when changes are costly to make, and compromises are made instead. However, agile development can significantly help to improve web accessibility due to its focus on regular testing [9]. Eklund and Levingston [6] and Ferreira et al. [10] argue for more frequent testing where more cost-effective methods are used several times throughout the project rather than relying on few but large and costly testing activities, such as hiring accessibility experts to do accessibility testing.

There is currently little research that offers concrete solutions for simple accessibility testing in agile settings; most current research discusses just the possibilities for accessibility testing in agile development. In this study, we have focused on giving accessibility testing some much-needed evaluation in an agile project. The fast and low-cost test methods in this study were perceived as useful and easy to use by the agile project members.

Next, as other research also has suggested [9, 26], we found that accessibility needs to be a team effort. Agile principles promote self-organization and communication within the development team and make it possible to inspect even the smallest of details when everyone is involved, instead of having only a few experts working on accessibility. Several of the methods we tested addressed many of these concerns. While some were easier to use and learn than others, they all were usable without extensive training and learning sessions. Our results showed that all three methods we tested, SiteImprove, the Cambridge glasses, and the dyslexia simulator, can be used across the development team and utilized in such a way that it becomes a team effort where testing can be commenced at regular but short intervals.

All three accessibility testing methods we used in this study were low-cost and perceived as very easy and quick to use. Most of them can be used very early in development, some even before any code is written, merely going by design drawings. There is no doubt that accessibility testing can be included early in agile software projects. Using any of the tools will enable testing to be done more often. The interviewees also suggested regular workshops at which the agile team members together could experience the solutions they made with different accessibility testing tools. Also, if there are formal requirements from the organization or customer, these issues could be discussed in planning and retrospective meetings and would probably be a more frequent theme in the daily-standup meetings.

SiteImprove was quick in producing results and is the method that would cover the broadest set of WCAG paragraphs in our study. One key factor in its success is the automation aspect of the tool. It dramatically reduces the time spent finding bugs, and the user is immediately presented with clearly defined statements of what is wrong and how one can improve. It was not surprising that the participants rated SiteImprove as easy to learn since most of the operations are provided automatically by starting the extension. We had expected a lower total score of SiteImprove since the tool uses many complicated terms and advanced terminology. A drawback with SiteImprove is that it cannot be used until a solution has been implemented, rendering it not as useful for designers or in the early phases. It is also limited by being able only to check what is programmatically possible.

The Cambridge simulation glasses were, along with SiteImprove, the method that worked well in many situations. It also worked well in cases where SiteImprove cannot help. Use of the glasses is not dependent on a solution having reached a certain level of development. The glasses can be used early in development on visual concepts, for example on sketches or prototypes. They are also platform-independent and can be used on any software or visual representation, making it a universal accessibility tool. One aspect remarked on by many of the participants who tested the method was that the glasses gave an overview of the product in its entirety. Being able to view the product from a higher perspective rather than fixating on small details also contributes to why so many liked to use the glasses.

We included the dyslexia tool because we wanted methods that covered cognitive impairment, and this method was one of the few testing methods that are low-cost and fast to test for this. The method was rated higher than we had foreseen, particularly because we expected more participants to misunderstand the idea behind the method. The tool received good results on the USE Questionnaire. However, with this tool, the testers have to interpret the results based on their knowledge of dyslexia. Some testers reported that the plugin could be helpful to discover text where long and complicated words were being used, and where the structure and layout were not organized. The improved accessibility by employing clear and concise language is an aspect not addressed by any of the other tools.

6.1 Threats to Validity

As with all empirical studies, there are some threats to validity that we need to consider. First, we used a single-case design and, as a result, have the possibility of bias in the data collection and analysis. Therefore, the general criticisms of single-case studies, such as uniqueness, may apply to our study. However, as the company had been using agile methods for many years, developing bank solutions for a wide variety of people, we found it to be a valuable case for investigating accessibility testing in agile software development. Furthermore, we triangulated the research question from multiple sources of evidence such as interviews, observations, and questionnaires to increase the quality of the case study [12].

Second, when using self-reported data to measure usability of tools, one might have the "social desirability bias" [27] where respondents respond more positively to rating questions because they unconsciously want to satisfy the facilitator giving them the questionnaire. To reduce this bias, following the advice of Albert and Tullis [25], we collected the responses anonymously on the web, and we did not look at the results until afterward.

6.2 Implications for Practice

Our results show that agile accessibility testing methods are not well-known among agile team members. Accordingly, agile projects should invest in simple tools that can be used by all roles, and project members should be informed about the techniques they can use. We found that the three tools tested were useful and should be used regularly in agile projects as they are also cost-efficient. For software developers who consider using accessibility testing tools, we suggest that Cambridge glasses be used early, as they do not require much effort from the agile developers. As the product becomes more stable, SiteImprove can be used regularly.

The methods and tools we have evaluated have been used with the intention of testing software and finding accessibility issues. In the larger scheme of accessible software, we suspect that using these tools, especially the ones that simulate an impairment, might have secondary benefits. Exposure to the type of simulation testing such as with the Cambridge glasses and the dyslexia simulator can give the tester a heightened sense of awareness of issues that could come into conflict with impaired users and foster more empathy and understanding.

Many comments were made that the testers had new insights and understanding. The new knowledge about how different users perceive software can give developers a subconscious ability to shape software in a more accessible direction, outside of directly applying accessibility methods. So, while the methods described in this paper might not be chosen to be used regularly, there can be a significantly insightful experience for agile developers to try these methods, and they can put that experience to use in later development.

There is still a way to go to more easily integrate accessibility testing into agile work processes. The existing tools should be more compatible with agile processes, and agile project members should have a wider variety of accessibility testing tools to aid them in making accessible software. Implementing this would reduce the resources needed for accessibility testing by continuing the work toward more lightweight and comprehensible tools, as well as making the surrounding issues with impairments more visible and the knowledge of how they affect software interaction more obtainable. This will aid in weaving accessibility into the development process.

Another barrier is that many testing tools are platform-dependent. Tools are not uniformly available on all operating systems, browsers, and developer tools. The different tools have their own characteristics, and integration and learning can be made more arduous because of this. Tools that support software not intended for web or mobile are also rare. The lack of diverse tools available on many platforms hampers any attempt to make accessibility a more uniform process as it now has to be individually tailor-made depending on the hardware and software available to developers, and without the right combination, it can be challenging to cover a wide range of impairments with tools.

7 Conclusion and Further Work

We have evaluated three different tools for accessibility testing, in addition to interviewing the participants and observing them in their daily work in software development teams. We argue that the methods we tested will help to discover accessibility issues while keeping costs low in an agile project. In our study, when introduced to the tools, the project members became more aware of how to make the software more accessible, and they had a positive attitude toward using the tools throughout their projects. The interviewees stated that they wanted accessibility work to be a team effort, rather than the responsibility of the UX designers or accessibility consultants.

Further work should test other accessibility tools such as screen reader, WCAG, and Personas to try to find an approach for these tools to be integrated into an agile development project. Furthermore, future work should investigate the connection between the cost of doing accessibility work throughout the agile process with the cost saved by fixing accessibility issues early.

References

1. Petrie, H., Bevan, N.: The evaluation of accessibility, usability, and user experience. In: Stephanidis, C. (ed.) The Universal Access Handbook, pp. 1–16. CRC Press (2009)
2. Sánchez-Gordón, M.-L., Moreno, L.: Toward an integration of Web accessibility into testing processes. Procedia Comput. Sci. **27**, 281–291 (2014)
3. Kane, D.: Finding a place for discount usability engineering in agile development: throwing down the gauntlet. In: Proceedings of the Agile Development Conference, pp. 40–46. IEEE (2003)
4. Zimmermann, G., Vanderheiden, G.: Accessible design and testing in the application development process: considerations for an integrated approach. Univ. Access Inf. Soc. **7**, 117–128 (2008)
5. Nielsen, J.: Return on Investment for Usability. Jakob Nielsen's Alertbox (2003)
6. Eklund, J., Levingston, C.: Usability in Agile Development, pp. 1–7. UX Research (2008)
7. Stray, V., Moe, N.B., Hoda, R.: Autonomous agile teams: challenges and future directions for research. In: Proceedings of the XP2018 Scientific Workshops, Porto, Portugal. ACM (2018)
8. Mikalsen, M., Moe, N.B., Stray, V., Nyrud, H.: Agile digital transformation: a case study of interdependencies. In: Proceedings of the Thirty Ninth International Conference on Information Systems (ICIS 2018), San Francisco (2018)

9. Luján-Mora, S., Masri, F.: Integration of web accessibility into agile methods. In: Proceedings of the 14th International Conference on Enterprise Information Systems (ICEIS 2012), pp. 123–127 (2012)
10. Ferreira, J., Noble, J., Biddle, R.: Agile development iterations and UI design. In: Agile Conference (AGILE), pp. 50–58. IEEE (2007)
11. Fuglerud, K.S.: Inclusive design of ICT: The challenge of diversity (2014)
12. Yin, R.K.: Case Study Research: Design and Methods. Sage, Thousand Oaks (2009)
13. Bias, R.G., Mayhew, D.J.: Cost-Justifying Usability: An Update for the Internet Age. Morgan Kaufmann Publishers Inc., San Francisco (2005)
14. Bai, A., Mork, H.C., Stray, V.: A cost-benefit analysis of accessibility testing in agile software development: results from a multiple case study. Int. J. Adv. Softw. **10**, 1 (2017)
15. Haskins, B., Stecklein, J., Dick, B., Moroney, G., Lovell, R., Dabney, J.: Error cost escalation through the project life cycle. In: INCOSE International Symposium, pp. 1723–1737. Wiley Online Library (2004)
16. Bordin, S., De Angeli, A.: Focal points for a more user-centred agile development. In: Sharp, H., Hall, T. (eds.) XP 2016. LNBIP, vol. 251, pp. 3–15. Springer, Cham (2016). https://doi.org/10.1007/978-3-319-33515-5_1
17. Chamberlain, S., Sharp, H., Maiden, N.: Towards a framework for integrating agile development and user-centred design. In: Abrahamsson, P., Marchesi, M., Succi, G. (eds.) XP 2006. LNCS, vol. 4044, pp. 143–153. Springer, Heidelberg (2006). https://doi.org/10.1007/11774129_15
18. Moreno, A.M., Yagüe, A.: Agile user stories enriched with usability. In: Wohlin, C. (ed.) XP 2012. LNBIP, vol. 111, pp. 168–176. Springer, Heidelberg (2012). https://doi.org/10.1007/978-3-642-30350-0_12
19. Meszaros, G., Aston, J.: Adding usability testing to an agile project. In: Agile Conference, pp. 289–294. IEEE (2006)
20. Bai, A., Fuglerud, K., Skjerve, R.A., Halbach, T.: Categorization and comparison of accessibility testing methods for software development. Stud. Health Technol. Inf. **256**, 821–831 (2018)
21. W3C Working Group Reading Level: Understanding Success Criterion 3.1.5. https://www.w3.org/tr/understanding-WCAG20/meaning-supplements.html
22. Stray, V., Moe, N.B., Sjøberg, D.I.K.: The daily stand-up meeting: start breaking the rules. IEEE Softw. (2018). https://doi.org/10.1109/ms.2018.2875988
23. Derby, E., Larsen, D., Schwaber, K.: Agile Retrospectives: Making Good Teams Great. Pragmatic Bookshelf (2006)
24. Edwards, R., Holland, J.: What is Qualitative Interviewing? A&C Black (2013)
25. Albert, W., Tullis, T.: Measuring the User Experience: Collecting, Analyzing, and Presenting Usability Metrics. Newnes (2013)
26. Constantine, L.: What do users want? Engineering usability into software. Windows Tech J. **4**, 30–39 (1995)
27. Nancarrow, C., Brace, I.: Saying the "right thing": coping with social desirability bias in marketing research. Bristol Bus. Sch. Teach. Res. Rev. **3**, 1–11 (2000)

Artifact-Facilitated Communication in Agile User-Centered Design

Andrei Garcia[1], Tiago Silva da Silva[2(✉)], and Milene Selbach Silveira[1]

[1] Faculdade de Informática, PUCRS, Porto Alegre, Brazil
andrei.garcia@acad.pucrs.br, milene.silveira@pucrs.br
[2] UNIFESP, Universidade Federal de São Paulo, São José dos Campos, Brazil
silvadasilva@unifesp.br

Abstract. One of the main challenges faced while establishing the integration of Agile and User-Centered Design is how to facilitate communication among the invariably distinct involved practitioners. Advocating the use of artifacts as enablers in this scenario, this paper aims to explore and understand the artifacts which can facilitate the communication between developers and designers in an Agile User-Centered Design approach. Drawing upon a netnography of a globally-distributed online community, we carried out community observation, data collection, and data analysis. The data analysis and interpretation pointed out two major themes: artifacts facilitate communication and artifacts support collaboration. Our paper provides an overview of the artifacts used for communication in Agile User-Centered Design and highlights how artifact-facilitated communication ensues in the industry through a perspective from practitioners.

Keywords: Agile User-Centered Design · Artifacts · Communication · Netnography · Online ethnography

1 Introduction

Agile User-Centered Design (AUCD) evolved from different motivations. On the one hand, Agile aims to satisfy customers through timely releases and responsiveness to change requests without compromising software quality. On the other hand, User-Centered Design (UCD) aims at ensuring appropriate usability of the implemented software, a characteristic that has not been sufficiently considered either in traditional plan-driven approaches nor in agile approaches. UCD addresses this issue but does not consider Agile principles [4]. There is an inherent tension between both schools of thought, and this tension is a core reason why researchers, seeing the value of both arguments, have been investigating how to integrate both approaches [9].

First concrete attempts to integrate Agile and UCD approaches were published about a decade ago. For instance, Sy [30], Fox et al. [12], Ferreira et al. [11], and da Silva et al. [8] came up with very similar proposals about the integration

P. Kruchten et al. (Eds.): XP 2019, LNBIP 355, pp. 102–118, 2019.
https://doi.org/10.1007/978-3-030-19034-7_7

between these two approaches. However, such interaction on a daily basis is still a concern, and one of its main problems is how to facilitate[1] communication between the invariably distinct involved practitioners aiming to build a shared understanding regarding the project context.

This shared understanding among Software Engineering (SE) and Human-Computer Interaction (HCI) individuals is critical to the success of several agile projects, but little has been known about how communication works [5]. Furthermore, the reliance on communication within agile teams is a fundamental characteristic [29]. In AUCD, designers and developers must be prepared to communicate and collaborate.

As Brhel et al. [4], we advocate the idea of artifact-mediated communication in this scenario. Aiming to identify and understand the artifacts used to facilitate the communication between designers and developers in an AUCD approach we carried out a netnographic study in a globally-distributed online community of agile practitioners.

To contextualize our findings, we present a general view of the artifacts used in AUCD (Sect. 2). Then, we detail how the netnographic study was planned and conducted (Sect. 3), and then we present our main findings (Sect. 4 and discuss (Sect. 5). Finally, we draw upon our findings to elaborate our conclusions (Sect. 6) and future work (Sect. 7).

2 Artifacts in AUCD

Salah et al. [24] conducted a systematic review to identify restriction factors regarding Agile and UCD integration and explored practices to deal with them. One of their findings in this review was about the dynamics between developers and designers which addresses the ongoing and continuous communication between the teams. Regarding sharing and understanding design tasks, some practices have been used, such as design studio, developers participating in User Interface (UI) specifications and shared artifacts within the team.

Brhel et al. [4] identified five principles for the integration of Agile and UCD in their study. The fifth one is: "artifact-mediated communication – in AUCD approaches, artifacts should be used to communicate, and document product and design concepts, and should be accessible to all involved stakeholders." For these authors, this principle consists of the use of tangible and up-to-date artifacts – accessible to all involved stakeholders – to document and communicate product and design concepts, which corroborates Schön et al. [26] that state that artifacts can also be used for communication, elaboration, validation, and documentation of requirements in agile environments.

Bearing in mind the importance of the artifacts for the Agile UCD integration, Garcia et al. [13] carried out a systematic mapping to identify which are the artifacts used and in which contexts they have been used to facilitate the

[1] Noteworthy, we are using 'facilitation' as a means of helping people to deal with a process or to reach an agreement or solution without getting directly involved in the process, discussion, etc.

communication in Agile User-Centered Design approaches. In this systematic mapping, the authors identified 20 different artifact groups that play a critical role as a communication facilitator. Prototypes and User Stories stand out as the most used artifacts. Besides, Personas, Sketches, Scenarios, and Wireframes also emerge as essential means for organizing communication and collaboration among AUCD team members.

This mapping study [13] also revealed five distinct events involving artifacts used as communication mediators – Discovery, Planning, Iterative Cycle, Review Meeting, and General Meetings. The Iterative Cycle was the event with the greatest sharing of artifacts, and, in this event, Prototypes, and User Stories once again were the most cited artifacts. Furthermore, artifacts are being used both in physical and electronic formats. Physical artifacts are commonly used throughout Planning and Discovery events; whereas the electronic ones are mostly used during the Iterative Cycle, often as a basis for development.

The importance of the role that artifacts play for AUCD is evident in the literature. However, while their importance is clear, there is no evidence concerning which artifacts are used for the communication between developers and designers, and how and in which ceremonies they are used.

Based on the studies analyzed – AUCD and Artifacts within this context – we can emphasize the importance of specific artifacts to improve teams' communication. Therefore, to understand – from a practitioners' perspective – how and when these artifacts have been used to promote communication within AUCD contexts, we carried out a netnographic study as described as follows.

3 Method

During the last two decades, online environments became rich and vital grounds for ethnographic studies [23]. In the same period, online communities have become one of the most popular forms of online services [21]. Online communities are essentially forums for meeting and communicating with others [2], or in a more detailed definition, online communities are web-based online services with features that make it possible the members to communicate with each other [21]. Along with online environments, the growth of online communities brought by Computer-Mediated Communications (CMC) established a solid research field for online ethnography studies [20].

Online ethnography adopts principles of ethnographic research molded in offline environments and applies them to online environments with necessary adjustments [23]. One of the online ethnography methods is netnography. Developed by Kozinets, netnography is a qualitative research method which adapts ethnography research processes to study cultures and communities that are emerging through CMC [17]. According to Kozinets [18], online ethnography is a generic term used when performing any type of ethnographic research using some sort of online method. Thus it is important to define netnography as a method by referring to a "specific set of related data collection, analysis, ethical and representational research practices" [18].

Thereby, we adopted the netnography method to identify and understand the artifacts used to facilitate communication between developers and designers. The netnography method performed in this study followed the steps of planning and entrée, community observation and data collection, data analysis, and reporting as per Kozinets guidance [18] on conducting netnography.

3.1 Planning and Entrée

This step involves the formulation of the research objective and questions, screening and identification of appropriate online communities. Furthermore, it is important to learn about the communities of interest and define the criteria to select the community that will be studied.

Definition of Research Questions. The goal of this netnographic study is to understand how artifacts are used to facilitate communication between designer and developer on AUCD approach according to practitioners, which participate in discussions on online communities. Therefore, we defined three research questions: *(RQ1) Which artifacts are used to facilitate communication between designer and developer? (RQ2) In what events are these artifacts being used?* and *(RQ3) What's the role the artifacts play?*

Identification of Online Communities. In order to discover appropriate online communities, we took into account the research goal, which led us to search for communities containing the terms "Agile", "User-Centered Design" or "Agile User-Centered Design". Ideally, the community should focus on AUCD, but since this is an approach that can be taken by Agile and UCD, all the three terms were included. Moreover, it is important to mention that in the industry the term User-Centered Design is widely known as User Experience Design, hence we also included this wording to search for communities of interest.

We performed this search using as base Facebook and LinkedIn groups as well as Slack communities. These revealed 36 communities that seemed relevant to the study. Communities containing the research topic but related to job offers, focused in a specific region or country and created for a particular company were not included.

Criteria Definition to Select the Community. The selection criteria were composed of seven factors including relevance, activity, interactivity, substantiality, heterogeneity, richness, and experientiality [18]. The relevance is the first and most important factor. For a community to be considered relevant it should have relation to the research focus and questions. The community needs to be active containing recent and regular communications. Interactivity factor is related to the flow of communication between members. Substantial factor regards to the mass of communicators and energetic feel. The heterogeneity factor concerns about either a variety of difference or a consistency of similar type of participants. The community should be rich in data offering more detailed or descriptive data. Finally, there is the experiential factor which is related to the experience that the community offers to the members.

Community Selection. Based on the selection criteria, and considering the relevance as the most important factor we selected the ***Scrum Practitioners*** LinkedIn Group. The decision to cherry-pick this community was based first on the relevance factor, once the community's topic was aligned with the research focus. In addition, the main purpose of this community is to help and spread the knowledge and implementation of agile for practitioners actively practicing the agile product development. Secondly, this community had the most activity containing the average of 2 posts (main threads) and 33 messages per day, the most interactive with the average of 18 comments per post, and therefore contained the most data. Moreover, the community was considered substantial containing 98431 members.

3.2 Community Observation and Data Collection

The second step of the netnographic research involves community observation and data collection [18]. Once we chose the community we could start collecting the data. However, foremost it is imperative to ensure ethical procedures for any online ethnographic study.

Ethical Procedures. Prior to the observation and data collection, ensuring ethical research must be an important part of the netnographic research planning. Therefore, to address the ethical issues we followed the procedures defined by Kozinets [18]: identifying the researcher profile and informing members about the research; asking for proper permissions; gaining consent when needed. Thus, we updated our user profiles containing the role as Researcher, additionally, we used the affiliation to openly, and accurately identify ourselves to the community and administrators.

Scrum Practitioners is a closed LinkedIn group with well-defined rules and two administrators. A group administrator is a legitimate gatekeeper who the researcher should approach prior to contacting other group members or collecting any data [18]. In LinkedIn Groups, gatekeepers assume the roles of Owner, Manager or Moderator and they are deemed a 'data controller' as stated by LinkedIn Groups Terms of Service [19].

Because of LinkedIn Groups terms, and considering the administrator as a gatekeeper, we properly asked the group's manager for permissions aimed at data analysis and interaction with the group. Besides, group members were informed about the research with an accurate description of the research focus and interest. No direct quotations were used in the report or publications to ensure the user's anonymity; once direct quotes are increasingly easy to identify through search engines. Also, all data were treated using pseudonyms for the group members.

Data Collection Strategy. Netnographic data can assume three forms [18]: archival data, which is already recorded and stored; communicatively co-created or elicited data; and, participative-authored field note data. Additionally, data collection has two elements, which are the data the researcher straight copy from online communities' platforms and the data the researcher writes in from their observations of the community.

Loanzon et al. [20] described that data collection in netnography usually is textual. As per observation, Scrum Practitioners group is mainly focused on textual communication, and their interactions happen through a post, that is usually a question from some agile professional, and the comments on this post from other members trying to collaborate with an answer. Based on LinkedIn Groups post structure, we collected textual data from posts and comments focused on the research questions. Thereby, the collected data derivate from historical posts (archival data), researcher interactions (elicited data), and researcher sketches as field notes (participative-authored data).

We collected archival data bearing in mind the research questions. Thus only posts related to the study topic were downloaded. LinkedIn groups keep all historical posts available, but only posts from March 2015 were gathered to have the most recent discussions. Furthermore, LinkedIn groups provide a search engine inside the community, which supported the archival data exploration. We performed the data collection from August 2017 to January 2018.

Posters Categorization. Posters are community members who interact with the group. According to Kozinets [17] they can be sorted in four categories: Tourists, Minglers, Devotees, and Insiders. To match the reality of this study, the description of each category was adapted to be aligned with the study's subject; thus instead of use "consumption activity" wording to define the member engagement, as originally stated by Kozinets, it was adapted to "group topic". Thus, all four categories are detailed next.

Tourists, who lack strong social ties, maintain a superficial interest in the group topic. They have shallow participation in the community, and potentially their participation in the group will not last very long. Tourists are in the community to get information [20]. Minglers, are members who have strong social ties but least interest in the group topic. They have high visibility but limited influence. Devotees are members who maintain a strong interest in group topic but few attachments to the online group. They do not participate actively in all posts, but only in some specific threads that they are interested. Insiders are the leaders of the community, they are both passionate about the group's topic and sensitive to the social welfare of the community. In other words, they have strong social ties and a high group's topic interest. They are well respected by other community members and have frequent and highly visible participation in almost all posts. Therefore, we categorized the members according to these four categories for all collected comments. Besides, we collected information related to the members' industry, job position, region, and skills to help contextualize their comments.

3.3 Data Analysis and Interpretation

Data collection and data analysis is a simultaneous process in qualitative researches [7]. Thus, this netnographic research step occurs concomitantly with community observation and data collection [17]. This step involves organizing, reading, coding, categorizing, and interpreting the data.

Data Analysis. We followed the data analysis approach from Creswell [7] through the six defined stages. The first stage commences with data organization and preparation for the analysis. The second stage regards to read and look at all data, in order to have a general sense of information and reflect on its overall meaning on the information collected from participants. Stage 3 addresses the data coding, which is the process of arranging the data by grouping and writing a word representing a category. Stage 4 concerns to generate a description of the setting or people, and also create categories or themes for analysis. Themes or categories can also use the approach of coding, and they are described as the major findings in a qualitative study. In stage 5, it is the moment to define how description and themes will be pictured. Stage 6 is the final step in data analysis, which involves an interpretation of the findings or results. Hence, we took advantage of these six stages approach to analyze the data. Also, we used the qualitative data analysis software QSR International's NVivo 11 [22] to perform the data analysis.

Data Organization. Whereas we used the software NVivo to analyze and code all the collected data, it is essential to describe how we organized it. First of all, we imported collected posts into the tool as internal sources and organized them as archival data or elicited data as previously mentioned. Each post was defined as a major case, and each member's comment was considered as an inner case, which was helpful for the coding process. Codes are treated as nodes on NVivo; consequently, we organized and created all codes under the nodes structure. Finally, we classified all inner cases containing the posters information and details according to the posters categorization.

Data Coding. Data coding is the process of organizing the data by grouping related data and labeling these categories with a term [7]. Since we have benefited from the results of Garcia et al. [13] we defined a preliminary codebook based on the theory which evolved during data analysis, ending up with 31 codes. From all codes, "Events" and "Artifacts" had sub-nodes that were used to break down the analysis per event and artifact. Furthermore, data coding was performed manually on text-based data since the collected data was textual.

4 Findings

The final set of collected data comprises six main posts, with a total of 134 comments, including archival and elicited data (Table 1). Most of the posts were from 2017, with no related posts between March 2015 and March 2017. Altogether 63 distinct members, from 18 different countries, participated in the posts discussions. The majority of the members who interacted in the collected posts were categorized as Devotees and Insiders due to the level of engagement in Scrum Practitioners LinkedIn group. From the 63 members, 49 were categorized as Devotees, 11 Insiders, and 3 Tourists. Summing up, 95,3% of the members who participated in the collected posts were Insiders and Devotees. According to Kozinets [17], preliminary research reveals that enthusiastic, devoted, energetically involved, and experienced user segments are represented by Insiders and Devotees in online communities.

Table 1. Collected data

Source	Data Type	Comments	Post Date	Collected Date
Post 1	Archival	6	03/12/2015	08/03/2017
Post 2	Archival	27	03/15/2017	08/05/2017
Post 3	Archival	13	08/23/2017	10/15/2017
Post 4	Elicited	30	10/19/2017	11/09/2017
Post 5	Archival	29	12/14/2017	12/17/2017
Post 6	Archival	29	12/18/2017	01/02/2017

Our first analytical lens was focused on answering the question *(RQ1) Which artifacts are used to facilitate communication between designer and developer?* Our findings reveal that seven distinct artifacts were mentioned by Scrum Practitioners community members as facilitators in communication between designer and developer. Moreover, the results from Garcia et al. [13] demonstrate that 20 artifacts accomplish this purpose. Therefore, to concentrate on the most used artifacts, we highlighted the intersection between this systematic mapping study and the findings herein presented (Fig. 1). The list of artifacts that were mentioned as communication facilitators includes user story, wireframe, prototype, mockup, sketch, and persona.

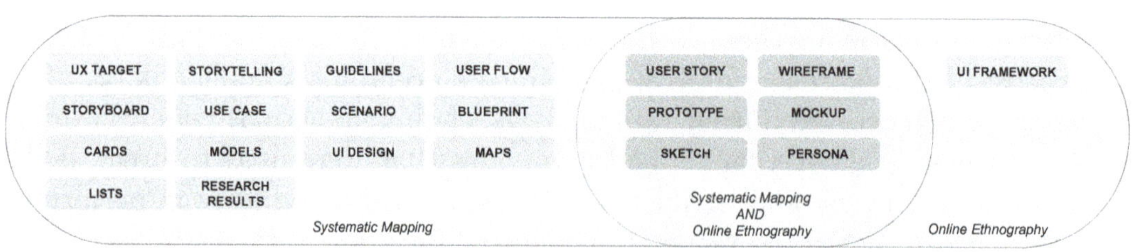

Fig. 1. Intersection between the Systematic Mapping and the Online Ethnography

All these artifacts may be used in different events of AUCD approach, which led us to answer the second question *(RQ2) In what events are these artifacts being used?* Our findings demonstrate that artifacts facilitate the communication throughout the AUCD events, starting with discovery sessions and going to the agile events including planning, iterative cycle, review, and backlog refinement.

For each event, the artifacts can be used for distinct purposes. The outcomes for question *(RQ3) What's the role the artifacts play?* disclosed that during discovery session artifacts as wireframes and prototypes are used to communicate and validate an idea, while personas delineate the user profile and create a shared understanding, as noted by some practitioners. User stories and wireframes were the most cited artifacts on Scrum Practitioners community, consolidating 50% of all artifacts references.

Users story helps to clarify what should be implemented. As Trenton[2] has noted, a well-written user story facilitates the communication, when the designer describes the interactions in the acceptance criteria, and the developers can estimate the effort necessary to implement the story *(Trenton, posted on Scrum Practitioners, March 15, 2017)*. These user story roles are also mentioned by Beyer et al. [3]. They state that user stories are shared with the development team and they can use them to estimate how much effort they require for the next iteration. User stories also facilitate discussions to define if a determined feature will deliver or not value for the product. This discussion also involves the breakdown of large user stories into thin vertical slices, which involves all architectural layers from the user interface to the backend code.

Wireframes support the description of a user story. They are used to support the acceptance criteria and communicate illustratively how a user interface should be structured. Since they illustrate high-level concepts and behaviors [15], wireframes complement user stories description and are necessary to define when a story is ready for development *(Ambrose, posted on Scrum Practitioners, December 17, 2017)*. An overview of all artifacts correlated with the events where they were mentioned and their roles are represented in Table 2.

5 Discussion

The qualitative data analysis and interpretation resulted in two major themes related to our research questions: (1) Artifacts Facilitate Communication and (2) Artifacts Support Collaboration. Nevertheless, before start addressing them, it is essential to discuss team structure. In all collected posts, there were discussions regarding where the designer should work, if as part of the Scrum Team or as part of a "Design Team". This discussion was generated because Scrum Guide [28] states that the Scrum Team consists of a Product Owner, the Development Team, and the Scrum Master, and has no citation to design discipline or designer role. However, the Scrum Guide also explains that Development Teams are cross-functional, containing all the necessary specialized skills to create a product increment. Thus, the community understanding is that the team must be cross-functional and the designer should be part of the team. Furthermore, considering

[2] As mentioned in the ethical procedures, we used pseudonyms to refer to members when discussing their comments.

Table 2. Overview of artifacts, events, and roles

Artifact	Events the artifacts were mentioned	Roles/Used to
User story	Planning	Clarify what should be implemented
		Estimate how much effort is required
		Clarify and communicate what will integrate an iteration
	Iterative cycle	Provide UI definitions
Wireframe	Discovery	Communicate illustratively how a UI should be structured
		Communicate and validate an idea
	Planning	Communicate the requirements
		Support the description and AC of a user story
		Help to estimate how much effort is required
	Review	Share results of the iteration
Prototype	Discovery	Verify the user interface
		Verify interactions feasibility in terms of technical support
	Planning	Communicate how the UI should be created
		Clarify and communicate what will integrate an iteration
	Iterative cycle	Foundation to create mockups
	Review	Share results of the iteration
Mockup	Iterative cycle	Communicate the UI details
	Review	Share results of the iteration
Sketch	Backlog refinement	Briefly describe a backlog item
Persona	Discovery	Delineate the user profile
		Create a shared understand
	Iterative cycle	Helps the team to focus and discuss core product functionalities
		Confirm the team is going in the right direction

the approach of AUCD, which has design discipline involved, the team must have a person with great skills in design as part of the team. Donnie has commented about having the designer as part of the team, stating that the designer sits with the team when he/she is not interacting with the end-users *(Donnie, posted on Scrum Practitioners, March 24, 2017)*. Donnie's comment was also supported by other members. Several citations of word "together" referring to the team, were encountered in the analyzed data, as displayed in the word tree (Fig. 2). Moreover, other synonyms were used to state that the designer should be part of the team, such as "along", "alongside", "part of", "sitting with", "whole", "integrate", "embedded", "jointly", and "work with".

5.1 Artifacts Facilitate Communication

Agile Manifesto asserts in the first sentence: "Individuals and interactions over processes and tools" [27]. Thus, interactions among professionals in the AUCD

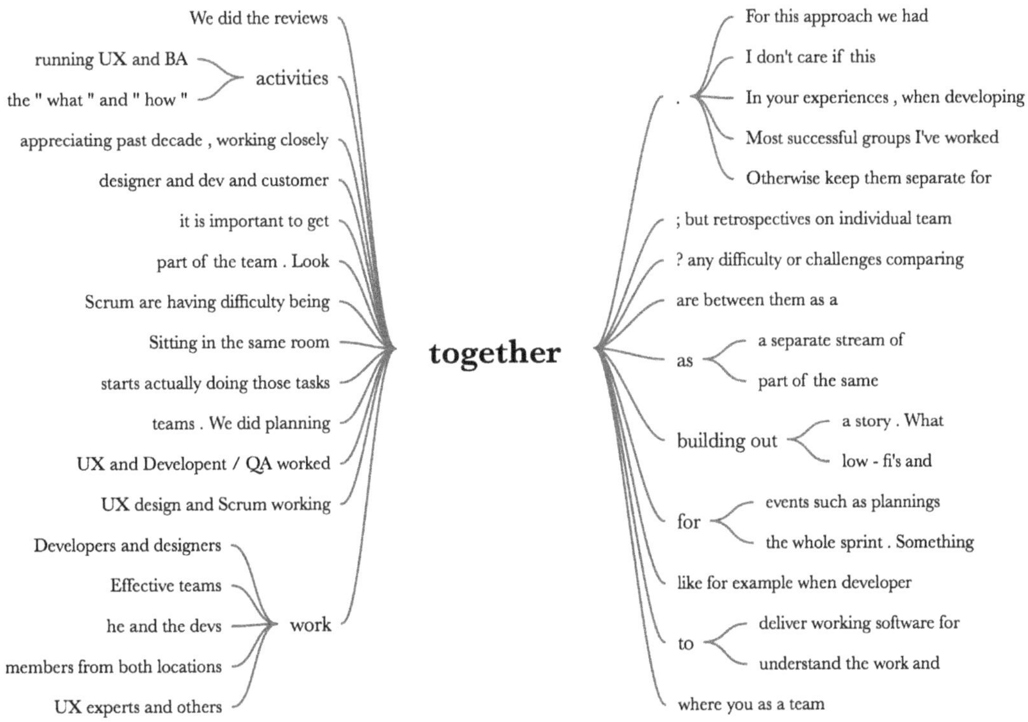

Fig. 2. Word tree generated from word "together"

approach are essential to conduct the product to the right course and deliver value. A common form of interaction is communication. Designers and developers communicate in different agile events using different artifacts as facilitators. The communication occurs throughout the entire AUCD flow, starting from discovery session, passing through all agile events including planning, iterative cycle, review, and backlog refinement.

As Mathew has noted, during discovery sessions the team, including developers, testers and designers, meet to create low fidelity prototypes to verify the User Interface and interactions feasibility in terms of technical support *(Mathew, posted on Scrum Practitioners, December 20, 2017)*. Thus, the team uses low fidelity prototypes to communicate how the User Interface should be created considering user experience and technical perspectives.

Wireframes and personas were also mentioned as communication facilitators through discovery sessions. Personas are used to delineate the user profile and create a shared understanding between the designer and the developer regarding the product focus. On the other hand, designers use wireframes to validate an idea with users and then employ these same wireframes to validate whether the development team can build it considering how much effort it takes in terms of feasibility and finances. Herman has mentioned that developers can understand what the requirements are, estimated how much effort it will take, and define how they will build them *(Herman, posted on Scrum Practitioners, December 19, 2017)*. Furthermore, Ambrose has commented that these resultant artifacts from discovery sessions are used as foundation to write user stories and/or refine the acceptance criteria of existing user stories that will feed the product backlog, ensuring that the highest priority backlog items are ready to be designed and built *(Ambrose, posted on Scrum Practitioners, December 17, 2017)*. Therefore, wireframes are used as a mean of communication to explain what are the user needs resulting from discovery sessions, as well as to validate and estimate how the requirements should be built.

Likewise, prototypes, as well as user stories, are relevant during planning events where they are used to define what will integrate an iteration. During the estimation process, designers use these artifacts to provide more details to developers for a more accurate estimation [10]. In general, at this event artifacts use to be more flexible and lightweight to facilitate face-to-face communication. Therefore, in the planning, the artifacts are intended for clarifying and sharing the work for the iterative cycle that is starting.

During the iterative cycle, the preliminary prototypes created throughout discovery sessions are used as a reference for designers to generate mockups. All along the iterative cycle, mockups are used to communicate how the user interface should look like, supported by the prototype and user story, which together define the user interface behavior *(Frederick, posted on Scrum Practitioners, March 18, 2017)*. Thus, mockups are important to communicate the user interface details such as colors, typography, and spacing, while prototypes and user stories provide the user interaction definitions. Personas were also mentioned as a communication facilitator during the iterative cycle. This artifact helps both designer and developer to focus and discuss the core product functionalities. Personas are used as means to confirm that the team is going to the right direction to implement the user stories, thus delivering value to the product *(Sophia, posted on Scrum Practitioners, December 15, 2017)*.

By the end of each iteration, there is the sprint review event. During this meeting, while the developers demonstrate the work that has been done, designers can show what is the result of parallel design track. Frederick has posted that wireframes, mockups, and prototypes are shown as result of designer's work in the sprint review, even knowing that these artifacts cannot be deployed as part of the product increment *(Frederick, posted on Scrum Practitioners, March 18, 2017)*. Thus, during sprint review designers can communicate what are the resultant artifacts, and use them to provide an overview of what will be possibly included in the next sprint.

Finally, before the succeeding sprint planning, it is time for product backlog refinement – also known as backlog grooming by practitioners. For the time of refinement, sketches are used to describe the backlog item quickly. They are used to add brief details to a user story, and the designer can easily communicate with the developers about what is expected from the user story even before to have a wireframe or a prototype. *(Tylar, posted on Scrum Practitioners, October 20, 2017)*. Therefore, sketches facilitate quick communication during refinement and help other team members to have a shared understanding.

5.2 Artifacts Support Collaboration

The collaboration between designers and developers should be supported by facilitating communication of design vision [25]. As mentioned by the authors, sharing an understanding of the design vision can be achieved via design thinking [6], engaging the whole team in design practices and UI specifications, and sharing design artifacts. Design thinking discipline creates an atmosphere of collaboration where the entire team, including designers and developers, can create low fidelity prototypes together to match users needs and technical feasibility *(Benjamin, posted on Scrum Practitioners, December 18, 2017)*. Consequently, the collaborative environment is extremely tied to the community understanding related to the team working as a whole. Figure 3, shows some excerpts considering the code collaboration, which corroborate the idea of close collaboration.

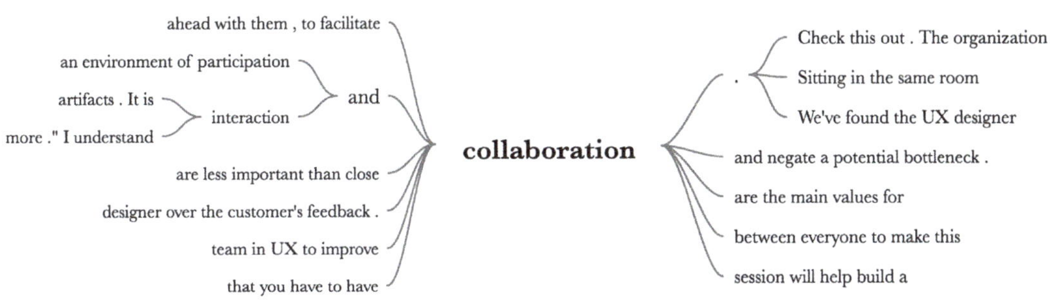

Fig. 3. Word tree generated from code “collaboration”

Moreover, InVision [16] and Confluence [1] were mentioned as collaborative tools. InVision provides a collaborative view where developers and designers can interact over shared mockups and prototypes, posting comments and defining the user interface *(Marianna, posted on Scrum Practitioners, October 22, 2017)*. Confluence provides a template where wireframes can be attached, and it also contains a section to add comments and discussions about the artifact *(Marlina, posted on Scrum Practitioners, October 21, 2017)*.

Another collaborative approach mentioned by the community was Lean UX. Lean UX stands on three foundations: design thinking, agile software development, and Lean startup method [14]. Since this approach stands on these three foundations, it also considers the team is working as a single unit, creating a collaborative environment. The author states that the artifacts such as stick notes, sketches, wireframes, and paper prototypes, created during kickoff and ideation sessions – also named discovery stage – are meaningful to the team since they created these artifacts together. Thus, Lean UX also defends the idea of using artifacts to support collaboration and creates a shared understanding necessary to create the team synergy.

6 Conclusion

Agile and UCD methods aim to design and produce quality software from different perspectives. Agile User-Centered Design approach attempts to close the gaps between these areas by bringing the most effective techniques, methods, and artifacts of each of them. Nonetheless, not only different aspects affect this integration, but also the communication between different professional profiles, such as designers and developers, have a high influence on it.

The study herein presented focused on the artifacts used to facilitate the communication between designers and developers in an Agile User-Centered Design approach. Through an online ethnography study applying a netnography method, it was possible to identify and understand the artifacts that facilitate communication, which event they are used, and what is the role they play to facilitate communication. The findings pointed out two major themes: (1) Artifacts Facilitate Communication and (2) Artifacts Support Collaboration. The themes interpretation and delineation show the usage of artifacts to facilitates teams' communication.

The outcomes of this study contribute to further studies regarding Agile User-Centered Design approach, integrating both Software Engineering and Human-Computer Interaction areas. Also, they highlighted how the artifact-facilitated communication ensues in the industry through a perspective of practitioners that participate in online communities.

Overall, contextual factors such as skill sets, experiences, and personalities of people involved impact on artifact-facilitated communication. Moreover, the choice of artifacts may vary over time, both as context change and as the team members learn what is effective for them. Additionally, team configuration and distributed teams influence on how the team's interactions and collaboration occurs, likewise including artifact-facilitated communication.

7 Future Work

A future study might extend the work presented in this paper. It became clear during the netnography analysis that communication factors impact the distributed teams, and artifacts that are used face-to-face cannot be applied to this team configuration. A member from the analyzed community even commented that distributed teams should be avoided whenever possible, due the complexity to manage communication between people *(Vicent, posted on Scrum Practitioners, March 1, 2015)*. Other members also commented that even the teams are distributed, it is important to get together for events such as planning and retrospectives, to work in the same space for some time, and to build a rapport among the team members.

Another point mentioned by several members is that planning meetings should involve the entire team, if possible in the same physical place if it is not possible video conferences can be used to have all team members understanding the work and sharing it. Thus, considering the distributed teams scenario, how are the distributed teams impacted by artifact-facilitated communication? Which are the applied artifacts when teams are distributed geographically?

Furthermore, it is possible to research the impact of different artifacts combination and interrelation; for instance, the sequence they are created and how they support the creation of new artifacts. Another perspective that can be studied is communication not only between developers and designers but also extended to reach the strategic levels of decision-making.

Acknowledgement. The authors would like to thank all the participants in this study. This research was achieved in cooperation with HP Brasil Indústria e Comércio de Equipamentos Eletrônicos LTDA. Using incentives of Brazilian Informatics Law (Law n° 8.2.48 of 1991).

References

1. Atlassian: Confluence (2018). https://www.atlassian.com/software/confluence
2. Bakardjieva, M., Feenberg, A.: Involving the virtual subjects. Ethics Inf. Technol. **2**, 233–240 (2001). https://doi.org/10.1023/A:1011454606534
3. Beyer, H., Holtzblatt, K., Baker, L.: An agile customer-centered method: rapid contextual design. In: Zannier, C., Erdogmus, H., Lindstrom, L. (eds.) XP/Agile Universe 2004. LNCS, vol. 3134, pp. 50–59. Springer, Heidelberg (2004). https://doi.org/10.1007/978-3-540-27777-4_6
4. Brhel, M., Meth, H., Maedche, A., Werder, K.: Exploring principles of user-centered agile software development: a literature review. Inf. Softw. Technol. **61**, 163–181 (2015)
5. Brown, J.M., Lindgaard, G., Biddle, R.: Collaborative events and shared artefacts: agile interaction designers and developers working toward common aims. In: Agile Conference, pp. 87–96 (2011). https://doi.org/10.1109/AGILE.2011.45
6. Brown, T.: Change by Design: How Design Thinking Transforms Organizations and Inspires Innovation. HarperBusiness, New York (2009)
7. Creswell, J.W.: Research Design. Qualitative, Quantitative and Mixed Methods Approaches, 4th edn. SAGE, Beverley Hills (2014). https://doi.org/10.2307/3152153
8. Da Silva, T.S., Martin, A., Maurer, F., Silveira, M.: User-centered design and agile methods: a systematic review. In: Agile Conference, pp. 77–86 (2011). https://doi.org/10.1109/AGILE.2011.24
9. Da Silva, T.S., Silveira, M.S., Maurer, F., Silveira, F.F.: The evolution of agile UXD. Inf. Softw. Technol. **102**, 1–5 (2018). https://doi.org/10.1016/j.infsof.2018.04.008
10. Ferreira, J., Noble, J., Biddle, R.: Agile development iterations and UI design. In: Agile Conference, pp. 50–58 (2007). https://doi.org/10.1109/AGILE.2007.8
11. Ferreira, J., Sharp, H., Robinson, H.: Values and assumptions shaping agile development and user experience design in practice. In: Sillitti, A., Martin, A., Wang, X., Whitworth, E. (eds.) XP 2010. LNBIP, vol. 48, pp. 178–183. Springer, Heidelberg (2010). https://doi.org/10.1007/978-3-642-13054-0_15
12. Fox, D., Sillito, J., Maurer, F.: Agile methods and user-centered design: how these two methodologies are being successfully integrated in industry. In: Agile Conference, pp. 63–72 (2008). https://doi.org/10.1109/Agile.2008.78

13. Garcia, A., Da Silva, T.S., Silveira, M.: Artifacts for agile user-centered design: a systematic mapping. In: Annual Hawaii International Conference on System Sciences (2016)
14. Gothelf, J.: Lean UX, Applying Lean Principles to Improve User Experience. O'Reilly Media Inc., Beijing (2015)
15. Hartson, R., Pyla, P.: The UX Book. Elsevier Inc., Waltham (2012). https://doi.org/10.1007/s13398-014-0173-7.2
16. InVision: InVision (2018). https://www.invisionapp.com/
17. Kozinets, R.V.: The field behind the screen: using netnography for marketing research in online communities. J. Mark. Res. **39**(1), 61–72 (2002). https://doi.org/10.1509/jmkr.39.1.61.18935
18. Kozinets, R.V.: Netnography: Redefined, 2nd edn. SAGE, Beverley Hills (2015)
19. LinkedIn: LinkedIn Groups Terms of Service (2017). https://www.linkedin.com/legal/more-groups-terms
20. Loanzon, E., Provenzola, J.P., Siriwannangkul, B., Al Mallak, M.: Netnography: Evolution, trends, and implications as a fuzzy front end tool. In: 2013 Proceedings of Technology Management in the IT-Driven Services (PICMET), PICMET 2013, pp. 1572–1593 (2013)
21. Malinen, S.: Understanding user participation in online communities: A systematic literature review of empirical studies. Comput. Human Behav. **46**, 228–238 (2015). https://doi.org/10.1016/j.chb.2015.01.004
22. NVivo: NVivo qualitative data analysis Software; QSR International Pvt. Ltd. (2017)
23. Rotman, D., Preece, J., He, Y., Druin, A.: Extreme ethnography: challenges for research in large scale online environments. In: iCOnference, pp. 207–214 (2012). https://doi.org/10.1145/2132176.2132203. http://dl.acm.org/citation.cfm?id=2132203
24. Salah, D., Paige, R., Cairns, P.: A practitioner perspective on integrating agile and user centred design. In: Proceedings of the 28th International BCS Human Computer Interaction Conference on HCI 2014 - Sand, Sea and Sky - Holiday HCI, pp. 100–109 (2014). https://doi.org/10.14236/ewic/hci2014.11
25. Salah, D., Paige, R.F., Cairns, P.: A Systematic Literature Review for Agile Development Processes and User Centred Design Integration. In: International Conference on Evaluation and Assessment in Software Engineering, pp. 1–10 (2014). https://doi.org/10.1145/2601248.2601276
26. Schön, E.M., Thomaschewski, J., Escalona, M.J.: Agile requirements engineering: a systematic literature review. Comput. Stand. Interfaces **49**, 79–91 (2017). https://doi.org/10.1016/j.csi.2016.08.011
27. Schwaber, K., Beedle, M.: Principles behind the agile manifesto (2001). http://agilemanifesto.org/principles.html
28. Schwaber, K., Sutherland, J.: The Scrum Guide. Scrum. Org and ScrumInc, p. 17 (2017). https://doi.org/10.1053/j.jrn.2009.08.012. http://www.scrumguides.org/docs/scrumguide/v1/Scrum-Guide-US.pdf
29. Sharp, H., Robinson, H., Petre, M.: The role of physical artefacts in agile software development: two complementary perspectives. Interact. Comput. **21**(1–2), 108–116 (2009). https://doi.org/10.1016/j.intcom.2008.10.006
30. Sy, D.: Adapting usability investigations for agile user-centered design. J. Usability Stud. **2**(3), 112–132 (2007)

Large-Scale Agile

The Product Owner in Large-Scale Agile: An Empirical Study Through the Lens of Relational Coordination Theory

Marthe Berntzen[1(✉)], Nils Brede Moe[2], and Viktoria Stray[1,2]

[1] University of Oslo, Gaustadalléen 23B, 0373 Oslo, Norway
{marthenb, stray}@ifi.uio
[2] SINTEF, Strindveien 4, 7465 Trondheim, Norway
{nils.b.moe, viktoria.stray}@sintef.no

Abstract. In agile software development, a core responsibility of the product owner (PO) is to communicate business needs to the development team. In large-scale agile software development projects, many teams work toward an overall outcome, but they also need to manage interdependencies and coordinate efficiently. In such settings, POs need to coordinate knowledge about project status and goal attainment both within and across the development teams. Previous research has shown that the PO assumes a wide set of roles. Still, our knowledge about how POs coordinate amongst themselves and with their teams in large-scale agile is limited. In this case study, we explore PO coordination in a large-scale development program through the theoretical lens of Relational Coordination Theory. Our findings suggest that (1) coordination varies depending on the context of each PO, (2) a focus on achieving high-quality communication changes coordination over time, and (3) unscheduled coordination enables of high-quality communication.

Keywords: Large-scale agile · Agile software development · Coordination · Relational Coordination Theory · Product owner

1 Introduction

Coordination is key to large-scale agile software development projects [4, 6]. In large-scale agile projects, the number of interdependencies requires the collective input of multiple teams and individuals, often with nonoverlapping knowledge sets. Because of frequent changes, size, and complexity, large-scale agile projects have a high level of uncertainty. In such high uncertainty contexts, it is more important to control output (e.g., by setting goals and targets) than to control behavior (e.g., through rules and programs). This can be achieved by relying on continuous feedback and mutual adjustment [20]. Furthermore, the high levels of uncertainty and dependencies in large agile projects require subcentral unscheduled coordination and the need for coordination mechanisms to continually emerge [22]. Additionally, delivering value frequently requires work and knowledge coordination on different levels (e.g., the program, project, and team levels). Teams need to manage dependencies with other teams, experts, managers and stakeholders [26]. To achieve effective coordination,

P. Kruchten et al. (Eds.): XP 2019, LNBIP 355, pp. 121–136, 2019.
https://doi.org/10.1007/978-3-030-19034-7_8

participants must be connected through relationships of shared goals, knowledge and mutual respect [12, 13].

Inter-team coordination is one mechanism for managing dependencies in large-scale agile. Dingsøyr et al. [6] described 14 inter-team coordination mechanisms in a large-scale software project, while Stray et al. [28] identified 20 mechanisms (11 synchronization activities and nine synchronization artifacts). Paasivaara et al. [24] found that the product owner (PO) and the PO team were critical in assisting with inter-team coordination. To understand coordination in large-scale agile, the PO role and the coordination mechanisms related to this role are crucial to understand. To the best of our knowledge, the existing literature does not address how POs coordinate work within and across teams in large-scale agile.

Motivated by the importance of coordination in large-scale agile and the need to understand the coordination in PO teams, our research question is as follows: *How do product owners coordinate work in large-scale agile?*

The study was conducted in a large-scale software development program, here referred to as the PubTrans program, where 13 development teams work toward the same overall goals. Here, the teams rely on agile methods of choice. Some use a Scrum-based approach, while others use Kanban or some combination of agile practices. As such, there is no one unified agile approach across the teams. Furthermore, while POs coordinate with a range of stakeholders, our focus in this paper is on how POs coordinate with each other and with their teams. The remainder of the paper is organized as follows. Section 2 outlines related work. In Sect. 3, we describe our research methodology. In Sect. 4, we present our findings, further discussed in Sect. 5 which also concludes the paper with a summary of major findings.

2 Background and Related Work

2.1 The Product Owner Role in Large-Scale Agile

Agile approaches focus on self-management, emergent processes, and informal coordinating mechanisms. The software team achieves coordination through the simple process of informal communication [8]. Large-scale projects, defined as projects with two to nine teams, or very large-scale projects, with more than 10 teams, introduce the need for new or adjusted agile practices [6]. When scaling up, several challenges arise, such as managing a larger number of stakeholders, keeping to the agile principles and coordinating the different teams while maintaining an informal approach to communication [4–6, 8]. In large software projects, informal communication can take place within teams, between groups of managers, or between groups of representatives acting on behalf of their teams.

Most agile methods are concerned with good customer relationships, where the customer should be involved, preferably on-site and co-located with the development teams and project management [1, 19]. In Scrum, the PO is defined as a person who gathers and prioritizes requirements and interacts with the customer [25]. In other agile approaches, such as Kanban and XP, the role is not defined [19], but similar activities are performed. In the PubTrans program, in which we conducted the study, the PO role is used, although the program does not use Scrum as the only agile approach. A PO needs to understand what should be developed and translate and communicate these business needs to the development team [1, 19]. The PO defines and prioritizes the features of the product, decides on release dates and content, and is responsible for the profitability of the product [29]. The development team is responsible for designing, testing, and deploying systems, while the PO knows what system should be built.

In large-scale agile, one strategy for scaling the PO function is for the POs to form teams to gather and prioritize inter-team requirements in the face of conflicting and competing business needs [1]. The POs on these teams can either share responsibility or be responsible for a subset of product features [24]. Bass [1] identified nine different functions that POs have in large-scale projects, which included architectural coordination, assessing risk, and ensuring project compliance with corporate guidelines and policies. As such, the PO role is a complex role with a broad set of responsibilities, which in large-scale settings may need to coordinate complex, interdependent tasks and team goals contributing to the overall goals of the software project.

2.2 Relational Coordination Theory

Relational Coordination Theory (RCT) is an established and empirically validated theory that originated from research conducted in the airline industry in the 1990s [12]. RCT holds that relationships are central to coordination toward common outcomes. An assumption is that relational coordination is stronger in more horizontally designed organizational structures [14], which is important to large-scale agile [7, 23].

Relational coordination is defined as "a mutually reinforcing process of interaction between communication and relationships carried out for the purpose of task integration" [13]. Gittell [12] proposed that relationships provide the necessary bandwidth for coordinating highly interdependent work in uncertain and time-constrained settings and that effective coordination in these settings is carried out through relationships of *shared knowledge, shared goals, mutual respect*, and *high-quality communication,* described in the below sections. These three concepts are mutually facilitated by frequent, timely, accurate and problem-solving communication [11, 12]. Because large-scale agile projects are characterized by high levels of interdependence, uncertainty, and time pressure, and because autonomy is a central tenet in agile [4], we believe RCT is an interesting theoretical lens for studying coordination in large-scale agile.

Shared knowledge informs participants of how their tasks, as well as the tasks of others, contribute to the overall work process [12]. However, individuals and groups working on different functional tasks often reside in different "thought worlds", which can hamper effective coordination because of the lack of insight about others' work [9]. Drawing on sensemaking theory [32] and transactive memory theory [18], RCT suggests that a shared understanding of the work process and a common understanding of each other's areas of expertise across roles facilitate the coordination of knowledge [12]. When participants know how their tasks fit with other tasks in the work process, they will better understand who will be impacted by changes; in other words, they will understand who needs to know what, why, and when [11].

In large-scale system development, no one can know everything. Therefore, teams' and peoples' knowledge networks are essential. Šmite et al. [26] found the size of teams' knowledge networks in a large-scale agile company to be dependent on the number of years the individual team members had been at the company, in addition to which forums the individual participated in.

Shared Goals. A goal may be seen as shared to the extent that employees across functional areas are aware of the same goals and have a similar understanding of why they are important [12]. Thus, they play an essential role in effective coordination by enabling people to accomplish a set of complex interdependent tasks [30, 31], a common characteristic in large-scale development projects, where autonomous teams work on different parts of an overall product.

In large-scale agile, the collective goal of the project or program can be broken down into a goal hierarchy. The goal hierarchy is important for teams in large-scale agile to share a distal goal while the individual teams pursue their more proximal goals. Nyrud and Stray [23] found that the demo meeting and backlog grooming were essential in this context because they provided an arena for creating common expectations and understanding the finished product – shared goals within and outside of the team. Moe et al. [21] found that when managers set goals in a large-scale project without involving the team, it resulted in team members being uncertain about the goal of the project.

Table 1. Elements of relational coordination based on the synthesis by Gittell [12].

Relational coordination	Definition	Specific examples
Shared knowledge	Informs participants of how their own and others' tasks contribute to the overall work process A shared understanding of the work process and others' areas of expertise facilitate knowledge coordination	Knowledge about overall delivery milestones; knowledge about which team is working on what, when
Shared goals	Direct the attention and effort of individuals and groups Transcend functional goals of different work units and enable unified effort toward a collective outcome	Keeping in mind overall program goals while working on team goals
Mutual respect	Valuing others' contributions and considering the impact of their own actions on the work of others	Considering the impact of one team's work on another; acknowledging differences in priorities; trusting others' decisions and work
High-quality communication	Communication that is frequent, accurate, timely and problem-solving in nature	Keeping meetings relevant, sending and receiving information at the right time with the right content; constructive feedback

Mutual Respect. Finally, for effective coordination to occur, employees should be connected by relationships of mutual respect between the coordinating parties. According to RCT, mutual respect reinforces the inclination to act in accordance with the overall work process by establishing a middle ground [12].

A study of large-scale Scrum found that responding respectfully to each other fostered psychology safety, which is important for agile teams [27]. In a study of a large-scale project Moe et al. [21] found that external stakeholders approached team members directly, despite members expressing that it disrupts the work. Bypassing the established process reduced team progress.

High-Quality Communication. According to RCT, shared knowledge, shared goals and mutual respect should mutually reinforce high-quality (that is, frequent, accurate, timely and problem-solving) communication [10–12]. This should, according to RCT, contribute to the overall quality of the coordination of the work process.

A survey on coordination in large-scale software teams found the importance of good personal relationships for coordination [2]. Dingsøyr et al. [6] found the importance of communication in large-scale agile to be both informal and formal, happening both in groups and by two people meeting. Furthermore, they found that an open work area supported fast communication in informal meetings. In relation to RCT, an open work environment enables high-quality communication, building shared goals, shared knowledge, and mutual respect in large projects.

Table 2. Data sources

Data	Description
Interviews	9 POs, 1 product manager, 1 development manager and 1 chief technology officer (CTO)
Observations	7 PO task board meetings (update task progress and discuss activities across teams), 2 PO weekly meetings, 5 weekly status meetings with one of the 13 teams, 2 retrospectives with one team, and one team leader retrospective. We facilitated one retrospective meeting during a PO workshop
Documents	Analyzed Slack logs from PO channel and one team channel

3 Method

We chose a case study approach [33], because case studies provide depth and detailed knowledge, and there is little research-based knowledge about how POs coordinate work in large-scale agile. We selected a case in which almost the whole development program was co-located in order to reduce the effects due to the distribution of teams. In the following, we refer to the case as the PubTrans program. The program started in 2016 and aims to develop a new platform supporting public transportation. The first author conducted fieldwork at the program and was given access to rich sources of data, including meetings, Slack[1] channels and documentation tools. In addition, the two other authors participated in site visits, workshops, and in two of the interviews.

[1] Slack is an electronic communication tool, trademark of Slack Technologies, www.slack.com.

3.1 Case Description

The PubTrans program has thirteen development teams ranging between five and fourteen team members working toward developing the same products. Each team is responsible for their part of the overall products. The PubTrans program can thus be classified as very large-scale agile [6]. In order to coordinate work within and across teams the program makes use of various electronic tools, such as Slack, Jira, and Confluence; material artefacts such as task boards; and various scheduled and unscheduled meetings. The development teams are autonomous to the extent that they may choose freely how they go about solving their tasks and rely on agile methods of choice. As such, there is no one unified agile approach across the teams. All teams include a team leader and a PO, but there is no defined Scrum Master role or any other roles specific to any one agile method. The POs are situated within each team and are considered part of the development teams in the PubTrans program. Seven of the POs have one team, whereas two have three teams each. The POs have varied backgrounds; some have a technical (e.g., engineering) background and have been working in the product domain for several years, while others came from industries such as marketing and business development.

3.2 Data Collection

We conducted twelve interviews in October 2018. The interviews were semi-structured, and we allowed the conversations to develop naturally as the participants unfolded their stories. The duration of the interviews was between 30 and 60 min (average of 40 min). All interviews were tape-recorded based on participants' consent and were later transcribed by the first author. We spent a total of eighteen days with on-site observation and participated in several PubTrans activities, described in Table 2.

3.3 Data Analysis

When analyzing the data material, we relied on data triangulation, including observation, interviews, and documentation as data sources (see Table 2). Our rationale for the choice of these data sources for the study of PO coordination was that by interviewing the participants, we gained access to their own understanding of their work routines. Analyzing the observations and documentation such as Slack logs shed light on the accounts given by the interviewees and provided context to their statements. As such, data triangulation was likely to contribute to strengthening our findings and conclusions through increased accuracy and compellability [33].

Through our engagement with the data, RCT emerged as an appropriate lens for examining PO coordination in a large-scale agile setting. This is because RCT is a suitable theory for organizational contexts characterized by high levels of interdependence, outcome uncertainty, and time criticality [11, 12] typical in large-scale development. We coded the data using Nvivo according to the coordination mechanisms used by the POs (Table 3) and how these mechanisms related to the RCT concepts defined in Table 1. The coding process proceeded as follows: First, all three authors coded parts of the material. Second, the authors discussed the material, resolving any disagreements. Third, the first author coded the material in more detail, followed by a second discussion of the analysis and results.

4 Results

Table 3 shows the main coordination mechanisms involving the POs. These were identified based on documentation of work routines from the PubTrans program, the interviews, and the authors' on-site observations. In the following, we describe a selection of these coordination mechanisms in relation to the relational coordination concepts of shared goals, shared knowledge, mutual respect, and high-quality communication.

Table 3. Product owner coordination mechanisms

Coordination mechanism	Between POs	PO and team
Product owner weekly meeting	x	
Product owner task board meeting	x	
Product owner workshop activities	x	
Unscheduled conversations	x	x
Slack	x	x
Jira	x	x
Confluence/wiki	x	x
Team status meetings		x
Team retrospectives		x
Internal team practices		x

4.1 Coordination Between POs

The weekly PO coordination meeting, facilitated by the product manager, enabled discussions on shared experiences and matters that came up during the previous week. For instance, POs discussed challenges with team processes or updated each other on external client issues. Having a weekly meeting contributed to communication that was problem-solving, accurate, and frequent. However, its content seemed to vary. One PO told us, "*There is no fixed, no defined agenda. We are supposed to talk about what is on our mind, and that is a very open question! [laughs]. It can be anything. So I think there have been some meetings that we have not gained so much from.*" The POs expressed different opinions regarding this weekly meeting. Some POs thought it was very useful, in particular for building shared knowledge and goals. Some thought that once a week was too frequent, because they wanted to spend more time with their team, whereas others felt there should have been more PO meetings like this because "*we don't have any places to meet to exchange experiences across teams, other than these Product Owner meetings.*" As such the meeting appeared to be an important coordination mechanism in relation to shared knowledge and goals.

Fig. 1. The PO task board meeting.

The bi-weekly task board meeting gathered the POs and relevant stakeholders. The meeting was typically facilitated by the product manager, CTO, or program management. All met in front of a large visual task board (Fig. 1) to update each other on their progress – current in-progress tasks and long-term delivery milestones. As such, this artefact provided all POs with shared knowledge of current goals and the status of the teams' various tasks.

The task board meeting was initially termed the "prioritization meeting," but according to the participants, this meeting did not meet its purpose. Rather than focusing on task prioritization, it was more of a reporting and updating meeting in which all POs simply reported on their teams' progress, and many talked for several minutes about their teams' internal tasks. Until recently, the meeting lasted one hour, and we observed how the POs struggled to pay attention to what others were saying as time went by. One PO said, "*If we compare hours spent [at this meeting] versus insights gained, it doesn't add up.*" Across several meetings, we observed that several sat down on the floor after a while, and some started looking at their phones, responding to messages and e-mails, rather than listening. During the interviews, some said that they felt bad for being disrespectful when they did not pay attention. Most of them, however, perceived the intention behind the meeting – updating each other on progress across teams – as useful and therefore wanted to keep the having meeting, but in a different format.

Unscheduled coordination between POs was common and was done just by walking over to each other in the open office environment. One PO explained, "*I seek out people at their desks… It is something about it, one thing is to communicate in writing [e.g., sending an email], but in my experience, you accomplish more by just talking to people.*" Sometimes a PO would also call a spontaneous meeting, inviting only those that needed to be part of the particular coordination activity.

Moreover, the POs have a dedicated Slack channel, created in March 2018, for knowledge sharing and quick updates regarding the goal attainment of the different POs' teams. During the interviews and from examining the Slack logs, it became clear that this channel was used to varying degrees by the different POs. Primarily, it was used for frequent and timely information updates, such as notifying each other of absence, or uploading documents such as plans and presentations, rather than for knowledge sharing and ensuring the attainment of shared goal across teams. For instance, one particular day in September 2018, two POs discussed whether to hold the weekly PO meeting:

PO 1: *"Does this mean you will not be here today either @PO 3? [PO 4] said he too would be absent today, and so is [the Product Manager], and when there is so few of us, is there a point in going through the things we agreed all of us should be part of? Should we skip the meeting?"*
PO 2: *"I'd like to meet those of you who are present, but we can postpone the planned common PO discussion theme"*
PO 1: *"We'll meet as planned then."*

The POs also use the Slack channel more informally. During a PO workshop, one posted, *"This is the smallest hotel room I ever saw! You'll find me in the bar."* This social and informal communication may indicate mutual respect and a sense of community among the POs, a mutual respect that is perhaps reinforced by the coordination activities they perform throughout the year.

The PO quarterly workshop gathers the POs normally overnight at an off-site location. Prior to these quarterly workshops, all POs attend a set of preparation meetings with the product manager. This is done to gain a sense of shared goals and knowledge before the workshop in order to work more efficiently together. As such, the quarterly workshop contributes to both shared knowledge and shared goals between POs at an overall program level, but it may also reinforce mutual respect between the POs as they get to know each other better. As stated by one of the POs, "*It is... both professionally useful, but it's also about getting together. It is rather social, actually."* The topics of the workshops depend on upcoming issues in the PubTrans program, for instance, discussing the potential implications of overall program strategies in relation to specific team and cross-team deliveries in the upcoming quarter. Another theme could be improving their own work processes, such as inter-team coordination.

In late fall 2018, two of the authors joined the POs for one such workshop with the product manager and eight of the nine POs. At this workshop, we facilitated a retrospective with the POs focusing on coordination efficiency. One outcome of this retrospective was four action points they believed would improve the coordination. First, in relation to the quarterly PO workshop, some POs expressed that they would prefer if the workshops were one full workday, with no overnight stay, as some felt it took up too much time. This led to some discussion, but eventually, although other POs appreciated the change of scenery, they agreed to try the next workshop as a one-day workshop. This demonstrates that although the POs do not always agree or have the same preferences, they are willing to adjust to each other, which may indicate mutual respect.

A second action point was to move all written communication to Slack rather than use it as a supplement to e-mail. After the workshop, we observed a change in the communication in the dedicated PO Slack channel. Communication in the channel became more frequent and contributed more toward shared goals and knowledge among the POs. For instance, the POs started to share "best practice" tips and work routines on Slack, as well as agenda points for the weekly PO meeting. A third action point was to increase the focus on a clearer agenda for the weekly PO meeting. As such, the communication at this meeting might have become more accurate, which in turn contributed to reinforcing shared knowledge and goals. Finally, the fourth action point was to reduce the length of the task board meeting from one hour to 20 min and to focus only on updates relevant for at least two thirds of the attendants. In the following three meetings, we observed that the new format led to communication that was more accurate and timely.

4.2 Coordination Between POs and Their Teams

We found differences in how the POs coordinate with their teams. Some POs have well-established practices and close, regular interaction with the team, while others have a more loosely defined approach with a high level of delegation. Regardless of their level of interaction with their team(s), the POs aim to communicate the vision and priorities for the teams' work such that all team members share knowledge about the team's own goal, as well as an understanding about other teams' work.

Coordination with the team leader was a key process for most POs. Several POs spoke respectfully about their team leaders, seeing them as having both good people skills and good technical skills. The POs described the team leader as an essential link for coordination with the team, who often joined the POs in the decision-making. One PO explained, "*We go through all priorities together. [...] we are rarely in disagreement. And if there is... it could, for instance, be that I have knowledge from the business side that calls for different priorities, then I make the decision, but normally we agree.*"

During a team retrospective, several team members expressed the importance of the PO and the team leader in shielding the team from external pressure and in making sure they knew which tasks to work on. This may indicate both the importance of these roles in relation to shared knowledge and what many POs found important: respect for the developers' time and their role in the overall goal attainment.

Stand-up meetings with the team varied in frequency. Some teams had stand-up meetings every day, others once or twice a week, and some on a more ad hoc basis, for instance through sharing task-related information on team Slack channels. The stand-up meeting was an important meeting for sharing knowledge and solving issues. A PO explained the challenge of just listening and then being an active participant in the meeting: *"I want to be part of the stand-ups, as I want to pay attention to what they are doing [...] but then they expect me to say something, and I feel that I have to, otherwise it is all 'top-down.'"* He further explained that he wanted to listen and learn from the team, but at the same time, he was not sure what he could bring to the meeting because he saw his work tasks as very different from the team's and did not find it relevant to talk about those tasks.

Retrospectives with the team varied in frequency and process. When the team members got together to discuss their work during the previous period, the meeting contributed to strengthening shared knowledge about the teamwork processes and shared team goals in that the teams analyzed, discussed, and adjusted their own practices. Mutual respect among the participants might also have been strengthened as they shared their thoughts and perspectives. Many POs left it up to the team leader to facilitate team retrospectives, while some took a more active role.

Furthermore, the retrospectives provided important information as to how the POs could adjust their coordination practices toward the team. One PO explained, *"I thought me and the team leader were good at bringing information back to the developers. As it turned out during our last retrospective…we were not! And we are going to do something about that."* This illustrates the importance of conducting retrospectives so that the team can mutually adjust to better accommodate each other. The willingness to adjust based on feedback may also indicate respect toward the team members through acknowledging the impact a lack of information could have on their work.

Unscheduled coordination with the team appeared important for fast decision-making. Much of the coordination with the team occurred during spontaneous conversations and meetings, and many decisions at the team level were made during such unscheduled conversations. According to one PO, *"If there are decisions to be made in relation to choice of technology or similar, normally it would be me, the team leader and some developer… we just decide then and there […]."* This illustrates how shared knowledge about decisions are reached through accurate, timely, problem-solving communication.

Slack was also extensively used among the teams in the PubTrans program; almost all teams appeared to have closed private channels where the whole team, including the PO, discussed internal matters. In addition, there was a range of public channels for different topics. While Slack was seen as an invaluable source of knowledge and information, for some it became overwhelming. One PO of three teams explained, "*I spent some time adjusting from e-mail to Slack. […] There are so many channels! It is so much to pay attention to and read, it can actually be a bit too much.*" The same PO further explained that Slack was not used for making larger decisions, but that overall, Slack was a great place to keep the discussion going on technical issues and everyday work-related matters.

5 Discussion and Conclusion

The PO has an important role in agile development, often performing a complex set of activities [1, 19]. Our findings underscore the importance of relationships for efficient coordination among POs and between the PO and the team. We have attempted to shed light on PO coordination through the concepts of RCT. We now turn to discussing our research question, "*How do product owners coordinate work in agile?*" Our analysis of PO coordination in a large-scale agile development company shows that (1) coordination varies depending on the context of each PO (type of team, experience, preferences), (2) a focus on high-quality communication changes coordination over time, and (3) unscheduled coordination enables high-quality communication.

5.1 Coordination Practices Varies Between the POs

During our observations and in the interviews, we noticed several differences in PO coordination both among each other and toward their teams. This may be due to differences in coordination preferences among the POs, as well as the number of teams a PO is responsible for. It may also be due to the autonomy the teams have in choosing their approach to agile methods leading to a variety in coordination mechanisms between the POs and their teams. The differences in routines on each team may have made it more challenging to coordinate across teams and between POs, and to ensure a shared understanding of goals among the POs and across and the different teams.

High-quality communication reinforces shared goals and knowledge [12–14]. The POs communicating frequently with their teams and with other POs, experienced such coordination to be beneficial, which then lead to even more frequent communication. Furthermore, how long the POs had known the teams and each other varied, which also might influence how frequent a PO communicate with other POs and their teams. In relation to this, Šmite et al. [26] found that the frequency of communication and the number of actors a person coordinated with depended on how long the person had been at the company. The longer the experience, the more frequent the communication, which indicates that coordination becomes more accurate because of knowledge about who knows what [26].

5.2 Changes in Coordination Over Time

Several of the coordination mechanisms involving the POs, such as the task board meeting and Slack communication, changed during the period of the study. Our findings are consistent with those of Jarzabkowski et al. [15], who argued that coordinating mechanisms do not appear as ready-to-use techniques but are formed as actors go about the process of coordinating. Furthermore, coordinating mechanisms are not stable entities but emerge through their use in ongoing interactions [15].

Throughout our data collection period, the main driver for change in a coordination mechanism was the focus on continuous improvement. During the retrospective, several action points were set, and we observed how coordination mechanisms were improved; for example, the task board meeting, was improved by more timely and accurate communication in that the meeting became shorter and more focused. We also observed a change in the PO Slack channel toward more frequent and problem-solving communication, for instance by using the channel to share agenda points for meetings and best practices from teams.

5.3 Unscheduled and Frequent Coordination Enables High-Quality Communication

As a supplement to the scheduled meetings, we found that unscheduled meetings appeared to be an important driver of high-quality communication in the PubTrans program for coordination on a daily basis. Our results indicate that unscheduled meetings and seeking out people at their desks are important for efficient day-to-day coordination. We also found that the use of Slack enabled timely, frequent, and unscheduled coordination between subsets of people, such as between the POs or within teams. As such, our results indicate that standardizing the communication channels on one digital platform contributes to shared knowledge across POs and teams.

Unscheduled conversations and meetings contribute to strengthening the shared knowledge and goals and can be seen as timely and problem-solving communication, in particular when only a subset of the POs needs to coordinate. In line with our findings, previous research supports the importance of both formal and informal communication, both in groups and by two people meeting, and that an open work area in large-scale agile supports fast communication in informal meetings [6].

5.4 Implications for Theory and Future Research

As can be derived from our results and this discussion, the elements of RCT are evident in the coordination mechanisms used by the POs in the PubTrans program. The theory, therefore, appears suitable for studying coordination in a large-scale agile setting. According to RCT, organizational change is seen as intertwined with the relationships between roles. Research that explores organizational change to further develop the theory has been encouraged [11]. Furthermore, according to RCT, relationships between roles are central for coordination [11–13]. In her work on the airline and health industries, which also represent large-scale settings, Gittell [12, 13] observed that the companies that performed best had higher levels of relational coordination between roles, which was explained by the differences between the studied companies in terms of shared knowledge, goals and mutual respect. In line with this, our results indicate that frequent communication and interaction between POs is important for coordination, also in the PubTrans program. Furthermore, our results indicate that coordination between the PO role and the team leader role is key for high-quality communication, knowledge sharing, and updates about goal attainment with the teams. While this study contributes to the understanding of PO coordination, this study is the first to utilize RCT in large-scale agile for understanding PO coordination. Therefore, more studies from other programs are needed to make comparisons between large-scale agile programs.

Future research could also investigate whether the number of teams for which the POs are responsible influences their coordination practices. It might be that the more teams, the more coordination is needed on each PO's part. Finally, while POs coordinate with a range of stakeholders, including customer representatives, management, and architects, our focus in this paper was on how POs coordinate with each other and with their teams. An interesting topic for future research would thus be to expand the focus to investigate how POs coordinate their work with other stakeholders.

5.5 Implications for Practice

We believe that our study has the following main implications for PO coordination. First, we recommend focusing more on unscheduled meetings rather than scheduled, time-consuming meetings, as also suggested by other research on large-scale agile [22, 28]. Established frameworks such as the Scaled Agile Framework and Large-Scale Scrum recommend a rather fixed meeting structure [16, 17]. In contrast, our results indicate that unscheduled meetings are important enablers of spontaneous coordination that contribute to shared goals, shared knowledge and mutual respect in large-scale agile. Such meetings are facilitated by open work spaces and co-located teams [6].

Second, we recommend agreeing on a common communication infrastructure, such as Slack, for swift communication and information sharing, but also for the POs to have their own space where they can discuss outside of the scheduled meeting arenas. Third, frequent meetings and workshops in which POs can discuss goals and share knowledge are necessary. However, such meetings should have a clear, predefined agenda to ensure efficient use of time and resources. Fourth, scheduled workshops throughout the year contribute to forming social bonds between the POs supporting relational coordination. Finally, we advise regular retrospectives focusing on improving coordination, strengthening shared knowledge and goals, and reinforcing mutual respect and trust within the PO group.

5.6 Limitations and Concluding Remarks

One limitation of our research is the reliance on a single case. As such, the general criticisms of single-case studies [3, 33] apply to our study. However, our rationale for choosing the PubTrans program as our case was that it represents a setting in which large-scale agile has been applied since the outset of the program in 2016. Furthermore, because the program is largely co-located and the POs are considered part of the teams, the case provided a unique setting for exploring how POs coordinate in large-scale agile settings. A further limitation relates to the reliance on semi-structured interviews as a major source of data collection and analysis [3]. However, data triangulation made it possible to study the phenomena of interest from different viewpoints, as well as during the changes we observed, which should serve to strengthen our results [33]. We facilitated a PO retrospective in which concrete action points were formed, indicating that we did affect how work processes are conducted in the PubTrans program, at least for the time being. However, the PubTrans program already had a high awareness of challenges with inter-team coordination before we started our research. Therefore, we do not believe our presence has biased the results.

On a concluding note, in this paper, we applied a relational coordination lens to the question of how POs coordinate work in large-scale agile system development. Our findings suggest that the PO contributes to shared knowledge and goals both within and across teams, and that efficient coordination also includes relationships of mutual respect and high-quality communication. This is in line with previous findings from research using RCT; however, this study is the first to investigate relational coordination in a large-scale system development setting. As such, this study makes way for future research that can contribute both to the further development of RCT as well as improving our understanding of coordination in large-scale agile development.

Acknowledgements. This research was supported by the Research Council of Norway through the research project Autonomous teams (A-teams) project, under Grant Number 267704.

References

1. Bass, J.M.: How product owner teams scale agile methods to large distributed enterprises. Empir. Softw. Eng. **20**(6), 1525–1557 (2015)
2. Begel, A., Nagappan, N., Poile, C., Layman, L.: Coordination in large-scale software teams. In: Proceedings of the 2009 ICSE Workshop on Cooperative and Human Aspects on Software Engineering, pp. 1–7. IEEE Computer Society (2009)
3. Diefenbach, T.: Are case studies more than sophisticated storytelling?: methodological problems of qualitative empirical research mainly based on semi-structured interviews. Qual. Quant. **43**(6), 875–894 (2009)
4. Dikert, K., Paasivaara, M., Lassenius, C.: Challenges and success factors for large-scale agile transformations: a systematic literature review. J. Syst. Softw. **119**, 87–108 (2016)
5. Dingsøyr, T., Moe, N.B.: Towards principles of large-scale agile development. In: Dingsøyr, T., Moe, N.B., Tonelli, R., Counsell, S., Gencel, C., Petersen, K. (eds.) XP 2014. LNBIP, vol. 199, pp. 1–8. Springer, Cham (2014). https://doi.org/10.1007/978-3-319-14358-3_1
6. Dingsøyr, T., Moe, N.B., Fægri, T.E., Seim, E.A.: Exploring software development at the very large-scale: a revelatory case study and research agenda for agile method adaptation. Empir. Softw. Eng. **23**(1), 490–520 (2018)
7. Dingsøyr, T., Moe, N.B., Seim, E.A.: Coordinating knowledge work in multi-team programs: findings from a large-scale agile development program. Proj. Manag. J. **49**, 64–77 (2018)
8. Dingsøyr, T., Nerur, S., Balijepally, V., Moe, N.B.: A decade of agile methodologies: towards explaining agile software development. J. Syst. Softw. **85**(6), 1213–1221 (2012)
9. Dougherty, D.: Interpretive barriers to successful product innovation in large firms. Organ. Sci. **3**(2), 179–202 (1992)
10. Gittell, J.H.: Coordinating mechanisms in care provider groups: relational coordination as a mediator and input uncertainty as a moderator of performance effects. Manag. Sci. **48**(11), 1408–1426 (2002)
11. Gittell, J.H.: New directions for relational coordination theory. In: Spreitzer, G.M., Cameron, K.S. (eds.) The Oxford Handbook of Positive Organizational Scholarship, pp. 400–412. Oxford University Press, Oxford (2012)
12. Gittell, J.H.: Relational coordination: coordinating work through relationships of shared goals, shared knowledge and mutual respect. In: Kyriakiduo, O., Ézbilgin, M. (eds.) Relational Perspectives in Organizational Studies: A Research Companion, pp. 74–94. Edward Elgar Publishing, Cheltenham (2006)
13. Gittell, J.H.: Relationships between service providers and their impact on customers. J. Serv. Res. **4**(4), 299–311 (2002)
14. Gittell, J.H., Douglass, A.: Relational bureaucracy: structuring reciprocal relationships into roles. Acad. Manag. Rev. **37**(4), 709–733 (2012)
15. Jarzabkowski, P.A., Lê, J.K., Feldman, M.S.: Toward a theory of coordinating: creating coordinating mechanisms in practice. Organ. Sci. **23**(4), 907–927 (2012)
16. Larman, C., Vodde, B.: Large-Scale Scrum: More with LeSS. Addison-Wesley Professional, Boston (2016)
17. Leffingwell, D.: SAFe 4.0 Reference Guide: Scaled Agile Framework for Lean Software and Systems Engineering. Addison-Wesley Professional, Boston (2016)
18. Liang, D.W., Moreland, R., Argote, L.: Group versus individual training and group performance: the mediating role of transactive memory. Pers. Soc. Psychol. Bull. **21**(4), 384–393 (1995)
19. Martin, A., Biddle, R., Noble, J.: An ideal customer: a grounded theory of requirements elicitation, communication and acceptance on agile projects. In: Dingsøyr, T., Dybå, T., Moe, N. (eds.) Agile software development, pp. 111–141. Springer, Heidelberg (2010). https://doi.org/10.1007/978-3-642-12575-1_6

20. Mintzberg, H.: Mintzberg on Management: Inside Our Strange World of Organizations. Simon and Schuster, New York (1989)
21. Moe, N.B., Dahl, B., Stray, V., Karlsen, L.S., Schjødt-Osmo, S.: Team autonomy in large-scale agile. In: Proceedings of the 52nd Hawaii International Conference on System Sciences, pp. 6997–7006 (2019)
22. Moe, N.B., Dingsøyr, T., Rolland, K.: To schedule or not to schedule? An investigation of meetings as an inter-team coordination mechanism in large-scale agile software development. Int. J. Inf. Syst. Proj. Manag. **6**(3), 45–59 (2018)
23. Nyrud, H., Stray, V.: Inter-team coordination mechanisms in large-scale agile. In: Proceedings of the XP2017 Scientific Workshops, p. 16. ACM (2017)
24. Paasivaara, M., Lassenius, C., Heikkila, V.T.: Inter-team coordination in large-scale globally distributed scrum: do scrum-of-scrums really work? In: Proceedings of the ACM-IEEE International Symposium on Empirical Software Engineering and Measurement, pp. 235–238 (2012)
25. Schwaber, K., Beedle, M.: Agile Software Development with Scrum. Prentice Hall, Upper Saddle River (2002)
26. Šmite, D., Moe, N.B., Šāblis, A., Wohlin, C.: Software teams and their knowledge networks in large-scale software development. Inf. Softw. Technol. **86**, 71–86 (2017)
27. Stray, V., Fægri, T.E., Moe, N.B.: Exploring norms in agile software teams. In: Abrahamsson, P., Jedlitschka, A., Nguyen Duc, A., Felderer, M., Amasaki, S., Mikkonen, T. (eds.) PROFES 2016. LNCS, vol. 10027, pp. 458–467. Springer, Cham (2016). https://doi.org/10.1007/978-3-319-49094-6_31
28. Stray, V., Moe, N.B., Aasheim, A.: Dependency management in large-scale agile: a case study of DevOps teams. In: Proceedings of the 52nd Hawaii International Conference on System Sciences, pp. 7007–7016 (2019)
29. Sutherland, J., Schwaber, K.: The scrum papers: nuts, bolts, and origins of an agile process (2007)
30. Saavedra, R., Earley, P.C., Van Dyne, L.: Complex interdependence in task-performing groups. J. Appl. Psychol. **78**(1), 61–72 (1993)
31. Wageman, R.: Interdependence and group effectiveness. Adm. Sci. Q. **49**(1), 145–180 (1995)
32. Weick, K.E.: The collapse of sensemaking in organizations: the Mann Gulch disaster. Adm. Sci. Q. **38**(4), 628–652 (1993)
33. Yin, R.K.: Case Study Research: Design and Methods. Sage, Thousand Oaks (2002)

Using Social Network Analysis to Investigate the Collaboration Between Architects and Agile Teams: A Case Study of a Large-Scale Agile Development Program in a German Consumer Electronics Company

Ömer Uludağ(✉), Martin Kleehaus, Soner Erçelik, and Florian Matthes

Technische Universität München (TUM),
85748 Garching bei München, Germany
{oemer.uludag,martin.kleehaus,soner.ercelik,matthes}@tum.de

Abstract. Over the past two decades, agile methods have transformed and brought unique changes to software development practice by strongly emphasizing team collaboration, customer involvement, and change tolerance. The success of agile methods for small, co-located teams has inspired organizations to increasingly use them on a larger scale to build complex software systems. The scaling of agile methods poses new challenges such as inter-team coordination, dependencies to other existing environments or distribution of work without a defined architecture. The latter is also the reason why large-scale agile development has been subject to criticism since it neglects detailed assistance on software architecting. Although there is a growing body of literature on large-scale agile development, literature documenting the collaboration between architects and agile teams in such development efforts is still scarce. As little research has been conducted on this issue, this paper aims to fill this gap by providing a case study of a German consumer electronics retailer's large-scale agile development program. Based on social network analysis, this study describes the collaboration between architects and agile teams in terms of architecture sharing.

Keywords: Large-scale agile development · Social network analysis · Agile architecture

1 Introduction

Emerging in the 1990s, agile methods have transformed and brought unprecedented changes to software development practice by strongly emphasizing change tolerance, continuous delivery, and customer involvement [1,2]. With these agile methods, self-organizing teams work closely with business customers in a single-project context, maximizing customer value and quality of delivered software

P. Kruchten et al. (Eds.): XP 2019, LNBIP 355, pp. 137–153, 2019.
https://doi.org/10.1007/978-3-030-19034-7_9

product through rapid iterations and frequent feedback loops [1]. The success of agile methods for small, co-located teams has inspired enterprises to increasingly apply agile practices to large-scale endeavors [2,3]. Since the initial application of agile methods was originally intended for small, co-located teams, many organizations are uncertain how to introduce them at scale and therefore face new challenges such as inter-team coordination, dependencies to other existing environments or distribution of work without a defined architecture [1,4,5]. The latter is also the reason why large-scale agile development has been subject to criticism since it neglects detailed assistance on software architecting [2,6]. Agile methods assume that architecture should evolve incrementally rather than being imposed by some direct structuring force (emergent architecture) [7]. However, the practice of this design is effective at team level but insufficient at large-scale. It causes excessive redesign efforts, architectural divergence, and functional redundancy increasing a system's complexity [7,8]. Therefore, an intentional architecture is required, which embraces architectural guidelines that specify inter-team design and implementation synchronization [7,9]. The effective evolution of a system's architecture requires the right balance of emergent and intentional architecture and a close collaboration between architects and agile teams [7,9,10].

Literature describing the collaboration between architects and agile teams in large-scale agile development is still scarce. This paper aims to fill this gap by providing a case study of a German consumer electronics retailer's large-scale agile development program. Based on this objective, our research question is:

How does the collaboration take place between architects and agile teams in a large-scale agile development program?

The remainder of this paper is structured as follows. In Sect. 2, we provide an overview of foundations and related works. In Sect. 3, we present the research approach of this paper. Section 4 describes the case study on the collaboration between architects and agile teams in the large-scale agile development program. We discuss our lessons learned in Sect. 5 before concluding the paper with a summary of our results and remarks on future research in Sect. 6.

2 Background and Related Work

In the following, the Scaled Agile Framework and Spotify Model are introduced, as the observed program has adopted these two scaling frameworks. Thereafter, the concept of communication networks is presented, which is essential for interpreting the results of the social network analysis in Sect. 4.

2.1 Scaled Agile Framework

The Scaled Agile Framework (SAFe), a widely used scaling framework [11], was first published by Dean Leffingwell in 2011. SAFe builds on existing lean and agile principles that are combined into a method for large-scale agile projects.

It provides a soft introduction to the agile world as it specifies many structured patterns. This introduction is needed for organizations moving from traditional to agile development environment [7]. The latest SAFe 4.6 version supports four out-of-the-box configurations: *Essential SAFe*, *Large Solution SAFe*, *Portfolio SAFe*, and *Full SAFe*. As the observed program uses Essential SAFe, we will subsequently focus on this. Essential SAFe is the simplest entry point for implementing SAFe and consists of team and program levels [7]. At team level, the techniques outlined are those used in Scrum. Each team consists of five to nine members, one scrum master (SM), and one product owner (PO). All teams are part of an agile release train (ART), a team of agile teams that delivers a continuous flow of incremental releases. Each team is responsible for defining, building, and testing stories from its team backlog in a series of two-week iterations using common iteration cadences [7]. At program level, the product management (PM) serves as the content authority for the ART and is accountable for identifying program backlog priorities. The PM works with POs to optimize feature delivery and direct their work at team level. A release train engineer (RTE) facilitates program execution, escalates impediments, manages risk, and helps to drive continuous improvement [7]. The system architect has the technical responsibility for the overall architectural design of the system and aligns the ART with the common technical and architectural vision [7].

2.2 Spotify Model

In 2012, Kniberg and Ivarsson [12] published Spotify's approach to scale agile methods over 30 teams across three cities. The Spotify Model emphasizes the importance of "aligned autonomy", i.e. the autonomy of agile teams with simultaneous collaboration and coordination to achieve the same goals. The basic unit of development is called a *Squad*, which is similar to an agile team in SAFe. Squads are self-organizing and autonomous teams that have all the skills to design, develop, test, and release for production. A *Tribe* is designed as a collection of squads working in related areas (correspondents to an ART in SAFe). Squads within a tribe are co-located. People with similar skills in the same competency area within the same tribe form a *Chapter*. A *Guild* is a community of people that share same interests and often includes all chapters working in this area (complies with a community of practice in SAFe) [12].

2.3 Communication Networks

According to Guo and Sanchez [13], communication is understood as the creation or exchange of thoughts, ideas, and emotions between senders and receivers. Communication can be decomposed into two types: inter-team and intra-team communication. The former stands for communication between several teams, the latter for communication within a team [14]. The flow of communication connecting senders and receivers are called communication networks [15]. Figure 1 depicts five common communication networks. The *wheel network* is the most centralized network pattern. In this network, each member communicates with

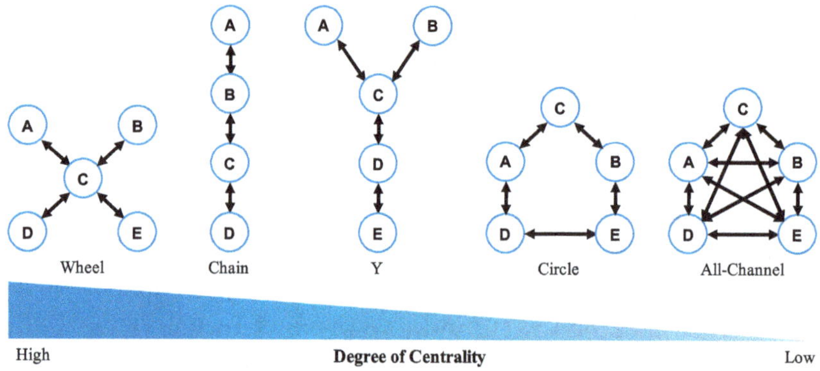

Fig. 1. Common communication networks [15]

only one other person. The superintendent C receives all the information from his subordinates A, B, D, and E and sends back information, usually in the form of decisions. The *chain network* is the second highest in centralization. Only two people communicate with each other, and they have only one other person to communicate with. The *Y network* is similar to the chain network except that two members are out of the chain. In the Y network, members A and B can send information to C but they cannot receive information from anyone else. Members C and D can exchange information. Member E can exchange information with member D. The *circle network* stands for horizontal and decentralized communication, which offers equal communication possibilities for every member. Each can communicate with one other to his right and left. Members have identical restrictions but the circle is a less restricted condition than the wheel, chain, or Y network. The *all-channel network* is an extension of the circle network and connects everyone in the circle network, as it permits each member to communicate freely with all other persons [15].

2.4 Agile Architecture

Angelov et al. [16] describe the role of architects and challenges they face in Scrum such as insufficient collaboration, lack of understanding of the value of architecture, and poor communication between team architects [16]. Bachmann et al. [17] and Nord et al. [18] present four tactics to achieve agility at scale by aligning the system architecture, organization structures and product infrastructures. These include vertical and horizontal system decomposition, matrix and augmented team structures, architecture and infrastructure runway, and deployability tactics and can be used in different phases in a system's life cycles. Uludağ et al. [10] describes how the adoption of domain-driven design supported a large-scale agile development program with three agile teams at a large insurance company. Uludağ et al. [10] report that agile teams and project managers involved in the program conceived that without any form of architectural guidance, large-scale agile development programs can hardly be successful. Dingsøyr et al. [19] investigated a large-scale development program with an extensive use of Scrum and a focus on customer involvement, inter-team coordination, and software architecture. Two key findings related to software architecture are the tension between up-front and emergent architecture and the demanding role of architects in large-scale agile development.

3 Case Study Design

A case study is a suitable research methodology for this paper, since it helps to study contemporary phenomena in a real life context [20]. We followed the guidelines described by Runeson and Höst [20].

Case Study Design: The main objective of this paper is to investigate the collaboration between architects and agile teams in large-scale agile development in terms of architecture sharing. Based on this objective, we defined one research question (see Sect. 1). The study is a an exploratory single case study, since this paper looks into an unexplored phenomenon and aims to seek new insights and generate ideas for future research [20]. The case was purposefully selected, because the studied company has successfully adopted SAFe for building complex software for the last one and a half years. The unit of analysis is the consumer electronics retailer's large-scale agile development program.

Data Collection: We used a mixed methods approach with three levels of data collection techniques [21]. As direct methods, we observed two Program Increment (PI) Planning events [7] with low degree of interaction by the researcher and low awareness of being observed [20]. These observations provided a deep understanding of the overall structure. With the help of seven semi-structured interviews, roles and practices related to architecture were identified and documented. Quantitative data was collected by the online-survey tool Questback for building the social networks and revealing the collaboration between architects and agile teams (see Sect. 4). Therein, we asked respondents how often they exchange architectural advice and decisions with their colleagues, how often they see their colleagues, and if they have suggestions on how to improve the exchange among team members (using a Likert scale). A total of 32 out of 62 available people from eight teams took part in the survey. Three persons were removed from the analysis because no clear assignment to these persons could be made. The response rate for the remaining 29 program members from eight teams is 47% with 758 connections for architecture sharing.

Data Analysis: Interviews and observation protocols were coded using a deductive approach as proposed by Cruzes and Dybå [22]. Qualitative data collected in interviews form the theoretical foundation for interpreting social relations between architects and agile teams. After initial coding, codes were refined and consolidated by merging related ones and removing duplicates. Quantitative data was analyzed through the use of social network analysis, which comprises a set of methodological techniques that aim to describe and explore patterns in relationships that individuals and groups form with each other [23].

4 Results

4.1 Case Description

In 2016, the case organization decided to relaunch a failed CRM project using agile methods. Due to the complexity of the project, the management decided to relaunch it with the help of a scaling framework. During early stages of research, the reasons for using Essential SAFe (from now on SAFe) became more apparent and convincing to the management. One reason for choosing SAFe was that it has proven itself in large organizations and offers comprehensive documentation. The adoption was initiated with a pilot project, which was geographically distributed. At the beginning, the pilot project faced a lot of problems. Thus, all involved employees were trained upon agile methods and SAFe by external agile coaches. After a few PIs, the responsible management team perceived that SAFe did not provide sufficient guidance on the coordination of their agile teams. Thus, the organization decided to combine SAFe with the Spotify Model. Within the transformation process, program members were divided into tribes, chapters, squads, and guilds. Figure 2 shows the current organizational structure of the observed program. Figure 2 also shows all 62 members forming a tribe. This tribe consists of a "scaled" team (Team A), which does not play a hierarchical superior, but a more coordinating role without personnel management, and four squads (Team B, Team C, Team D, and Team E). Team F, Team G, and Team H, which are not shown in Fig. 2 constitute representatives of three suppliers that provide external support for their third-party systems. The tribe is divided horizontally into nine chapters for: (1) the chief product owner (CPO) and POs, (2) RTE and SMs, (3) IT project managers (IT-PMs), (4) quality analysts and test managers (QAs & TMs), (5) data analysts (DAs), (6) solution architects (SAs)[1], (7) business process architects (BPAs), (8) product reliability engineers (PRE), and (9) developers (Devs). Each SA is assigned to a squad and takes care of the overall system architecture with its subsystems and interfaces. The team concentrates on the cross-system data flows and processes related to the integration of the architecture. These data flows and processes are used to define minimum interface requirements that all teams must meet. In contrast to SAs, who represent technical architects, BPAs are functional architects that are also dedicated to squads. The responsibilities of BPAs are not really known yet, as their role has been added to the program just recently. However, both architect roles should play a dual role within their squads by making architectural decisions and guiding them to fulfill the required architectural standards. Due to ongoing transformation, guilds have not yet been established but will be organized soon. In the following two sections, the inter- and intra-team exchange of architecture-related information of the observed program will be presented.

[1] The role of the SA in the case organization correspondents to the role of the system architect as described by SAFe [7]. For reasons of consistency, we use the same terminology as the case organization.

4.2 Inter-Team Architecture Sharing

Figure 3 provides an overview of how architecture-related information is shared across all teams. An interesting finding here is that the scaled team is located in the center of the graph. This indicates continuous communication and coordination between the scaled team and the four squads on architectural topics. Figure 3 also shows a close collaboration between Team B and Team E and between Team B and Team D, which is due to architectural dependencies between the systems on which they work. Figure 3 also provides an overview of roles that are inten-

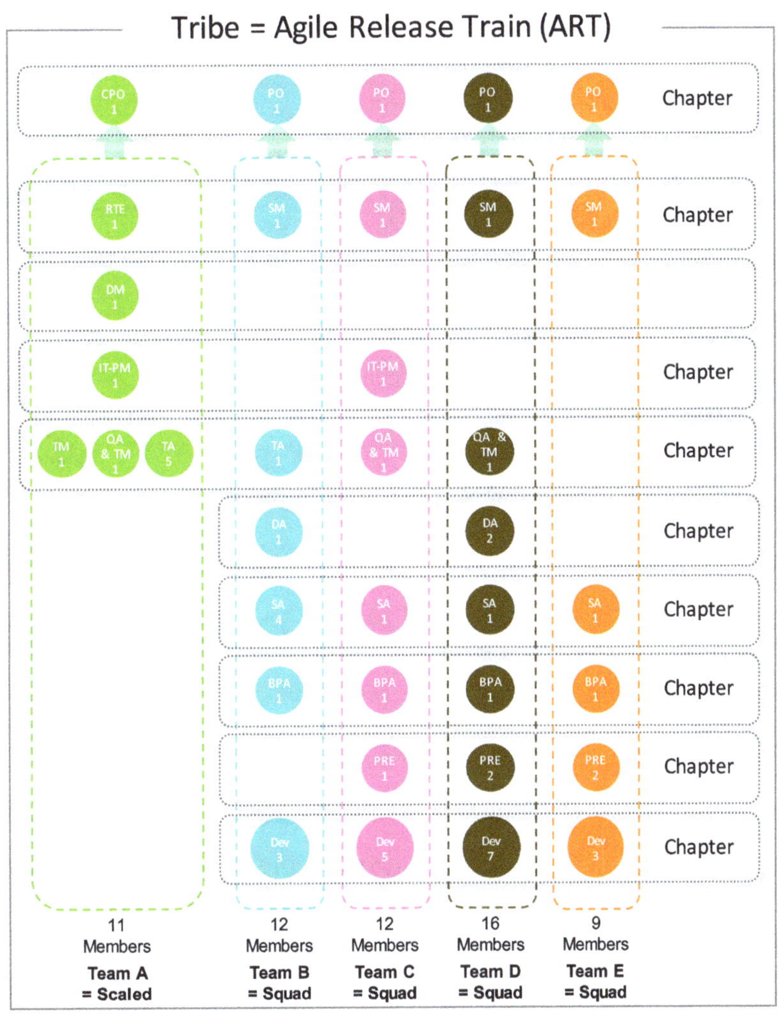

Abbreviations	
BPA - Business Process Architect	PRE - Product Reliability Engineer
CPO - Chief Product Owner	QA & TM - Quality Analyst & Test Manager
DA - Data Analyst	RTE - Release Train Engineer
Dev - Developer	SA - Solution Architect
DM - Delivery Manager	SM - Scrum Master
IT-PM - IT Project Manager	TA - Test Analyst
PO - Product Owner	TM - Test Manager

Fig. 2. Organizational structure of the observed large-scale agile development program

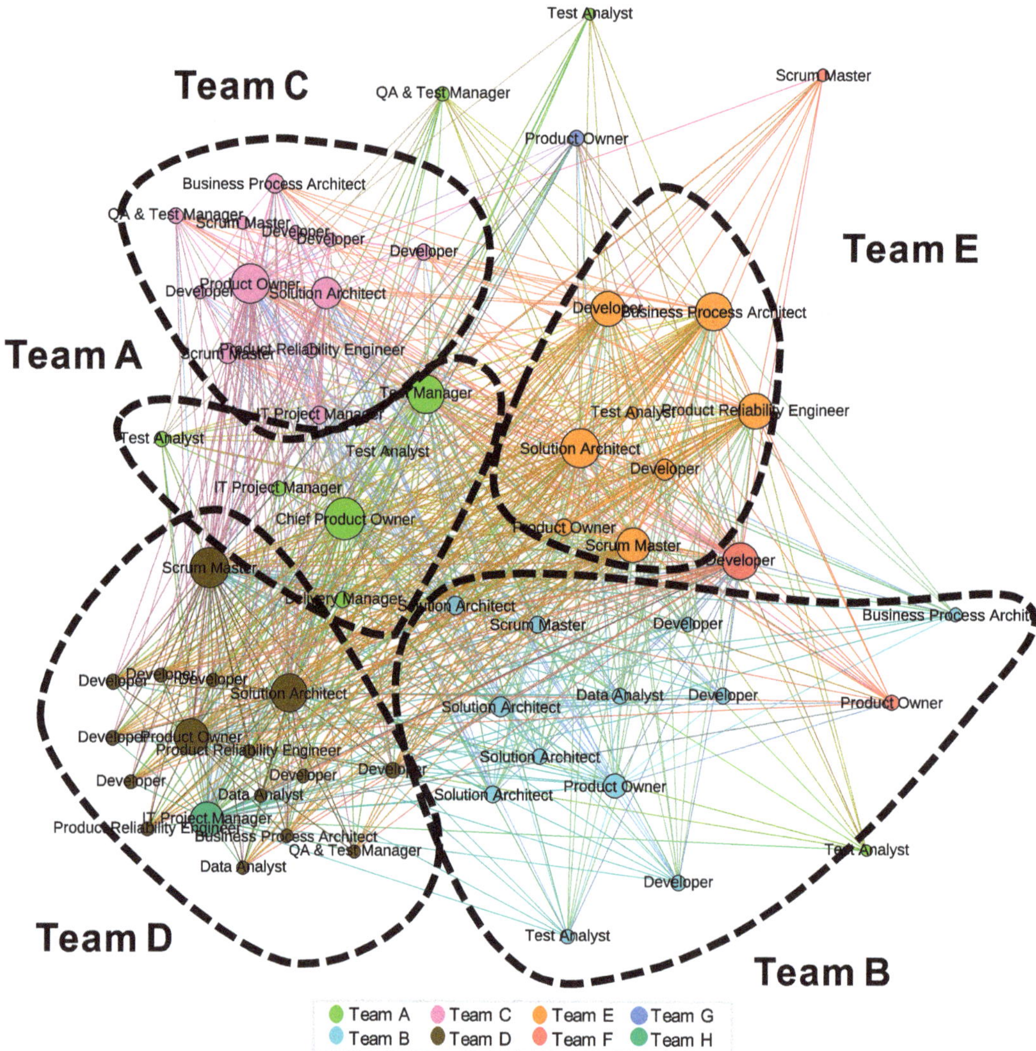

Fig. 3. Social network of eight teams including salient roles that are intensively involved in inter- and intra-team architecture-sharing

sively involved (large nodes) in architecture sharing. First, it shows that the CPO of Team A (CPO_A) is the most outstanding node in the inter- and intra-team exchange of architecture-related information. Second, SAs also form relatively large nodes compared to other roles. This observation confirms the importance of SAs for the exchange of inter- and intra-team architectural information. Figure 3 also shows that the TM_A also plays an important role in architecture sharing. Table 1 presents top 10 stakeholders involved in inter-team sharing based on the normalized degree centrality[2] measure. Table 1 shows that the CPO_A has a normalized degree centrality value of 1,0, which indicates that he/she is sharing information with all stakeholders involved in the observed program. The SA_E

[2] The normalized degree centrality is defined as the number of links of an stakeholder divided by the maximal possible number.

Table 1. Top 10 stakeholders involved in inter-team architecture sharing based on normalized degree centrality

Rank	1	2	3	4	5	6	7	8	9	10
Role	CPO_A	SM_D	PO_C	SA_E	SA_D	TM_A	BPA_E	Dev_F	PRE_E	PO_D
Value	1,0	0,95	0,93	0,92	0,90	0,90	0,89	0,87	0,84	0,82

and SA_D have normalized degree centrality values of 0,92 and 0,90 indicating high involvement in inter-team sharing.

The PI planning event of SAFe is a face-to-face event [7] that aims to align all agile teams within the ART to share the common mission and vision by creating iteration plans and team objectives for the upcoming PI. It is conducted every two and a half months and offers a platform for the exchange of general and architectural information across teams, since all members of the ART are present in one location. Figure 4(a) shows that SAs and BPAs have a very strong sharing with other teams during the PI planning. Figure 4(d) reveals a chain communication between the SA_B, SA_C, SA_D, and SA_E on a daily basis. In particular, the chain is composed as follows: SA_E exchanges information with SA_B, who exchanges information with SA_D, who shares information with SA_C. This communication pattern characterizes a centralized communication between SAs. The chain communication pattern can also be observed with SA_B, SA_D, and SA_E. Figure 4(e) shows that SA_B, SA_D, and SA_E constantly[3] exchange information and that the SA_C is no longer involved in an exchange with other SAs. Figure 4 shows that SAs form a decentralized all-channel communication pattern. This means that each SA speaks with all other SAs. The overall comparison also shows that the three external SA of Team B are less participating in the inter-team exchange than the rest of internal SAs involved in the program. Other roles such as SM, TM, PO, and CPO are also heavily involved in exchange of information within the PI planning. The shorter the observed time intervals become, the more dominant the SA becomes with regards to the inter-team sharing.

4.3 Intra-Team Architecture Sharing

The exchange of architectural information in Team B shows a central wheel communication pattern between SAs, since external SAs are guided by the internal SA, who represents the intra-team lead architect (see Fig. 5(a)). Figure 5(a) also shows that SAs form the core of the team. Moreover, Fig. 5(a) shows that BPA_B only exchanges information with another role. A decentralized all-channel communication pattern can be observed in Team C (see Fig. 5(b)). This means that other non-architectural roles exchange information without necessarily involving SA_C. Nevertheless, SA_C plays the most central role, since the SA frequently communicates with all team members. Compared to BPA_B, BPA_C plays a more central role, as he/she shows a close collaboration and communication with his/her

[3] Constant exchange means that it takes place more than once a day.

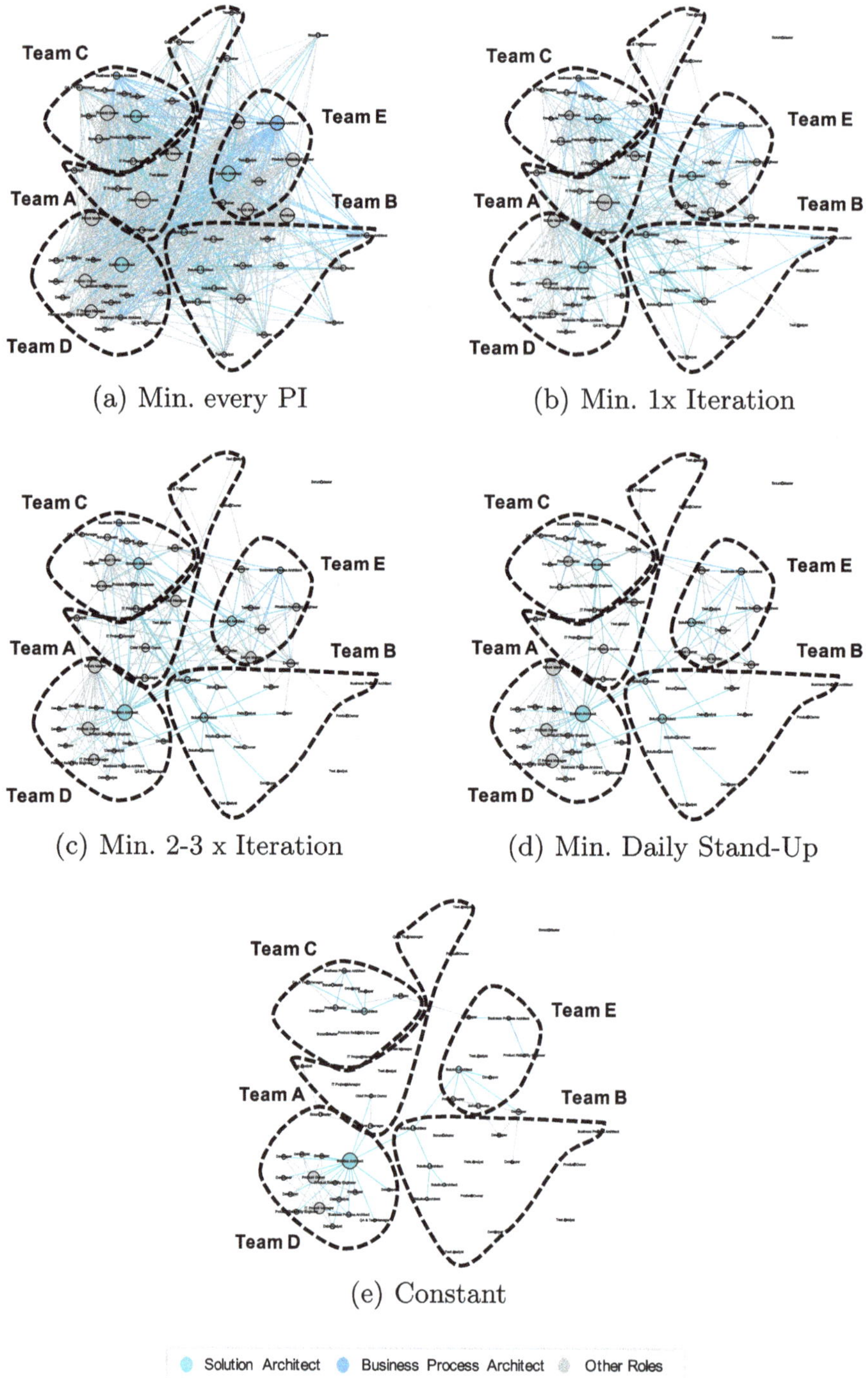

(a) Min. every PI (b) Min. 1x Iteration

(c) Min. 2-3 x Iteration (d) Min. Daily Stand-Up

(e) Constant

Fig. 4. Social networks focusing on SAs and BPAs with regards to the frequency of inter- and intra-team architecture sharing

squad (see Fig. 5(a) and (b)). The comparison of the two figures also shows that SA_C and BPA_C exchange information more frequently than SA_B and BPA_B. Figure 5(b) shows a decentralized all-channel communication pattern between architects and other team members of Team D. Similar to BPA_C, BPA_D often

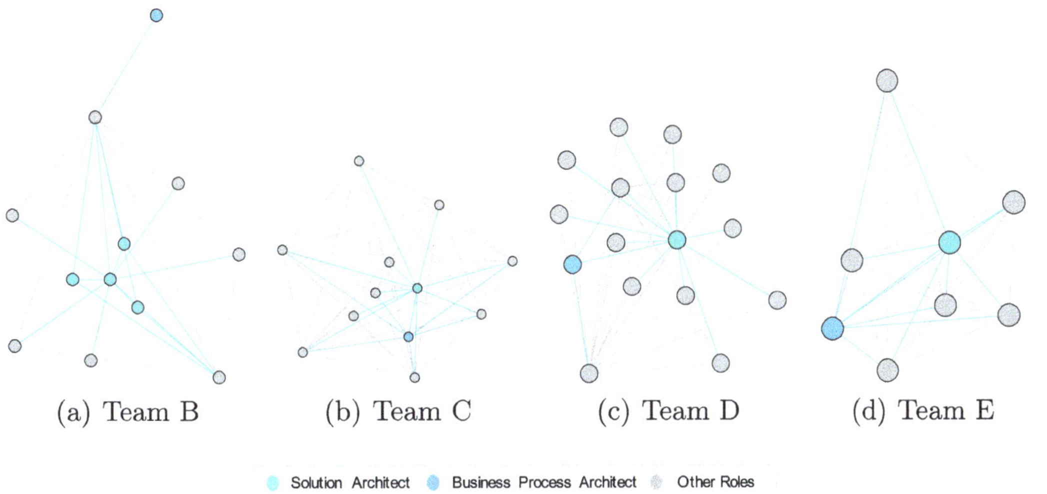

Fig. 5. Social network of the four squads focusing on SAs and BPAs involved in intra-team architecture-sharing

Table 2. Normalized degree centralities of architects in intra-team architecture sharing

	Team B	Team C	Team D	Team E
SA	0,91	1,0	1,0	1,0
BPA	0,09	0,64	0,2	1,0

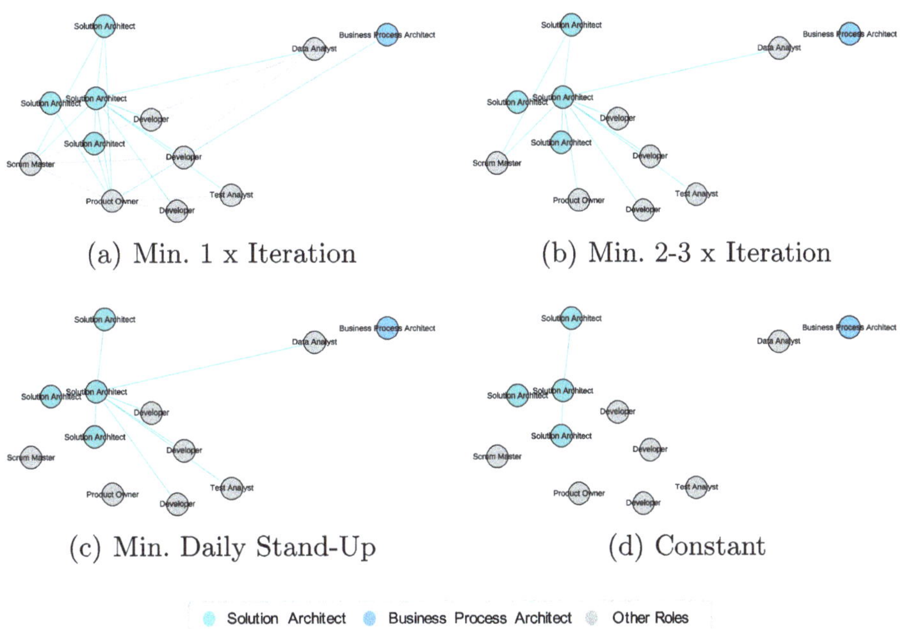

Fig. 6. Social network of Team B focusing on SAs and BPAs with regards to the frequency of intra-team architecture sharing

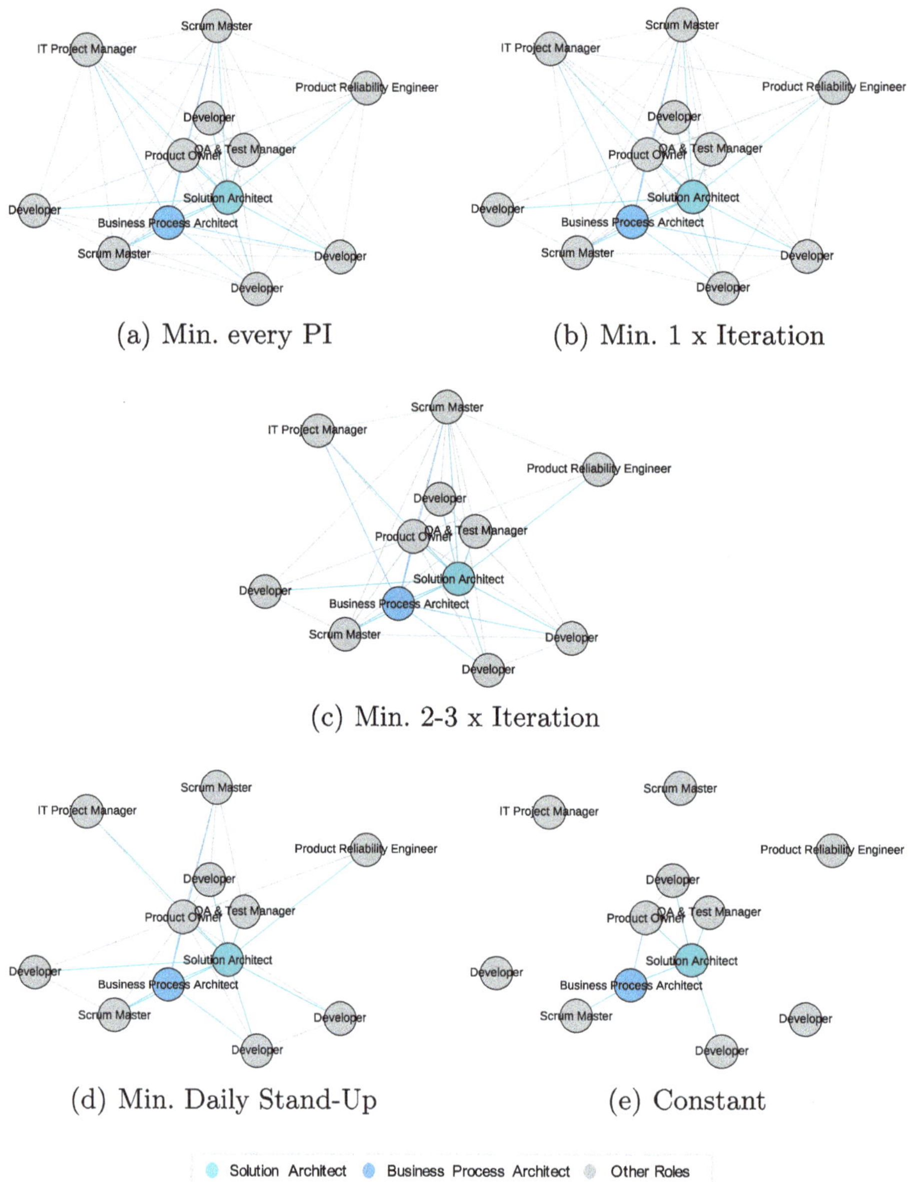

Fig. 7. Social network of Team C focusing on SAs and BPAs with regards to the frequency of intra-team architecture sharing

exchanges architecture information with team members. Table 2 shows the normalized degree centrality values of SAs and BPAs involved in intra-team architecture sharing. 75% of the SAs possess a normalized degree centrality value of 1,0 indicating that they share information with all squad members. Comparing SAs with BPAs, Table 2 shows that SAs have a stronger exchange of information with their squad members than BPAs (except Team E).

Figure 6 shows how Team B's intra-team sharing changes at four distinct time intervals. For instance, Fig. 6(a) shows that BPA_B only exchanges information with one Dev_B once per iteration. Figure 6(b) shows that the exchange of information between SAs and non-architectural roles mostly takes place two to three

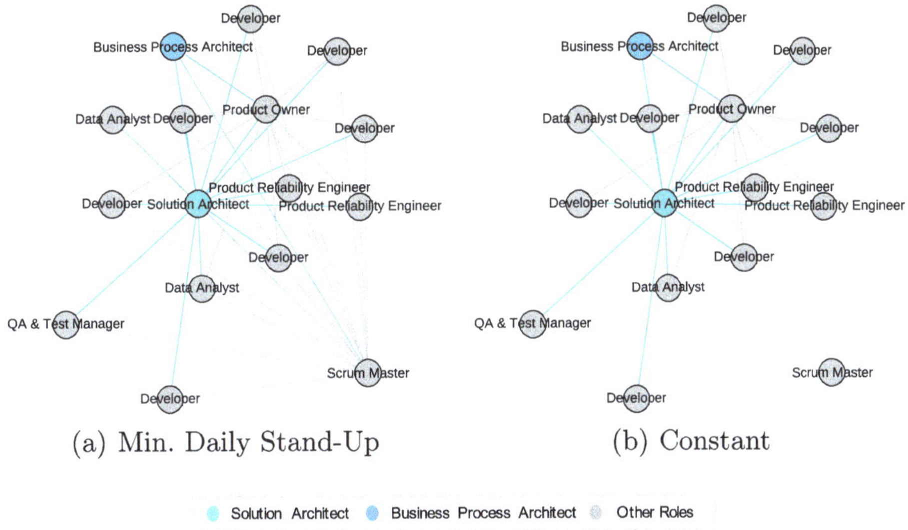

(a) Min. Daily Stand-Up (b) Constant

Fig. 8. Social network of Team D focusing on SAs and BPAs with regards to the frequency of intra-team architecture sharing

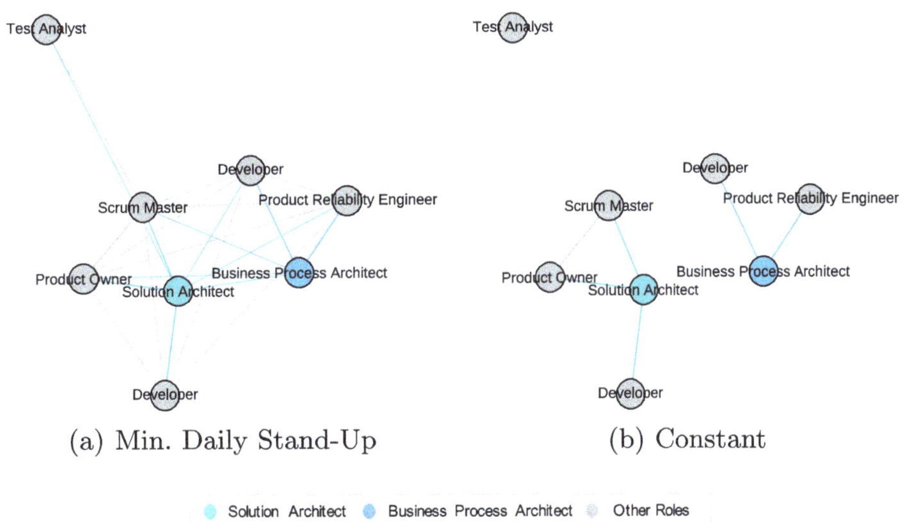

(a) Min. Daily Stand-Up (b) Constant

Fig. 9. Social network of Team E focusing on SAs and BPAs with regards to the frequency of intra-team architecture sharing

times per iteration, while the sharing between SAs takes place constantly (see Fig. 6(d)). Similar to Figs. 6, 7 shows Team C's intra-team architecture sharing. The exchange in the team usually takes place two to three times per iteration (see Fig. 7(c)). Sharing between architects and non-architectural roles takes place on a daily basis (see Fig. 7(d)). In contrast to Team B, Fig. 7(e) shows that SA_C and BPA_C constantly communicate together. Figure 8(a) shows that the exchange between architects and non-architectural roles as well as among architects mainly takes place on a daily basis. SA_D and BPA_D constantly exchange architectural information (see Fig. 8(b)). Figure 8(b) also shows that other members such as DA_D, QA & TM_D, PRE_D, and PO_D constantly exchange architectural information. The intra-team exchange of Team E takes place mainly on a daily basis (see Fig. 9(a)). SA_E and BPA_E communicate on a daily basis (see Fig. 9(b)). Architecture sharing between architects and non-architectural roles takes place on a daily basis. Figure 9(b) shows that two groups are formed during the constant exchange of information. The first group includes SA_E, SM_E, Dev_E, and PO_E, while the second group constitutes Dev_E, BPA_E, and PRE_E. Table 3 provides a summary of the social network analysis with identified communication patterns and frequencies.

5 Discussion

5.1 Key Findings

Both architectural roles, i.e. SAs and BPAs, and other roles, e.g. TMs, SMs, and POs, are involved in inter- and intra-team architecture sharing. In particular, the CPO plays one of the most salient roles. An all-channel communication network can be observed in each squad. SAs enable a decentralized exchange so that other team members can exchange architecture-relevant information without necessarily involving SAs. This observation coincides with the values and principles of agile software development. Both SAs and BPAs prefer face-to-face communication with their team members and do not exchange information by including bridging roles. Each squad is accompanied by at least one SA and BPA. Both architects play a dual role in their squads. On the one hand, they make architectural decisions and iteratively create architecture models. On the other hand, they provide guidance and support their squad in meeting architectural standards. With this setup, the observed program aims to increase development speed by balancing emergent and intentional architecture. In all social networks, SAs form central nodes in inter- and intra-team sharing.

Table 3. Summary of the social network analysis

	Team A	Team B	Team C	Team D	Team E
Overview (communication network)	decentralized; -	decentralized; all-channel	decentralized; all-channel	decentralized; all-channel	decentralized; all-channel
Architects with other roles (communication network)	not applicable	decentralized; all-channel	decentralized; all-channel	decentralized; all-channel	decentralized; all-channel
Architects with other roles (frequency of sharing)	not applicable	mostly 2-3x pro iteration (except BPA)	mostly daily basis	mostly daily basis	mostly daily basis
Between architects (Communication Network)	not applicable	centralized; wheel (between SAs)	not applicable	not applicable	not applicable
Between architects (frequency of sharing)	not applicable	constant (except BPA)	constant	constant	mostly daily basis

5.2 Threats to Validity

We discuss potential threats to validity along with an assessment scheme as recommended by Runeson and Höst [20].

Construct Validity: This aspect reflects to what extent operational measures that are studied really represent what the researcher has in mind [20]. Two countermeasures were taken for construct validity. First, interview protocols were coded by the author of this paper and reviewed by a second researcher. Second, a key informant of the organization has reviewed the analyses of this paper.

Internal Validity is irrelevant, as this study was neither explanatory nor causal.

External Validity: This aspect of validity concerns to what extent the findings can be generalized, and to what extent the findings are of interest to other persons outside the case under investigation [20]. This paper focuses on analytical generalization [20] by providing a detailed description of the case. It provides empirical insights that allow for a profound understanding on the collaboration between architects and agile teams. The shown findings should be viewed as valuable insights for other organizations that adopted Essential SAFe.

Reliability: This validity is concerned with to what extent the data and the analysis are dependent on the specific researcher [20]. To mitigate this threat, two countermeasures were taken. First, the case study has been designed so that the large number of interviewees and multiple interviewers allowed data and observer triangulation. Second, a case study database was created, which includes case study documents such as audio recordings protocols, and field notes of observations.

6 Conclusion and Future Work

In this paper, we described the collaboration between architects and agile teams in a large-scale agile development program of a German consumer electronics retailer. Due to the complexity and extent of the CRM product, each squad is guided and supported by at least one SA and BPA. Each SA is responsible for the architecture of a subsystem and ensures that the respective squad complies with defined architectural requirements. The observed program also introduced the new role of the BPA that is responsible for developing the functional architecture of the subsystem. To understand the role of SAs and BPAs and their collaboration with squads, we investigated social networks of one scaled team and four squads. We learned that intra-team architecture sharing is usually facilitated by SAs. Comparing the social networks with common communication networks, we discovered that SAs and BPAs prefer direct communication. For the most part, architects share information on a daily basis with their teams. The intra-team sharing between architects and their teams is characterized by an all-channel communication network.

As future work, we will continue to study the large-scale agile development program of the German consumer electronics retailer. First, we will research how the current state of architecture sharing is perceived by the stakeholders and how it could be improved by the use of various coordination mechanisms such as ad hoc meetings, co-location or communities of practices. Second, as the squads in the large-scale agile development program become more mature and evolve towards feature teams, we will investigate the architectural decision-making process of squads. We hope to gain a better understanding of the collaboration between architects and squads regarding the distribution of their responsibilities for architectural issues.

References

1. Kettunen, P.: Extending software project agility with new product development enterprise agility. Softw. Process: Improv. Pract. **12**(6), 541–548 (2007)
2. Dingsøyr, T., Moe, N.B.: Towards principles of large-scale agile development. In: Dingsøyr, T., Moe, N.B., Tonelli, R., Counsell, S., Gencel, C., Petersen, K. (eds.) XP 2014. LNBIP, vol. 199, pp. 1–8. Springer, Cham (2014). https://doi.org/10.1007/978-3-319-14358-3_1
3. Alqudah, M., Razali, R.: A review of scaling agile methods in large software development. Int. J. Adv. Sci. Eng. Inf. Technol. **6**(6), 28–35 (2016)
4. Dikert, K., Paasivaara, M., Lassenius, C.: Challenges and success factors for large-scale agile transformations: a systematic literature review. J. Syst. Softw. **119**, 87–108 (2016)
5. Uludag, Ö., Kleehaus, M., Caprano, C., Matthes, F.: Identifying and structuring challenges in large-scale agile development based on a structured literature review. In: IEEE 22nd International Enterprise Distributed Object Computing Conference (EDOC) 2018, pp. 191–197. IEEE (2018)
6. Rost, D., Weitzel, B., Naab, M., Lenhart, T., Schmitt, H.: Distilling best practices for agile development from architecture methodology. In: Weyns, D., Mirandola, R., Crnkovic, I. (eds.) ECSA 2015. LNCS, vol. 9278, pp. 259–267. Springer, Cham (2015). https://doi.org/10.1007/978-3-319-23727-5_21
7. Leffingwell, D.: SAFe® 4.5 Reference Guide: Scaled Agile Framework® for Lean Software and Systems Engineering. Addison-Wesley Professional, Boston (2018)
8. Mocker, M.: What is complex about 273 applications? untangling application architecture complexity in a case of european investment banking. In: 2009 42nd Hawaii International Conference on System Sciences 2009, HICSS, pp. 1–14. IEEE (2009)
9. Waterman, M.: Reconciling agility and architecture: a theory of agile architecture, Ph.D. thesis, Victoria University of Wellington (2014)
10. Uludağ, Ö., Hauder, M., Kleehaus, M., Schimpfle, C., Matthes, F.: Supporting large-scale agile development with domain-driven design. In: Garbajosa, J., Wang, X., Aguiar, A. (eds.) XP 2018. LNBIP, vol. 314, pp. 232–247. Springer, Cham (2018). https://doi.org/10.1007/978-3-319-91602-6_16
11. Uludağ, Ö., Kleehaus, M., Xu, X., Matthes, F.: Investigating the role of architects in scaling agile frameworks. In: 2017 IEEE 21st International Enterprise Distributed Object Computing Conference (EDOC), pp. 123–132. IEEE (2017)
12. Kniberg, H., Ivarsson, A.: Scaling agile @ spotify (2012)
13. Guo, L.C., Sanchez, Y.: Workplace communication. Organizational behavior in health care, pp. 77–110 (2005)

14. Presbitero, A., Roxas, B., Chadee, D.: Effects of intra- and inter-team dynamics on organisational learning: role of knowledge-sharing capability. Knowl. Manag. Res. Pract. **15**(1), 146–154 (2017)
15. Lunenburg, F.: Network patterns and analysis: underused sources to improve communication effectiveness. Nat. Forum Educ. Adm. Super. J. **28**(4), 1–7 (2011)
16. Angelov, S., Meesters, M., Galster, M.: Architects in scrum: what challenges do they face? In: Tekinerdogan, B., Zdun, U., Babar, A. (eds.) ECSA 2016. LNCS, vol. 9839, pp. 229–237. Springer, Cham (2016). https://doi.org/10.1007/978-3-319-48992-6_17
17. Bachmann, F., Nord, R.L., Ozakaya, I.: Architectural tactics to support rapid and agile stability. Technical report, Carnegie-Mellon University Pittsburgh PA Software Engineering Institute (2012)
18. Nord, R.L., Ozkaya, I., Kruchten, P.: Agile in distress: architecture to the rescue. In: Dingsøyr, T., Moe, N.B., Tonelli, R., Counsell, S., Gencel, C., Petersen, K. (eds.) XP 2014. LNBIP, vol. 199, pp. 43–57. Springer, Cham (2014). https://doi.org/10.1007/978-3-319-14358-3_5
19. Dingsøyr, T., Moe, N.B., Fægri, T.E., Seim, E.A.: Exploring software development at the very large-scale: a revelatory case study and research agenda for agile method adaptation. Empirical Softw. Eng. **23**(1), 490–520 (2018)
20. Runeson, P., Höst, M.: Guidelines for conducting and reporting case study research in software engineering. Empirical softw. Eng. **14**(2), 131 (2009)
21. Lethbridge, T.C., Sim, S.E., Singer, J.: Studying software engineers: data collection techniques for software field studies. Empirical softw. Eng. **10**(3), 311–341 (2005)
22. Cruzes, D.S., Dyba, T.: Recommended steps for thematic synthesis in software engineering. In: 2011 International Symposium on Empirical Software Engineering and Measurement (ESEM), pp. 275–284. IEEE (2011)
23. Scott, J.: Social Network Analysis. Sage, Thousand Oaks (2017)

How Are Agile Release Trains Formed in Practice? A Case Study in a Large Financial Corporation

Abheeshta Putta[1(✉)], Maria Paasivaara[1,2], and Casper Lassenius[1,3]

[1] Department of Computer Science, Aalto University, Espoo, Finland
{abheeshta.putta,casper.lassenius}@aalto.fi
[2] IT University of Copenhagen, Copenhagen, Denmark
mpaa@itu.dk
[3] Simula Metropolitan Center for Digital Engineering, Oslo, Norway

Abstract. The Scaled Agile Framework (SAFe) is currently the most widely adopted framework for scaling agile in the software intensive industry. Despite this, there exists very little scientific research on the transformation process, as well as on the challenges and success factors of using SAFe in large-scale organizations. To start filling in this research gap, we conducted a case study by investigating the formation of agile release trains and the related challenges in a large financial organization adopting SAFe. We conducted 24 interviews with 27 interviewees, after which we analyzed the transcribed interviews using open and axial coding.

The SAFe transformation started by forming a pilot train with teams that already had experience in agile practices. The success of the pilot led to the launching of new release trains. The forming of new agile release trains was challenging due to politics, difficulties in identifying the value streams, and the avoidance of a radical restructuring of the organization. These challenges led to opting for an organic way of transformation.

Management organized several workshops to identify stakeholders for the second train. This was followed by team members choosing their teams based on skills and interests. The last two trains were formed using Lego workshops. The most significant challenges after forming the release trains at the case organization were struggles with existing projects and challenges due to inter-train dependencies.

Keywords: Agile release trains · Scaled Agile Framework · SAFe · Challenges

1 Introduction

The agile software development methods were originally designed for small co-located teams. However, with the success of agile methods in small teams, organizations started adopting them also in large and distributed environments [1].

P. Kruchten et al. (Eds.): XP 2019, LNBIP 355, pp. 154–170, 2019.
https://doi.org/10.1007/978-3-030-19034-7_10

To support this, practitioners have proposed different scaling frameworks such as the Scaled Agile Framework (SAFe) [2], Large Scale Scrum (LeSS) [3] and Disciplined Agile Delivery (DAD) [4]. According to the 12th *State of Agile Survey* [5], SAFe seems to be currently the most popular scaling framework, with 29% of respondent organizations reporting the adoption of SAFe.

Researchers have identified the lack of research, and emphasized the need for scientific studies on the adoption of scaling frameworks [6,7]. A recent multivocal literature review (MLR) on SAFe identified only six scientific studies published on the framework [8]. Most of the published information related to SAFe consists of the experience reports written by practitioners. These reports are available on the SAFe homepage [2]. The MLR also identified a need for research-based evidence related to the transformation process to SAFe [8].

In this paper, we describe a part of the transformation process in a large traditional organization in the financial sector. We focus on the formation of *agile release trains (ARTs)*, a central construct in the SAFe framework, and the related challenges experienced in case the organization.

The paper is structured as follows: In the next section, we describe how value streams are identified and ARTs formed according to the SAFe framework. Then, we present the previous literature on the formation of ARTs and the related challenges. In Sect. 3, we describe our research methodology and present the case organization. Section 4 provides out results. In Sect. 5, we discuss the results and finally, in Sect. 6, we conclude the paper and suggest directions for future research.

2 Related Work

2.1 The Scaled Agile Framework: Identifying Value Streams and Agile Release Trains

The Scaled Agile Framework[1], introduced in 2011 [2], integrates practices from lean and agile to support scaling to the enterprise level. The framework has four different levels: portfolio, large solution, program and team [9]. Each layer has a set of activities, roles, and processes to support and build solutions.

One of the critical moves during adoption of SAFe is the identification of *value streams*, which are defined as *"the sequence of steps used to build solutions that generates continuous customer value. They may deliver either direct customer value or may support internal processes"* [10].

When the value streams have been identified, teams are grouped into ARTs, which are *long-lived organizational structures, composed of agile teams, key stakeholders, and other resources* [2]. An ART typically includes 50–125 people, and delivers solutions incrementally using time-boxed Program Increments (PIs) [11]. The *Program Increments* are typically eight to twelve weeks long, and are preceded by a *PI planning*. The PI planning meetings, in which all teams in an ART meet face-to-face, typically last two days, and serve as the heartbeat of

[1] See https://www.scaledagileframework.com/ for more information.

the ART, helping to align the teams to a common vision [12]. During a program increment, agile teams work on their backlogs using either Scrum or Kanban.

The SAFe implementation road-map [13] gives a detailed description on how to identify the value streams and form the release trains [10]. The SAFe framework defines two types of value streams: *operational* and *development*. An operational value stream is a set of steps taken in order to provide services to the customer [10]. A development value stream supports operational value streams by developing new products or services. Initially, the organization starts by identifying the operational value streams. SAFe provides a *template* to help organizations to define them.

After identifying the *operational value streams*, the next step is to identify the systems that support the value streams and the people who develop these systems. Then, the development value streams are identified. The organization might have one or several development value streams. The development value streams need to be *mostly* or *wholly* independent, in order to deliver the value without having many *inter-value stream dependencies* [10].

When the value streams have been identified, ARTs are formed to realize the identified development value streams. SAFe defines the following set of attributes of an effective ART: (1) consisting of 50–125 people, (2) focus on a complete system or a related set of products or services, (3) long lived and stable teams that deliver value constantly, and (4) deliver independently by having a minimum number of dependencies with other ARTs [13].

Depending on the number of people in the ARTs, different designs are possible: *"a single ART delivering a single value stream"*, *"a single ART delivering multiple value streams"*, *"multiple ARTs delivering a single large value stream"* [10]. When having multiple ARTs delivering a single large value stream, there are typically a lot of dependencies between them. In this case, the ARTs can be designed into *feature ARTs* or *subsystem ARTs*. Typically, a large system might require both types of ARTs. When developing a segment inside large value streams, ARTs may not be *end-to-end*. However, in reality, the beginning and the ending of a value stream are quite relative to each other [10]. The inputs, values and systems may vary for each different segment that in fact creates a *logical diving line* for the ARTs [10]. In practice, other factors like geography, spoken language, and cost centers might influence the ART design, but these are considered less desirable [10].

2.2 Overview on Release Train Formation and Its Challenges

The existing literature contains very little information on how organizations define value streams and form ARTs in pratice. Below, we summarize the reported information on value streams and release train formation.

During their transformation to SAFe, organizations start to identify the value streams [14–16]. Some mapped the existing value streams [17] during different workshops like management [15] and leadership workshops [14]. One organization reported arranging a *value stream mapping event* by bringing different Scrum teams together [18].

Organizations formed release trains by combining the existing product clusters, Scrum teams and component teams [19], or system teams, development teams and cross-functional roles [20]. Some cases structured release trains around the current products and web portals [21], product streams [22], utilities [21], platforms [21,23], markets [14] and business programs [24]. In one case [22], the software development domain was divided into eight ARTs, while in another case [25] several domains, *"commercial, cargo, flight and ground operations, engineering and maintenance, finance, human resources"*, were combined to form the release trains. This setup bought in value for all the domains.

Challenges related to defining and structuring the organization around value streams have been reported by several cases [14,21,26]. In [21], it was difficult to figure out the domain of the ART. Struggles with handling cross-team dependencies between ARTs and integrating teams with less dependencies into ARTs was reported in [27]. Resistance to be a part of the ARTs was also reflected in [19].

Even though the above mentioned literature touches the topic, in-depth information on the formation of release trains in practice is lacking both in the grey and in the scientific literature, grey literature providing more information on the topic compared to the scientific literature.

3 Research Methodology

3.1 Research Goals and Questions

The objective of our research was to investigate the SAFe transformation in a large, traditional financial corporation. In this paper, we focus on the formation of ARTs and related challenges in the case organization, as this rose as a central theme during the interviews. The case organization was purposefully selected, as it provided an opportunity to perform an information rich case study [28]. Additionally, it is one of the largest corporations in Denmark that has implemented the SAFe framework.

We approached this case in an exploratory manner, and formulated the following research questions:

RQ1: How did the ART formation proceed at the case organization?
RQ2: What were the challenges of forming ARTs at the case organization?

3.2 Case Description

The case organization is a financial corporation developing large and complex pension and insurance products. At the time of the study, the organization consisted of 1300 persons, of which 300 people (32 teams) were involved in software development. The development was distributed to two sites: *Denmark and Poland*, the main part of the development taking place in Denmark, while consultants were hired from Poland making up ca 10–15% of the headcount.

Before agile, the organization used the sequential PRINCE 2 process model, and was *siloed* and *hierarchical* with a *command and control* leadership style. In 2015, the organization got a new CEO, who brought a modern way of leading to the organization. A strategy to change the traditional mindset at the organization was developed, but people were not ready to embrace the strategy, due to the lack of resources and the right infrastructure. They were struggling with long queues and capacity allocation. The organization started a *Kanban initiative* in the beginning of 2016, introducing lean projects to optimize the way of running projects. At this time, a group of 20 persons working on front-end development started using agile practices.

In the end of 2016, a new CIO was appointed. He gathered many directors and C level leaders to start an agile pilot. The organization established an *agile pilot* with front end teams. During this time, the organization studied different scaling frameworks and models, including SAFe, the Spotify model, DAD and LeSS, finally settling on SAFe. A significant force behind this decision was the new CIO, who had an ambition to implement SAFe, as he had positive experiences from a SAFe transformation from his previous company. Furthermore, SAFe provided a top-down approach that helped to get management buy-in. A further supporting fact was that SAFe had been taken into use by many other financial organizations, making it easy to recruit coaches with framework experience.

At the time of the interviews, the case organization had four ARTs, see Fig. 1. Along with the trains they also had formed six Centers of Excellence (CoEs): Project and Program CoE, DevOps CoE, Lean and Agile CoE (LACE), SAP CoE, Integration and BPM CoE, and Test CoE.

The organization had approximately 30 projects running at the time of interviews. These projects were running in parallel with the release trains.

In the beginning, the organization had quarterly releases. Besides the quarterly releases, a few small releases happened every week. Finally, the organization moved to *monthly releases*.

3.3 Data Collection

We collected data by conducting 24 semi-structured interviews, during a 3-month period from February to April 2018. We collected data on different topics, for example: transformation reasons; transformation process; success factors, benefits and challenges of adopting SAFe; lessons learned; recommendations for future adopters; what could have been done differently in the transformation; and future steps at the case organization.

In this paper, we only focus on the formation of ARTs and the challenges faced after forming them. The interview data was complemented by observations of two PI planning meetings, in February and April 2018.

We interviewed a total of 27 people from different roles, including developers (4)[2], Product Managers (2), Project Managers (2), Product Owners (2), people from different Centers of Excellence (5), Project and Program (1), DevOps

[2] Number in the bracket indicates number of people interviewed.

(1), Integration (1), Test (1), Scrum Masters (2), Release Train Engineers (2), requirement analyst (1) and person from Service Oriented Architecture (SOA) (1).

We collected the data from the two longest running trains (DCE and DBI trains), as they were the pioneers in the SAFe journey. The other two trains (IP and DM) were only recently formed. All interviews were conducted face-to-face with two interviewers present, one being the primary interviewer, while the other was taking detailed notes and asking complementary questions. In one interview three persons were interviewed at the same time and in another interview two persons. In the rest of the interviews only one interviewee was present at the time.

The interviews were semi-structured and conversational to help in adapting to different roles and to understand individual opinions and perceptions. Each interview lasted 1–2 h, with an average of 90 min.

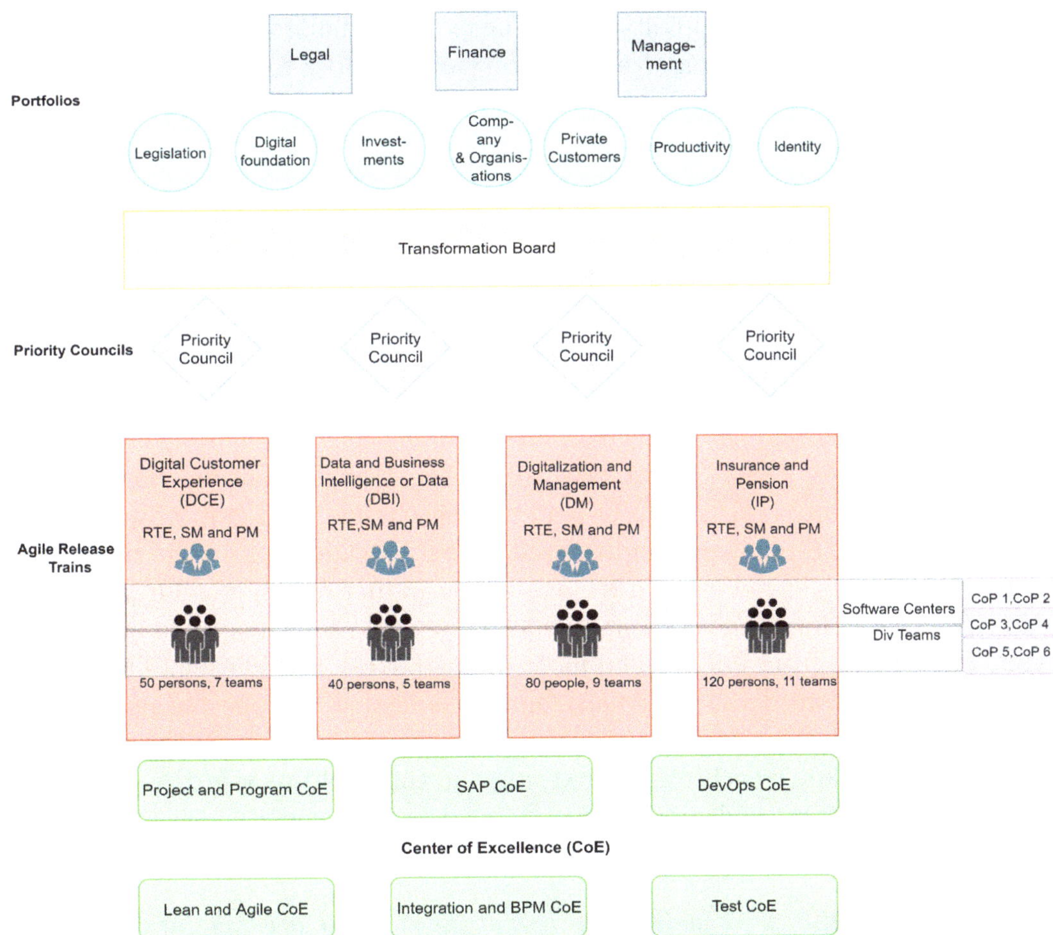

Fig. 1. Organizational structure after transition to SAFe

3.4 Data Analysis and Validation

All interviews were recorded and transcribed, and analyzed using the qualitative coding tool Nvivo 12 [29]. We followed the guidelines from [30] for coding. The first author started with *open coding* and compared the similarities and differences among the open codes and clustered them together into *axial codes*. During the process of axial coding, the authors discussed the clustering and naming. Based on the discussions, a few codes where modified or renamed. We identified the following high-level codes from the analysis: opinions on the SAFe framework, transformation reasons, transformation process, success factors of the adoption, challenges of the adoption, future steps for the case organization, recommendations for future adopters, lessons learned, and things that could have been done differently during the transformation.

After the analysis, the results were presented in a feedback session at the case organization in June 2018. All interviewees were invited. Twelve persons attended the session, most of which were interviewees. At the end of the session we discussed with the participants about the existing challenges and the changes they made in the organization after the interview period, i.e after April. Nobody disagreed with our results.

4 Results

4.1 The Formation of ARTs (RQ1)

In this section we describe how the case organization formed the ARTs, and the different negotiations that took place and compromises that were done.

Piloting and the First Train. As this SAFe transformation started from the IT management, with the CIO leading the change, and not from the top management, the IT managers had to "sell" the SAFe adoption to the rest of the organization: to developers, business people and higher managers. They decided to do that by starting a pilot through which they could show concrete benefits of SAFe. The pilot, a front-end development area (portal), was chosen. There were several carefully considered reasons behind this choice: (1) the teams working in this area had already started using agile and lean practices, (2) the people in this area already knew each other, lowering the threshold to join the pilot, and finally (3) in the front-end area it was deemed to be easy to show results and business value with help of short iterations and frequent deliveries.

> *"It was the easiest one, we had the people that used to work together. And because it was front-end development mainly, it was easy to show something. It is much more difficult when you do back-end development to show results, right? So they could actually, quite fast show business value."*
>
> — A Coach

The pilot train was called DCE, for *"Digital Customer Experience"*. The team formation was led by the front-end department leader and a project manager from the digital area. In the pilot phase, the train consisted of four teams. Later on, after some reorganization, a fifth team was added.

The pilot was commenced by a kick-off event. The event program included communicating the reasons behind the agile transformation and the selection of SAFe as a framework, explaining how the transformation will be started, as well as presenting the management ambitions for the release trains. The kick-off was followed by a PI planning session at the end of March 2017.

The pilot organization faced problems when trying to collaborate with the rest of the organization, as the surrounding parts were not ready to support the pilot as quickly as required by the agile way of working. People outside the pilot commented that they would not like to change their ways of working just for the sake of this pilot. As, after all, it was just a pilot that would be over after some time. Thus, our interviewees explained that being called as a "pilot" was not purely positive.

> *"... start with one train to experiment with, but never call it a pilot. Make sure it is something that is going to stay forever, because then, all the other departments, the operations, and so on, they need to recognize it and say, oh, then we need to change some of our processes to help them and support this department"*
>
> — A coach

Despite these problems, the pilot ended up being successful, and after less than six months the next train was launched, with the pilot train stabilizing its position as the first train.

An Organic Way of Transformation. After the success of the pilot, management planned to launch new release trains. However, they faced three major challenges: (1) political issues, (2) difficulties in identifying and separating value streams, and (3) avoiding a big restructuring of the organization.

Political Issues: Before moving to SAFe, the organization was *siloed*, with each director owning a pool of resources. Thus, it was crucial to get buy-in from the directors to allocate their resources in the release trains. Initially, none of the directors wanted to lose power by allocating resources into the release trains, as the power of each director was measured by the number of full-time employees overseen. Therefore, management wanted to create a *comfortable set up* for directors to willingly allocate their resources into the trains. Thus, they had to make compromises while designing the trains: the trains were almost *vertically sliced*, instead of horizontal slicing, to retain their old silos. This structure helped getting the business buy-in needed for the formation of the release trains.

Difficulties in Identifying and Separating Value Streams: The organization struggled to identify the relevant value streams, due to the presence of tightly coupled systems with a significant amount of cross-system dependencies. The same specialized persons participated in the development of several systems. For example, there were discussions on splitting up the *pension and insurance* products into two different value streams. However, splitting them and making them full stack was considered extremely difficult due to the lack of resources and the competence profile of people, i.e, very specialized competencies working on both products. Therefore, these two product groups were finally put into one joint train.

Avoiding a Big Restructuring of the Organization: The management was not ready to radically restructure the entire organization and invest in new resources for getting enough of the currently scarce resources (that were now working with several products) to each value-stream based train. As the SAFe transformation was not initiated by top management, the managers driving the transformation felt that they had to start from somewhere, first making easier changes that provide benefits and show the potential of SAFe. Then, after gaining experience of working with this framework, they would gradually start moving people from one train to another, slowly making the trains end-to-end and based on real value streams. A few interviewees called this plan an *organic way* of transformation, as the following quote explains:

> *"So that is part of why it is a journey and not just a destination... you can do it as a big bang decision, but then you have to do it as a complete, almost organizational re-engineering exercise, where you significantly restructure and probably invest in new resource pools at the same time. And we were not ready to do that, because we were doing it a bit more organically, you could say. So I think the way I succeeded in doing this discussion was that I actually made most of the executives, at least those close to the transformation, aware that we are now doing a compromise. And thus, I have opened up the thinking that probably we have to reorganize this within a year or perhaps one and a half. When we increasingly have gotten maturity in this way of working."* — A Coach

Transformation Teams. The high level design of the trains was lead by the main agile coaches. This design included figuring out what will be part of each train and what is left outside, by discussing details like, *what is the focus of each train, how big are the trains, and which groups of people are part of each train.* After that, the coaches formed transformation teams for each train. Each team was composed of people from business and different departments, and included line mangers and specialists. Each transformation team had approximately, 10 to 20 people, as the coaches wanted to involve all key stakeholders to make them to commit to the train design.

The designing of the trains was carried out iteratively: line managers from the transformation teams presented the designs to the employees by going to each department and talking to them. They collected feedback on the design and afterwards made a few changes to the structure of the trains to achieve the best possible solutions.

> *" So we used a lot of time figuring out what is part of this train, what is not part of this train. How many people, which people, and then, how to design the teams. And*

> *we have really used a lot of time for that, designing all those teams and finding out which people should be in them and what is the focus, and all that"* — A coach

Forming the Second Train. Every business area in the organization had their own *data department*. The organization had a need to centralize the people working on data by aligning different data related initiatives, such as data warehouse solutions or data for artificial intelligence. Thus, people working on data were allocated to a second train, the "Data Train", officially *"Data and Business Intelligence"*.

The coaches facilitated the designing of the train. They conducted workshops by bringing together all people, who were identified as key stakeholders. Initially, a design workshop was conducted to figure out the purpose of the train and who should be a part of the train. This train had many departments involved and people did not share similar qualifications. Again, full-stack teams were not seen as possible in this train. Thus, they ended up with a component team type of structure.

> *"So we started having the design workshop, saying what should the train do, who should be part of which teams, who should have in the leading roles and actually the PM and the system architect, trying to figure that out, trying to figure out which departments, who bought in the idea about a data train, where could we get people, from which business areas could we have people in the teams."*
> — A Product Manager

In another workshop the coaches and the train management described a vision for each team and chose the Product Owners for the teams.

In the next couple of workshops the team members could put their names in teams based on their skill set and interests. Later on, the coaches and the train management made only a few adjustments on the teams. Finally, five Scrum teams were formed and the Data Train started in August 2017.

Forming the Third and Fourth Trains. The last two trains were formed in March 2018. The trains were called *"Pension and Insurance Products"*, and *"Digitalization and Management"*. The Pension and Insurance Product train included the company's core products and their further development. The Digitalization and Management train concentrated on future areas, like digitalization of the different work processes in the company's business, like digitalization of administrative processes, as well as new directions, like robotics and artificial intelligence. These trains had eleven and nine Scrum teams when started.

Again, a series of strategic discussions were held to decide the boundaries between ARTs, in terms of systems, business processes and resources, which ended up to a rough draft on the philosophy of what kinds of ARTs will be designed. This draft was further worked in a workshop between business, IT and team leaders where it was described what kind of teams these ARTs need. The designing of teams inside the trains was realized by using *"Lego-blocks"*. Different coloured legos were used for different roles, e.g., core developer with *blue colour*

Legos. Some of the Lego blocks had names on them to represent the limited resources. Every manager had a certain number of Lego blocks representing a role. They aimed to make the teams as cross-functional as possible.

> *"It was really fun. So we were presenting different kind of roles. So each colour is a kind of role. So it is a portal developer and so on. And then, we put it together as Legos, [...] we are moving people around with Legos"* — A Coach

4.2 Challenges of Forming the ARTs (RQ2)

Besides the challenges mentioned in the previous section: political issues, difficulties in identifying and separating the value streams and not wanting to start a big restructuring of the organization, we identified several other challenges the case organization faced while adopting SAFe. To answer the second research question, we chose to present a couple of the most significant challenges faced by the organization while forming the ARTs: (1) project related challenges and (2) challenges due to dependencies.

Project Related Challenges. *Complex Projects:* Before the transformation, the development work in the organization was purely based on projects that were tightly controlled by the project managers. When the transformation started, the projects still kept running and the project managers kept their role in controlling the projects. Even though the idea was to finally get rid of the projects, this could not be done suddenly. Thus, the projects were running in parallel with the trains, with each project having work items in several trains.

The organization did not implement the portfolio layer with epics, but instead had projects. The projects were mentally transitioned into epics, i.e, *product epics.* These projects, running in parallel with the release trains, required detailed resource allocation and long term planning. Many interviewees mentioned that projects were not suitable for the release trains, as they had strict deadlines and large tasks, which cannot be delivered in small bits. Projects were so complex that they required detailed analysis phase before putting into the release trains. These project tasks were put into release trains in the form of features and user stories. In many cases, one task in a project required more than one train to realize it. This brought communication and coordination challenges between the four release trains. Moreover, the project managers felt helpless when they were responsible for the projects, but at the same time not able to control the work done in the trains.

Aligning Project and ART Releases: The projects had a different planning horizon than the release trains. The projects employed release management, which required details of the releases two months in advance. The release cycles of the projects *were not synchronized* with the PI release cycle used by the release trains. Thus, only the release trains were working in an agile way, and the rest of the organization was still waterfall driven. It was difficult to figure out how to align the project release cycle with the PI cycle of release trains.

Prioritization Challenges: The project tasks were distributed between the four trains due to lack of full stack trains. The priority of the project tasks differed between trains due to the lack of alignment between the trains. The trains had different PI cycles, i.e., they lacked PI cadence. They did not have joint PI planning, nor joint prioritization. One of the project managers mentioned that, they need to have some kind of planning where they can continue the prioritization or have some common prioritization session. While some other interviewees hoped for a portfolio layer to have continuity in the prioritization and to make sure the related tasks have the same priority between the trains.

For example, if project tasks were allocated between two trains, a task in train one is prioritized as *one* and in train two a related task as *ten*. If there is a delay, then the train two may move the task to the next PI, which causes a delay in the delivery of the project, which has a strict deadline. This also created additional coordination overhead between the trains to ensure the other tasks related to a certain priority, e.g., *"one"*, also have the same priority *"one"* between all four trains.

Challenges Due to Dependencies. *External Dependencies:* The tasks and features done in trains had several dependencies to the organizational units external to the trains. Many interviewees reported that every task or feature that was supposed to be delivered by a release train had lots of dependencies outside the trains. Additionally, the organization had separated the operations (Ops) and testing from the release trains by forming separate centers of excellence (CoE) for DevOps and Testing. This created further delays and dependencies between the trains and CoEs.

The organization found it impossible to form full stack trains by having all the competencies and people working full-time for the trains also from the external units. These dependencies between the trains and external units caused a lot of delays to the deliveries.

Inter-train Dependencies: The train design still had the old silo structure, i.e., the trains were responsible only for their own silo. The *front-end* and the *back-end* work was distributed between two different trains. Most tasks required data from the back-end to change something in the front end. This caused a lot of dependencies and coordination needs between the trains and finishing a task during the same period was challenging.

Many people argued these dependencies between the tasks were already present while running the projects, but there were project managers to coordinate the dependencies. After SAFe, the coordination of dependencies was pushed down to the team level. Teams were good at identifying the dependencies, but they were not good at acting on them. The project managers, who were not part of trains, were trying to coordinate between the trains, even though the teams should coordinate themselves according to agile and SAFe.

> *"A lot of these coordination things has been done by a project manager, before it hits the train. It is a lot bigger challenge, when you have to do it on the fly. [...]*

And that is where the silo is a problem. If you have full-stack, then it is internal, and then you can solve it internally in the different tracks, but when you have the silos, you have to talk across. And that is a challenge." — A Project Manager

Some of the interviewees, especially at the team level, expressed the need to bring in the portfolio and large solution layers to deal with the coordination between the ARTs. At the end of our study period, the coaches were planning the portfolio layer.

5 Discussion

5.1 RQ1: How Did the Release Train Formation Proceed at the Case Organization?

The SAFe transformation was initiated by launching a pilot with the teams that already had experience with agile practices. The SAFe implementation road-map [13,31] does not explicitly mention piloting as a starting point for the SAFe transition. However, it recommends the organizations to *"pick up one value stream and one ART"* and then, suggests to make a preliminary implementation plan for launching the next successive ARTs [31]. The same scenario was observed in our case, as they started with a pilot and then launched three more new ARTs. Several such instances of starting a pilot were identified in the literature [32–37].

After the success of the pilot, the organization was not ready for a radical and organization-wide restructuring for launching the new release trains that would be based on value streams. Instead, the old silo structure was retained to gain political acceptance for the transformation. Thus, an *organic way* of forming the release trains was initiated without having *"rigid value streams"* in the beginning, but planning to change the trains gradually towards real value streams. Likewise, several organizations in the existing literature struggled to identify the right value streams [14,21,26].

The road-map says [13] breezing or attempting a shortcut for identifying value streams is considered as *"putting your foot on the brake at the same time you are trying to accelerate"* [10]. This statement seems to be true within our case, as several challenges arose due to compromising for the train structure by designing them around silos instead of value streams. However, this compromise helped, according to our interviewees, the organization to gain acceptance for the transformation and to get more business resources into trains, which might not have happened by aiming for rigid value streams. This case adopted several innovative approaches for designing the teams for next three trains, such as *design workshops and Lego workshops.* We could not find detailed information on experiences of forming ARTs and teams in the existing literature.

5.2 RQ2: What Were the Challenges of Forming Release Trains at the Case Organization?

The case organization retained its *old silo structure* even after forming the release trains, due to political struggles and the desire to avoid big restructuring. Managing dependencies between the four silo based release trains was a significant challenge, which created coordination overhead. The same was reflected in [27], regarding managing the cross-team dependencies across release trains. Additionally, several other cases of adopting agile at scale reflected challenges with cross-team dependencies [1].

Our case struggled with complex projects that were hamstrung with deadlines and large tasks, as existing projects continued and their tasks were just distributed to different trains. Project managers continued their work, but did not have a say in the prioritization of the tasks distributed to different trains. We did not find similar cases from the literature.

5.3 Limitations

We identified the following threats to validity [28].

Construct Validity: This treat is concerned with how well the case study reflects reality. We carefully selected a rather large number of respondents representing various roles jointly with the organization to facilitate respondent triangulation. Initially, we made a list of potential interviewees, during a PI planning session at the case organization. This list was checked by one of the core member of the transformation team, who also suggested other people for getting the desired information for the study. There is a treat to misunderstand and misinterpret the questions, this was mitigated by conducting the interviews in a conversational manner, that helped interviewees to clarify the questions, in case of ambiguity. All interviews were conducted by two researchers, who also actively discussed the analysis.

External Validity: The external validity is concerned with the ability to generalize the results to other contexts. While it is difficult to explicate the exact context variables that facilitate generalisation, we compared our results with other SAFe case studies [2], with the SAFe implementation road-map [13], as well as with general studies of large-scale agile adoption [1].

Reliability: This threat is concerned with replication of the study. There is a threat of researcher bias in interpretation of the data. To mitigate this threat, we collected data from multiple sources, to ensure correctness of data. The results of coding process were validated by conducting a feedback session at the organization, and by discussing the analysis among the researchers.

6 Conclusions

The number of organizations adopting SAFe is increasing, but despite this, scientific studies on adopting this framework are scarce. Moreover, the published studies contain no in-depth information on the transformation process. This paper makes a contribution by describing the formation of ARTs and the challenges faced while forming them, as part of a SAFe transformation.

SAFe is not a silver bullet to all the scaling problems encountered by large-scale organizations. It can only be a starting point for scaling, and cannot solve all the challenges involved. Several organizations have reflected the struggles to form the release trains and to identify suitable value streams, especially those that develop multiple and tightly coupled systems. In this specific case we could see that turning a silo based traditional organization with projects into a SAFe organization that would have value stream based agile release trains was not possible overnight. The steps towards the goal required compromises, which caused a lot of challenges.

The current literature lacks in-depth information on how to form release trains and value streams in real complex organizations. Since several organizations have reflected such challenges, it is crucial to conduct more in-depth research on how to form release trains in practice and how to mitigate the challenges encountered to provide guidance to the practitioners. We welcome case studies, especially from matured organizations, that have taken SAFe into use for more than three years ago and that could give detailed information on the mitigation strategies adopted for the challenges faced during their SAFe adoption.

References

1. Dikert, K., Paasivaara, M., Lassenius, C.: Challenges and success factors for large-scale agile transformations: a systematic literature review. J. Syst. Softw. **119**, 87–108 (2016)
2. Scaled Agile, Inc.: SAFe Home Page. https://www.scaledagileframework.com/
3. The LeSS Company B.V.: Large Scale Scrum. https://less.works/case-studies/index.html
4. Ambler, S.W., Lines, M.: Disciplined Agile Delivery: A Practitioner's Guide to Agile Software Delivery in the Enterprise. IBM Press, Indianapolis (2012)
5. VersionOne: State of Agile Survey. https://explore.versionone.com/state-of-agile/versionone-12th-annual-state-of-agile-report
6. Moe, N.B., Olsson, H.H., Dingsøyr, T.: Trends in large-scale agile development: a summary of the 4th workshop at XP2016. In: Proceedings of the Scientific Workshop Proceedings of XP2016, p. 1. ACM (2016)
7. Moe, N.B., Dingsøyr, T.: Emerging research themes and updated research agenda for large-scale agile development: a summary of the 5th international workshop at XP2017. In: Proceedings of the XP2017 Scientific Workshops, p. 14. ACM (2017)
8. Putta, A., Paasivaara, M., Lassenius, C.: Benefits and challenges of adopting the scaled agile framework (SAFe): preliminary results from a multivocal literature review. In: Kuhrmann, M., et al. (eds.) PROFES 2018. LNCS, vol. 11271, pp. 334–351. Springer, Cham (2018). https://doi.org/10.1007/978-3-030-03673-7_24
9. Scaled Agile, Inc.: Description of Framework. https://www.scaledagileframework.com/what-is-safe/
10. Scaled Agile, Inc.: Identifying Value Streams and Agile Release Trains. https://www.scaledagileframework.com/identify-value-streams-and-arts/
11. Scaled Agile, Inc.: Agile Release Trains (ART's). https://www.scaledagileframework.com/agile-release-train
12. Scaled Agile, Inc.: Program Increment Plannings (PI's). https://www.scaledagileframework.com/program-increment/

13. Scaled Agile, Inc.: Implementation Roadmap. https://www.scaledagileframework.com/implementation-roadmap/
14. Crudup, R.F.: SEI Case Study. https://www.scaledagileframework.com/wp-content/uploads/delightful-downloads/2017/09/SEI_Agile_Case_Study.pdf. Accessed 09 Jan 2018
15. Scaled Agile, Inc.: EdgeVerve Case Study (2018). https://www.scaledagileframework.com/case-study-edgeverve-systems/. Accessed 28 Mar 2018
16. Scaled Agile, Inc.: Thales Case Study (2017). http://www.scaledagileframework.com/thales-case-study/. Accessed 09 Jan 2018
17. Richards, M.: Big IT Shop Case Study (2013). http://www.agilenotanarchy.com/2013/02/scaled-agile-framework-applied-25.html. Accessed 09 Jan 2018
18. Scaled Agile, Inc.: Northwestern Mutual Case Study (2017). http://www.scaledagileframework.com/northwestern-mutual-case-study/. Accessed 09 Jan 2018
19. Janisse, J.: TomTom Case Study (2016). https://www.scaledagileframework.com/wp-content/uploads/delightful-downloads/2017/09/Driving-SAFe-at-Tomtom1.pdf. Accessed 09 Jan 2018
20. I.J.I. Scaled Agile: Nordea Case Study. https://www.scaledagileframework.com/wp-content/uploads/delightful-downloads/2017/09/Nordea-Case-Study.pdf (2015). Accessed 09 June 2018
21. Holdorf, C.: John Deere Case Study. http://www.scaledagileframework.com/john-deere-case-study-part-3/. Accessed 09 Jan 2018
22. Pries-Heje, J., Krohn, M.M.: The safe way to the agile organization. In: Proceedings of the XP2017 Scientific Workshops, p. 18. ACM (2017)
23. Scaled Agile, Inc.: Case Study Australian Post (2017). http://www.scaledagileframework.com/case-study-australia-post/. Accessed 20 Nov 2018
24. Auret, C., Froville, J., Levaslot, M.: Pole Emploi Case Study (2016). https://www.scaledagileframework.com/wp-content/uploads/delightful-downloads/2017/09/Pole-Emploi-SAFe-Case-Study-V1.1.pdf. Accessed 09 Jan 2018
25. Scaled Agile, Inc.: KLM Air France Case Study (2018). https://www.scaledagileframework.com/case-study-air-france-klm/. Accessed 28 Dec 2018
26. Gusch, L., Herbai, P.: Elekta Case Study (2018). http://www.scaledagileframework.com/?ddownload=35393. Accessed 09 Jan 2018
27. Brenner, R., Wunder, S.: Scaled agile framework: presentation and real world example. In: 2015 IEEE Eighth International Conference on Software Testing, Verification and Validation Workshops (ICSTW), pp. 1–2. IEEE (2015)
28. Yin, R.K.: How to do better case studies. In: The SAGE Handbook of Applied Social Research Methods, vol. 2, pp. 254–282 (2009)
29. QSR International: Coding Tool for Qualtitaive Analysis. http://www.qsrinternational.com/nvivo/support-overview/downloads
30. Corbin, J.M., Strauss, A.L.: Basics of Qualitative Research: Techniques and Procedures for Developing Grounded Theory, 3rd edn. Sage Publications Inc., Los Angeles (2008)
31. Scaled Agile, Inc.: Creating implementation roadmap. https://www.scaledagileframework.com/create-the-implementation-plan/
32. Scaled Agile, Inc.: SK Hynix Case Study. http://editor.scaledagileframework.com/hynix-case-study/. Accessed 09 June 2018
33. Rutzen, A.: Waterfall to Agile Case Study (2014). https://www.scaledagileframework.com/wp-content/uploads/delightful-downloads/2017/09/1434405855wpdm_Waterfall_to_Agile_A_Case-Study.pdf. Accessed 22 Feb 2019

34. Scaled Agile, Inc.: Pole Emploi Case Study. http://www.scaledagileframework.com/pole-emploi-case-study/. Accessed 09 June 2018
35. Scaled Agile, Inc.: NHS Case Study (2017). http://www.scaledagileframework.com/nhs-case-study. Accessed 09 June 2018
36. R Software: BMC Case Study (2007). http://www.scaledagileframework.com/wp-content/uploads/delightful-downloads/2017/09/Case_Study_BMC10.pdf. Accessed 22 Feb 2019
37. Scaled Agile, Inc.: Royal Philips Case Study (2016). http://www.scaledagileframework.com/royal-phillips-case-study/. Accessed 09 June 2018

Agility Beyond IT

Corporate-Level Communities at Ericsson: Parallel Organizational Structure for Fostering Alignment for Autonomy

Darja Šmite[1(✉)], Nils Brede Moe[1,2], Jonas Wigander[3], and Hendrik Esser[3]

[1] Blekinge Institute of Technology, Karlskrona, Sweden
Darja.Smite@bth.se
[2] SINTEF, Trondheim, Norway
[3] Ericsson, Stockholm, Sweden

Abstract. Organizational management traditionally has taken care of all the important strategy, structure, and work-design decisions, as well as most of the ongoing decisions about work procedures. In large-scale corporations with many geographically distributed sites and high divisional detachment, such strategies are yet doomed to result in implementing irrelevant work methods and procedures that conflict with the local interests. As Tayloristic habits are disappearing, organizations willingly or unwillingly change their decision-making approaches to enable more participation and influence from the performers. These trends are associated with the rise of participation-based parallel structures, such as quality circles, task forces or communities of practice. In this paper, we present our findings from studying corporate-level communities by the means of a multi-case study at Ericsson. We found that the main hindrances are related to the limited decision-making authority of parallel structure, member selection and achieving representation across the organizational units. Our results suggest that parallel structures highly depend on the authority of the members within their local communities, and their ability to not only channel the dialog between the units they represent and the community, but also enable the active engagement of the unit in the community studies. As such, we believe that special attention shall be put on the ambassador role of the community members.

Keywords: Large-scale agile · Organizational agility · Bottom-up governance · Communities · Parallel structures · Alignment for autonomy · Empirical

1 Introduction

The sweet spot of agile methods is small-scale software development, and the vast majority of agile methods are intended to improve efficiency and effectiveness of small agile teams. Yet, adoption of agile principles on a corporate level and for large-scale contexts is gaining a lot of attention [1]. The paradigm shift towards increased agility on all levels in the organization has motivated major organizational transformations and puts the traditional hierarchical view on decision-making in question. In fact, along

P. Kruchten et al. (Eds.): XP 2019, LNBIP 355, pp. 173–188, 2019.
https://doi.org/10.1007/978-3-030-19034-7_11

with agile transformations on the development levels, large organizations are increasingly adopting alternative organizational models to circumvent the challenges of traditional hierarchies, top-down management structures, and centralized decision-making, and focus on self-management, autonomy and decision-making as a shared process, even though these efforts are associated with many challenges [2–4].

To become more flexible, large-scale organizations seek new ways to combat their inefficiencies. Centralized decisions in large organizations significantly slow down decision-making, and, to function faster, such organizations increase autonomy through decentralization at the divisional level, while keeping the technostructure at corporate headquarters [5]. However, such work systems are often associated with divisional detachment and increased coordination challenges [6], as well as varying quality and efficiency across the different units. It is not uncommon that different organizational units simultaneously would spend effort on attacking the same problems, or in the worst case even developing competing products. Thus, large organizations often depend on their ability to standardize the outputs and process [5] through coordination and alignment.

In a large-scale agile organization, where work is organized in programs and teams situated in different geographic locations and often belonging to different organizational units, there is a need to align a lot of decisions, e.g. the vision, mission and strategy, development tools to use, methods and processes. Standardizing the processes and tools will also help the organization in keeping track of the state of practice across the organization, to share good practices and knowledge across the organizational units. At the same time, rigid control impairs necessary local optimizations and ability to see creative solutions to local problems [7]. To succeed, organizational units need the freedom to choose the best processes and tools to solve their problems in their particular context. This leads to a paradoxical challenge of how to standardize as little as possible to benefit from organizational alignment and not impair the autonomy and flexibility.

One of the known answers to this challenge is fostering organization-wide participation in leading the alignment efforts with the means of structures parallel to the traditional organization. Parallel structures are permanent or temporary structures that are established to supplement the regular organization by performing functions that it does not perform or is ill-suited to perform well [8]. Some examples of parallel structures include quality circles [9] and communities of practices [10]. In this paper, we present our findings from studying corporate level communities in Ericsson, a large international company headquartered in Sweden, one of the worldwide leaders in the telecommunication market. Ericsson can be seen as an organization compound of many geographically distributed research and development centers united in thirteen product development units (each of which may include multiple geographic locations). Ericsson has started the World Class Development program in 2014 to improve the ways of working across the whole organization, and multiple workgroups were created to formulate corporate-level strategies and standards within selected subject areas. Members for the work groups were chosen from different parts of the organization, to find ideas and solution candidates already existing in the organization, and to increase the buy-in. These work groups were coordinated by the Software Systems community, the first corporate-level community that later initiated the transformation of the short-term working groups into long term communities that support the organizational units in the deployment of established standard approaches, and lead the continuous improvement of these standard approaches.

As a form of parallel organizations, communities have their strengths and weaknesses. Lawer and Mohrman [9] have observed that such company-wide mechanisms are said to attract a lot of attention and enthusiasm in their startup phases but then require significant effort to sustain them over several years. Similarly, not all Ericsson communities turned out successful in the long run. A few years after the implementation of the parallel structures, the community leaders recognized that achieving an agreement and commitment to the concept of corporate communities across the organization is challenging. The organization continuously changes and the community leaders have to keep all the managers from different organizational units aware of the community mission and work. This was challenging because collaboration over boundaries in a fragmented organization is a very formidable task, and because this initiative is still looked at as being driven from "above". Our research is thus driven by the need to better understand what makes or breaks the implementation of parallel organizational structures that are introduced to increase the agility in the large. In our research we thus aim at answering the following questions:

RQ1: What hinders participation-based parallel structures in a large-scale distributed agile organization?
RQ2: How to strengthen such parallel structures to maximize their benefits?

The rest of the paper is organized as follows. In Sect. 2, we summarize the existing research related to the participatory mechanisms for organizational alignment. Section 3 outlines the empirical background of our work, and the applied research methodology. Section 4 contains the results, which are discussed in Sect. 5, followed by conclusions in Sect. 6.

2 Related Work

Parallel organizational structures can be seen as a part of corporate governance, elements of the system relating to the management and control of an organization. As a governance structure, it should specify the distribution of rights and responsibilities, and arrange the rules and procedures governing decision-making processes. Although the area of organizational governance is a well-developed research field, studies on participation-focused parallel structures used for governance tasks in large-scale agile software organizations are scarce.

Participation and involvement have been one of the most important foundations of organizational development and change and has always been a central goal and one of the pillars of organizational learning [11]. When members of an organization feel they are excluded from participation by the leadership, they will find ways, often unhealthy, to express themselves [12]. Participation is also highly valued in software companies [13] and specifically in agile software development. Therefore, organizations need to provide a climate of participation if they are to remain healthy. By doing so, they increase not only the learning capacity of employees, but also their ability to influence organizational outcomes. Another potential effect of participation is increased emotional attachment to the organization, resulting in greater commitment, motivation to perform and desire for responsibility. As a result, employees care more about their work, which may lead to greater creativity and helping behavior, higher productivity and service quality [14]. However, participation is a challenge when the scale is large, even in agile organizations, where thousands of developers are scattered across multiple locations. Further, participation itself does not ensure that an organization will be successful in achieving its goals, and participation includes some degree of risk, as seen by management. For participation to be successful, the members of an organization must know how to participate effectively [12].

So, how does a large-scale agile organization achieve participation? Several techniques have been proposed to foster participation in organizations. Cotton et al. [15] found that long-term forms of participation appear to be more effective than short-term forms. For example, search conferences [16], survey feedback [17], autonomous work groups [18], quality circles [9, 18], process workshops [19], and learning meetings [20] are all predicated on the belief that increased participation will lead to better solutions and an enhanced organizational problem-solving capability.

Self-organizing groups that transcend official organizational structures have proven to be key enablers for success in the kinds of environments, where top-down organizational alignment, standardization and control are unwanted or difficult to operate [2]. A **quality circle**, for example, is an organizational structure composed of volunteers who arrange regular meetings to look at productivity and quality problems and discuss work procedures [9]. The strength of such circles is that they allow employees to deal with improvement issues that are not dealt with in a regular organization. The solutions proposed by the quality circles may or may not be implemented by the organization [18], since they are formulated as recommendations further discussed with and approved by the management. As such quality circles have a participatory rather than delegated decision-making [9]. Similarly, **communities of practice** that are traditionally suggested for their ability to foster knowledge sharing within an organization, and help individuals expand skills and expertise [21, 22], are also cultivated for their potential to help organizations improve coordination and standardization across units [10].

Both quality circles and communities of practice are well researched parallel structures. There are also examples of related research in the context of large-scale agile, including project level communities such as communities used for inter-team coordination in an agile program [23], communities using open space technology as a participation technique similar to a search conference [16] that served as a forum to discuss challenges and improvement initiatives [24], experience forums focusing on improving the development methods in a large-scale program [25] and communities that primarily target knowledge culture in organizations [22]. At the same time, corporate-level structures especially in the large-scale agile context are not well understood. Lawer and Mohran [9] mention **task forces** that broaden the quality circle structure by including the authority to look into policies, organizational design and other organizational issues. Kahkonen proposed three agile methods developed at Nokia that use facilitated workshops to solve multi-team issues and cultivate communities of practice that amass people from different parts of organizations to perform a specific well-defined task [2].

Finally, it is fair to assume that research proposing recommendations for well-functioning parallel structures enabled on the operational level such as the task forces, quality circles and communities of practice, are also applicable on a corporate level. According to Lawer and Mohran [9] and Wenger et al. [10], to succeed with the implementation of parallel structures, an organization shall pay attention to:

- Designing the existing organization to support the parallel structure by ensuring the needed decision-making authority and means of getting the needed support in implementing decisions;
- Involving a broad part of the organization by allowing open participation of various forms and promoting a high level of participation and representativeness across the organizational units;
- Delivering the value for the organization and the participants. This often means that a parallel structure shall be equipped with the competence needed to make good suggestions and decisions from practical and economic points of view, taking into account overall strategy and business objectives;
- Ensuring the visibility of the achieved results and value created for everyone.

3 Research Methodology

Since the goal of this research is to explore and provide insight into the participation-based parallel organizational structures in large-scale agile software development, it is important to study such structures in practice. In this study, the focal point is corporate-level communities that are introduced to improve work processes, methods and tools in the areas of organizational importance, where coordination and alignment across organizational units is seen as a source of performance and cost benefits.

To address our research questions, we designed a holistic multiple-case study [25] of seven communities in one company, Ericsson, which had been using agile for more than 10 years. According to Yin, case studies are the preferred research strategy when a "…question is being asked about a contemporary set of events over which the investigator has little or no control" [25].

Our sample contained seven out of eight communities; all available for study (C1–C7, see Table 1). Our research was performed in two steps. First, we contacted community leaders to learn and describe how the corporate level communities operate (October 2017). Then, we performed a detailed study of two selected communities focusing on the challenges and improvement recommendations from the point of view of the community members (November 2017 – March 2018).

3.1 Data Collection

In the first step, we interviewed the leaders of all seven communities. We conducted eight semi-structured interviews (one leader was interviewed twice), which aimed at capturing community's mission, authority, membership and repertoire. All interviews were approximately 1 h long, conducted in English and recorded with the help of AudioNote. Most of these interviews were held in person, but some via Skype due to unavailability of the interviewees in the office.

Based on the first step, leaders of two communities (C3 and C5, see Table 1) volunteered for detailed analysis, during which the researchers observed online community meetings and interviewed community members. In both C3 and C5, we started by interviewing the leader (one in C3 and 2 interviews with the leader of C5). The leaders helped us select six members (passive, active and new) for further interviews. We also observed community meetings at two occasions in each of the communities and wrote detailed minutes. All interviews in the second stage were held electronically via Skype, conducted in English and recorded with the help of AudioNote.

3.2 Data Analysis

The data collected from 23 interviews and four observations was analyzed in iterations. All interviews were recorded using AudioNote which is a tool for writing notes during the recording. The notes are then connected to the actual part of the interview. During the data analysis, we listened to the interviews and extended the notes. Through our engagement with the data, the success criteria for implementing organizational parallel structures emerged as an appropriate lens for examining participation in a large-scale agile setting. Thus, when analyzing the data, we used the success criteria from related research [9] as input and sought to understand the hindrances.

When analyzing the data, we relied on data source triangulation. Our rationale for the choice of interviews, observations and documentation as data sources for the study of communities as an example of participation and parallel organization is that by interviewing members, we gained access to their own understanding of the communities. Analyzing the observations and documentation shed light on the reasons given by the interviewees and provided context to their statements. As such, data triangulation is likely to have strengthened our findings and conclusions by increased accuracy.

4 Results

In this section, we describe our results from studying corporate-level communities at Ericsson and how they enable organizational agility and participation in a large-scale distributed organization. As described in the related work, to succeed with the implementation of parallel structures, an organization shall pay attention to [9, 10]:

- Ensuring the needed authority;
- Involving a broad part of the organization;
- Supporting value creation for the organization and the participants;
- Ensuring visibility of the achieved results for everyone in the organization.

In the following, we describe how the studied communities are set up (see Table 1), their mission and scope, and how they operate according to the above success criteria, and what are the main hindrances.

4.1 Mission and Scope

Ericsson has started their agile transformation more than 10 years prior to our investigation. However, the maturity of the new ways of working significantly differs across the organizational units and geographic locations. Corporate-level communities were implemented partly to support the agile transformation and the acceptance of the agile principles, and partially to foster the participative culture across the organization. Each of the studied communities focused on a selected strategic area (see Table 1). The prime purpose of these communities can be seen as standardization [27]. As an interviewee described: "*When we got 100 [agile] teams in eight countries we need to agree on some common tools*". Based on a high level of participation, communities are responsible for keeping track of the state of practice across the organization, communicate the corporate strategy, get feedback on the feasibility of the needed changes, enable autonomy and support the units in their efforts towards alignment. As explained by an interviewee *"It is about just-enough alignment, maximum autonomy and maximum participation.... We call it a self-organizing eco-system"*.

Table 1. Overview of the studied communities. "X" in the table denotes characteristics present in a community.

	C1	C2	C3	C4	C5	C6	C7
Focus areas and characteristics	Continuous analysis	Software development	Performance management	Tools	CI and test	Capability management	Software development system
Mission and scope							
– Strategy development				X	X		X
– Standardization	X			X	X		X
– Support with alignment			X		X	X	
– Status monitoring	X		X	X	X		
– Knowledge sharing	X	X	X	X	X	X	X
Authority							
– Makes a decision			X	X	X		X
– Makes a recommendation	X				X	X	
– Unclear		X					
Membership							
– Open	X	X	X			X	X
– By appointment	X		X	X	X		X
– No of members	30	30–40	13	31	30	30+	25–30
Representation							
– Represented units	10	Unknown	13	13	12	13	11
– Unrepresented regions	Asia, USA		USA			Asia, India, USA	Asia, India
Meetings							
– Duration	1 h	1 h	1–1,5 h	3 h	1,5 h	30 min	1,5–2 h
– Frequency	monthly	biweekly	biweekly	biweekly	every 3rd week	biweekly	monthly

While standardization and corporate-level alignment is the essential mission of the studied communities, knowledge sharing is also an important emergent task. Most of the communities dedicate time for sharing experience across the organizational units.

Knowledge sharing is often fostered by community leaders, who seek interesting topics and contributions from more mature units and request to demonstrate locally developed tools, practices, and lessons learned, such as the advances in continuous integration or continuous testing. This is said to be of great value for less mature organizational units.

To keep track of what is going on across the organization, discuss the needed improvements to the corporate strategies and share the knowledge across the units, the studied communities hold regular planned meetings. These meetings are on average 1,5 h long (between 30 min and 3 h) and are typically held on a biweekly basis. Since all communities have representatives from different geographic locations, community meetings are held electronically, typically using audio channel only. Some communities happen to have several co-located members who gather in the same meeting room and connect to the rest of the members via a phone conference.

The vast majority of community meetings follow a structured agenda, proposed by the leader. From observing community meetings, we found that the meeting in one of the communities was about reporting and informing, and it's mostly the leader talking. The other observed community had more interaction and discussion.

Beside the meetings, members are required to read material before the meetings, answer questions, elicit feedback or seek approval locally in their units, prepare presentations on the status in their units, and pursue the units to engage in field studies, i.e. testing community ideas, piloting new ways of working.

4.2 Decision-Making Authority

We found a great variance among the corporate-level communities with respect to their decision-making authority, as well as commonly recognized challenges. First of all, we found that most of the communities make recommendations to management, based on their work, similarly to the quality circles [9] which means they do not have unlimited decision-making authority. Among seven communities, the leaders from only three communities had a strong belief they have the power to drive the strategy or change the existing standards in their areas. This means that the targeted cross-organizational alignment becomes a result of a dialog between the units, the community and the corporate management. The leaders of other communities mentioned that they either did not have the power to make certain decisions or have never used it. In some communities, the alignment directives are driven from the top down, in which case members of the community develop an action plan on how to comply with the corporate directions and follow up on the progress across the organizational units.

One particular challenge related to authority many communities face is their limited ability to implement the standards across the organization units. Some of the community recommendations might conflict with the interests of particular organizational units. As one member explained: *"What is a good practice in one [organizational unit] is not a good practice in another"*. Since communities are not equipped with policing functions, but focus on the status gathering and support, the perceived authority of the communities to purse the organizational units is low. As such, some leaders said that when organizational units disagree with the alignment requests, they can simply not follow the community recommendations. In addition, communities cannot request the units to apply or implement their proposals, because communities do not have any dedicated budget, and any community-related field work ultimately depends on the ability of local representatives to find and approve the use of resources within that unit.

Challenge: When corporate interests are in conflict with the local interests, community recommendations may be ignored due to a lack of formal authority.

While some community leaders and members perceived missing a formal decision-making authority as a problem, others explained that the formal authority was not that important. For the parallel structure to influence the established organization, several interviews claimed that it was more important to have a dialogue with the key management in the local organizations. One community member explained: *"To make a change you need to discuss [it] with management that got decision-making authority.... I therefore conducted 30 min interviews with key stakeholders in the line organization to understand their perspective and to create a good relationship. Then I use my social network to influence their decisions"*. This community member was successful in implementing decisions made by the community and to share knowledge from the community. He called himself a "diplomate". However, not everyone had such a strong network and were able to influence others.

Challenge: While the lack of authority can be to a degree addressed by a strong local social network, community members that are new or weakly integrated in the organizational networks are not able to have any local influence.

4.3 Breadth of Involvement

We found that all but one community (Software Developer community that was open to anyone) are designed to have permanent members representing each organizational unit. Some of these communities are also open for additional members. At the moment of our study, the number of community members varied from 13 to 40 with the average of 28 members. The units could be represented by one or several members and could bring guests to particular meetings. One community maintained an information channel open for subscription with over 90 subscribers.

All community leaders agree that broad involvement from the units is important for the corporate-level communities to be able to make good decisions and make sure that recommendations do not conflict with local interests of a unit. At the same time, having too many representatives can also cause challenges. Communities with too many people involved in approving ideas makes decision-making process slower. As the leader of the CI and test community explained: "The wheel is too big to turn. It can take months". To ease the process of feedback elicitation and speed up decision making, some communities publish working material in the community spaces and used Yammer[1] functionality for online discussions, where the members can trace all questions and comments, and make changes before meeting and discussing the decisions.

[1] Freemium enterprise social networking service used for private communication within organizations.

Challenge: Achieving an agreement across all organizational units takes time.

Another challenge that impacts the efficiency of decision-making is the coverage of the units in the community. Three of the studied communities reported that they do not have representatives from all units or locations. This mean that decisions taken in the community might not reflect the actual situation in the whole distributed agile organization, and that decisions need to be revisited if people of the missing units join.

Furthermore, some community leaders said that the organizational units do not always make a good selection of representatives. As the CI and test community leader explained, communities need to get the right people to represent the organizational units, and thus it is important to seek the best suited experts instead of formal appointment. These people shall have local authority and a contact network, to be able to elicit fast feedback from the unit on the decisions discussed in the community. Another community member verified this view: *"How successful we are depends on who are the members and how well they are connected to the local organization"*.

In addition, some of the organizational units are so large (see Fig. 1) that one representative is not always aware of the processes and happenings across the whole unit he or she represents. One of the members from the CI and test community described that his unit is a merger of two different product development organizations spanning several geographical locations. Each of the product development organizations had their own methods, processes, and tools, and subsequent interests. Thus, he thought that ideally more representatives were required to represent the possibly varying interests.

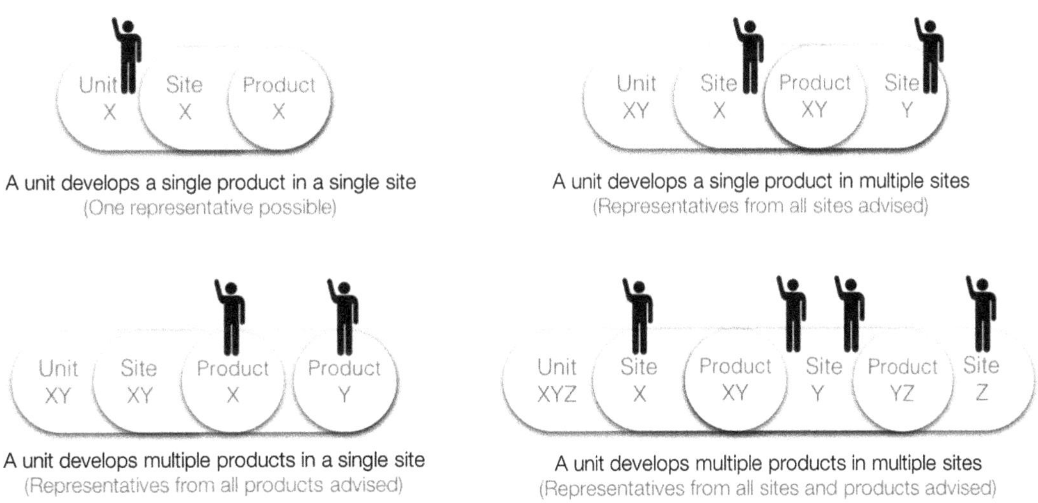

Fig. 1. Structures relevant for selection of unit representatives.

Challenge: Selecting one permanent member to represent an organizational unit is insufficient in large distributed units.

The ability of communities to make the interests of particular organizational units heard was also affected by the level of attendance of the meetings. Some organizational units are represented, but the members either do not attend meetings, or remain inactive. Community leaders estimate that on average about 40% of all members participate in meetings. The community with the highest attendance reported 2/3 of the members to be present regularly, while the community with least attended meetings reported about 1/5 of the members. Notably, only 1/3 of the members present in the meetings is said to actively engage in discussions or ask questions.

Challenge: Poor attendance and activity of the members negatively influence their ability to voice the interests of particular units in the community.

To understand what influences the level of engagement, we elicited opinions from the members of two communities. The following circumstances increased participation:

- Personal contact and familiarity among the members;
- Personal interest and competence in the topic;
- Leader's effort in engaging members.

We also learned that participation decreased when:

- Organizational unit's competence is much higher than that of others member represented units (perceived ability to learn from others is low);
- Only the leader on the agenda, so others are reluctant to engage;
- Members are new to the community and have not been properly onboarded;
- Organizational units do not prioritize or recognize community work.

4.4 Value and Results

We found that communities generated value on three levels – corporate level, unit level and individual level of the members. On the corporate level, the recognized benefits are primarily related to the ability of the communities to drive the execution of strategic plans, capacity for knowledge-development projects and form knowledge-based alliances, and enabling coordination, standardization and synergies across organizational units. On the unit level, the benefits seem to be twofold. For more mature units, participation in communities provides opportunities to influence the corporate strategies and promote their local advances in an area to the corporate level. Meanwhile less mature units can benefit from getting access to the advances from across the organization. Finally, on the individual level, the interviewed community members mentioned to benefit from participation in the community through the ability to deepen their understanding of the standards, find solutions to own problems and learn from others, and from networking with key experts across the organization.

4.5 Visibility in the Organization

Sharing experience among units and disseminating community work results, including conclusions based on cross-unit field studies and investigations, was seen as an important mission for all communities. The main means to achieve this included communication among the members and with their local peers, communities and management, and sharing results through a community web page that is available for everyone in the company. One particular community enabled a number of means of communication with the community for the rest of the potential users (see Fig. 2): anyone accessing this web page can ask questions about the community, see the results from community work, and community plans (e.g. backlog and task list).

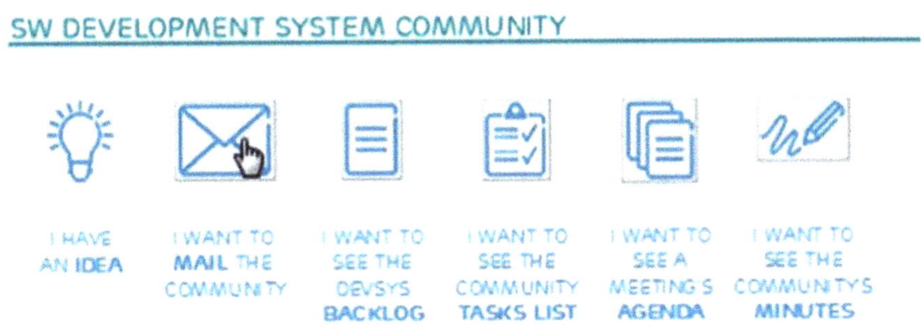

Fig. 2. A snapshot of a part of the Software Development System's community web page.

Some members complained that their communities were not well recognized or even known to their peers in respective organizational units, while others said that their communities were well-recognized for their work. We found that in many cases, the visibility of the community was again directly related to whether the individual members are well connected in their local units. One of the community members explained, *"In some cases I have used own distribution lists. In other cases I go directly to persons I know are affected, sometimes I set up a meeting with whoever should be aware of [the results]... I am using the established forum where product, processes, methods and tools [-related] meetings we have, where I can present this kinds of stuff".*

Challenge: Community work visibility across the whole organization highly depends on the connections of the community members in local units' networks.

5 Discussion

In this paper, we presented our findings from studying corporate-level communities by the means of a multi-case study at Ericsson. These structures at Ericsson are regarded as important elements of the self-organizing eco-system. We now discuss our results in light of our research questions: *What hinders participation-based parallel structures in a large-scale distributed agile organization?* and *How to strengthen these parallel structures to maximize their benefits?*

5.1 Hindrances in Corporate-Level Parallel Structures

To understand what hinders corporate-level parallel structures at Ericsson, we have analyzed their characteristics in the light of the success factors proposed in related research [9, 10]. A successful parallel organizational structure is said to have support from the organization in terms of the needed decision-making authority, to involve a broad part of the organization, to deliver value for the organization and the members, which is also recognized within the organization.

With respect to the organizational support, we found that not all Ericsson communities have received the needed decision-making authority. Our results suggest that some communities still act upon top-down directives, and have limited decision power, while others drive the strategy and improvements in their area. Furthermore, we found particular challenges with the ability to pursue and engage the organizational units in community studies and initiatives. Corporate support was insufficient and whenever community recommendations conflicted with the local organization, communities were perceived as a burden, as suggested in related research [9].

With respect to the involvement in the large-scale distributed context, we further found that the studied communities had a broad coverage of the organizational units. While voluntary participation is often seen as a weakness of community structures [10], mandatory unit representation ensured a reasonable representativeness, even though some units were not represented in some communities. The main challenge with respect to involvement was to sustain high levels of member participation in meetings. Similarly to related research [9] we found symptoms that the enthusiasm when the initial work groups were launched has decreased over time, and some of the previously active members have become less active. We also found that achieving a valid representation of all locations and programs in large units was important (see Fig. 1), since each might have their own work processes, tools and/or local improvement initiatives. As such, we found that the success of communities highly depends on whether the members are well connected in their local networks and the level of their awareness of what is happening across the unit they represent.

Most of the communities seemed to work successfully towards their goals, i.e. coordinated the deployment of the standards and policies supporting agile software development and balancing the corporate need for alignment and the local need for unit autonomy. As such, the organization represented by the Software Systems community, has recognized the value of enabling community-based parallel structures. The individual members also benefitted from their membership in terms of access to the knowledge and a company-wide expert network. As such, our study confirms the ability of parallel structures to create value on an organizational and individual levels [10, 21]. Furthermore, we learned that those who seem to benefit the most from community membership were the representatives from the organizational units with less mature ways of working or limited knowledge in an area of community concern.

Finally, community leaders have complained about the lack of visibility of their results across the organization, and the lack of understanding of the value for the units. In fact, many community leaders and community members commented on the lack of dedicated time for community work given to the unit representatives (a common problem in communities of practice [22, 27, 28]), and the lack of recognition of the importance of unit representation.

5.2 Strengthening Corporate-Level Communities

Our findings suggest that parallel structures might be doomed to take a back seat when it comes to power and decision-making mandate in comparison with official organizational structures. Therefore, we would like to emphasize the importance of the personal authority and connections of the individual unit representatives in their local organizations. In contrast to communities of practice, in which membership is voluntary and internal structures evolve organically [10], parallel structures similar to the studied communities at Ericsson will need mandatory membership in addition to the open one, and careful selection. We believe that the key to strengthening the corporate-level communities is related to finding **ambassadors** well anchored in their local organizations. Our findings suggest that even if a community would have no authority mandated by the corporate management, it would still be able to drive initiatives, if the individual unit representatives had local authority. Furthermore, it seems that the number of representatives does not matter, if the member present is well connected. This is why we believe that local authority and the amount of connections in the organizational unit's should be the prime characteristics for member selection.

At the same time, our findings suggest that member participation and unit engagement play a critical role when it comes to the value created by the communities. All of the identified benefits of the studied communities relate to learning, discussion, networking or coordinating with others. If the number of participants is low, naturally the benefits provided by participation in the community are decreasing. Larger participation seems to increase the potential to provide more benefits. In particular, it increases the chances of spreading the good practices and improving coordination and alignment. The only drawback could be perhaps when organizational units have too diverse practices and strive for more autonomy. In this case, increased participation might lead to increased disagreements.

Other recommendations based on our findings and related research include:

- Enabling decision-making in the community [9, 10, 27, 28];
- Welcoming different level of participation [10, 27] to increase the level of participation, as well as the transparency and visibility of community work;
- Allocating the needed resources for community work [22, 27, 28], (members and unit engagement in locally run activities);
- Strengthening external image of the community [9, 10], e.g. by making community work results publicly available.

6 Conclusions

Several studies show that participation is not only an agile value but is important for any software company to be successful [13]. We have given examples on how a large software company has used corporate-level communities for achieving long-term participation across a number of organizational units in enabling alignment and autonomy in large-scale agile organization.

We found communities that had the power to define the strategy, and others that worked with the implementation of a management strategy. Some communities made decisions themselves, others provided recommendations to the management. As such, there were examples of top-down, bottom-up and sandwich decision-making approaches.

We found a number of hindrances that lowered the ability of communities to impact the organizational units. We have listed recommendations for strengthening the communities, with community member selection being the key one to compensate for the common deficiency of mandate given to a community. We conclude that members of parallel structures shall be well-anchored ambassadors, having close contact with practitioners in a selected area, being aware of what is happening across the whole unit, and having a strong network and local authority to deploy the community work.

We will continue to study how both new and old participation techniques are used in Ericsson, and the balance between autonomy and alignment in large-scale agile. We will also study how other large companies can achieve a higher level of participation in agile software development, particularly at the team, project and program level.

References

1. Moe, N.B., Dingsøyr, T.: Emerging research themes and updated research agenda for large-scale agile development: a summary of the 5th international workshop at XP2017. In: Proceedings of the XP2017 Scientific Workshops, p. 14. ACM (2017)
2. Kahkonen, T.: Agile methods for large organizations-building communities of practice. In: Proceedings of the XP Conference, pp. 2–10. IEEE (2004)
3. Olsson, H.H., Bosch, J.: No more bosses? In: Abrahamsson, P., Jedlitschka, A., Nguyen Duc, A., Felderer, M., Amasaki, S., Mikkonen, T. (eds.) PROFES 2016. LNCS, vol. 10027, pp. 86–101. Springer, Cham (2016). https://doi.org/10.1007/978-3-319-49094-6_6
4. Moe, N.B., Aurum, A., Dybå, T.: Challenges of shared decision-making: a multiple case study of agile software development. Inf. Softw. Technol. **54**(8), 853–865 (2012)
5. Mintzberg, H.: Mintzberg on Management: Inside Our Strange World of Organizations. The Free Press, New York City (1989)
6. Ingvaldsen, J.A., Rolfsen, M.: Autonomous work groups and the challenge of inter-group coordination. Hum. Relat. **65**(7), 861–881 (2012)
7. Takeuchi, H., Nonaka, I.: The new product development game. Harvard Bus. Rev. **64**(1), 137–146 (1986)
8. Mohrman, S.A., Edward E.L.: Parallel participation structures. Public Adm. Q. 255–272 (1989)
9. Lawler, E.E., Mohrman, S.A.: Quality circles - after the honeymoon. Organ. Dyn. **15**(4), 42–54 (1987)
10. Wenger, E., McDermott, R.A., Snyder, W.: Cultivating Communities of Practice: A Guide to Managing Knowledge. Harvard Business Press, Boston (2002)
11. Dybå, T.: An empirical investigation of the key factors for success in software process improvement. IEEE Trans. Softw. Eng. **31**(5), 410–424 (2005)
12. Zajac, G., Bruhn, J.G.: The moral context of participation in planned organizational change and learning. Adm. Soc. **30**(6), 706–733 (1999)

13. Moe, N.B., Dybå, T.: Improving by involving: a case study in a small software company. In: Richardson, I., Runeson, P., Messnarz, R. (eds.) EuroSPI 2006. LNCS, vol. 4257, pp. 159–170. Springer, Heidelberg (2006). https://doi.org/10.1007/11908562_15
14. Fenton-O'Creevy, M.: Employee involvement and the middle manager: evidence from a survey of organizations. J. Organ. Behav. **19**(1), 67–84 (1998)
15. Cotton, J.L., Vollrath, D.A., Froggatt, K.L., Lengnickhall, M.L., Jennings, K.R.: Employee participation - diverse forms and different outcomes. Acad. Manag. Rev. **13**(1), 8–22 (1988)
16. Purser, R.E., Cabana, S.: Involve employees at every level of strategic planning. Qual. Prog. **30**(5), 66–71 (1997)
17. Baumgartel, H.: Using employee questionnaire results for improving organizations: the survey "feedback" experiment. Kansas Bus. Rev. **12**, 2–6 (1959)
18. Guzzo, R.A., Dickson, M.W.: Teams in organizations: recent research on performance and effectiveness. Annu. Rev. Psychol. **47**, 307–338 (1996)
19. Dingsøyr, T., Moe, N.B.: The impact of employee participation on the use of an electronic process guide: a longitudinal case study. IEEE Trans. Softw. Eng. **34**(2), 212–225 (2008)
20. Dybå, T., Dingsøyr, T., Moe, N.B.: Process Improvement in Practice - A Handbook for IT Companies. Kluwer, Boston (2004)
21. Millen, D.R., Fontaine, M.A.: Improving individual and organizational performance through communities of practice. In: Proceedings of the 2003 International ACM SIGGROUP Conference on Supporting Group Work, pp. 205–211. ACM (2003)
22. Oliver, S., Reddy Kandadi, K.: How to develop knowledge culture in organizations? A multiple case study of large distributed organizations. J. Knowl. Manag. **10**(4), 6–24 (2006)
23. Paasivaara, M., Lassenius, C.: Communities of practice in a large distributed agile software development organization–case Ericsson. Inf. Softw. Technol. **56**(12), 1556–1577 (2014)
24. Dingsøyr, T., Moe, N.B., Seim, E.A.: Coordinating knowledge work in multiteam programs: findings from a large-scale agile development program. Project Manag. J. **49**(6), 1–14 (2018)
25. Moe, N.B., Dingsøyr, T., Rolland, K.: To schedule or not to schedule? An investigation of meetings as an inter-team coordination mechanism in large-scale agile software development. Int. J. Inf. Syst. Proj. Manag. **6**(3), 45–59 (2018)
26. Yin, R.K.: Applications of Case Study Research, 2nd edn. Sage Publications, Thousand Oaks (2003)
27. Šmite, D., Moe, N.B., Levinta, G., Marcin, F.: Spotify guilds – cultivating knowledge sharing in large-scale agile organizations. IEEE Softw. **36**, 51–57 (2019)
28. Millen, D.R., Fontaine, M.A., Muller, M.J.: Understanding the benefit and costs of communities of practice. Commun. ACM **45**(4), 69–73 (2002)

Scaling Agile Beyond Organizational Boundaries: Coordination Challenges in Software Ecosystems

Iris Figalist[1(✉)], Christoph Elsner[1], Jan Bosch[2], and Helena Holmström Olsson[3]

[1] Corporate Technology, Siemens AG, 81739 Munich, Germany
{iris.figalist,christoph.elsner}@siemens.com
[2] Department of Computer Science and Engineering, Chalmers University of Technology, Hörselgången 11, 412 96 Göteborg, Sweden
jan.bosch@chalmers.se
[3] Department of Computer Science and Media Technology, Malmö University, Nordenskiöldsgatan, 211 19 Malmö, Sweden
helena.holmstrom.olsson@mau.se

Abstract. The shift from sequential to agile software development originates from relatively small and co-located teams but soon gained prominence in larger organizations. How to apply and scale agile practices to fit the needs of larger projects has been studied to quite an extent in previous research. However, scaling agile beyond organizational boundaries, for instance in a software ecosystem context, raises additional challenges that existing studies and approaches do not yet investigate or address in great detail. For that reason, we conducted a case study in two software ecosystems that comprise several agile actors from different organizations and, thereby, scale development across organizational boundaries, in order to elaborate and understand their coordination challenges. Our results indicate that most of the identified challenges are caused by long communication paths and a lack of established processes to facilitate these paths. As a result, the participants in our study, among others, experience insufficient responsivity, insufficient communication of prioritizations and deliverables, and alterations or loss of information. As a consequence, agile practices need to be extended to fit the identified needs.

Keywords: Large-scale agile software development · Inter-team coordination · Software ecosystems

1 Introduction

Agile practices in software development have been around for quite some time and originally emerged due to the need to adapt faster to changing customer

P. Kruchten et al. (Eds.): XP 2019, LNBIP 355, pp. 189–206, 2019.
https://doi.org/10.1007/978-3-030-19034-7_12

requirements [1]. Developing in iterations provides the required flexibility and enables agile projects to "identify and respond to changes more quickly than a project using a traditional approach" [1]. With the focus being on "individuals and interactions over processes and tools" [2], preferably through face-to-face communication, agile practices initially aimed at small, local teams. However, as agile development became more popular, larger organizations adapted certain practices as well [3]. As a result, large-scale agile frameworks, such as SAFe [4] and LeSS [5], were developed to provide guidance to large organizations. The application of scaled agile methods has already been investigated to a great extent, e.g. in [3,6–10], and [11]. The focus, however, lies mostly on large-scale projects or multiteams within one organization. This lead us to the question: How to scale agile even further, beyond organizational boundaries?

Software ecosystems can be defined as "the interaction of a set of actors on top of a common technological platform that results in a number of software solutions or services. [...]" [12]. Opening up a platform to external developers enables platform operators to expand their offerings and provide further functionalities that they would not have been able to develop themselves, thereby providing more value to the customer but at the same time requiring additional coordination efforts [13,14].

In large-scale distributed, agile teams, inter-team coordination has previously been identified as a major challenge [8]. As large-scale software ecosystems differ from traditional organizations in various ways, these challenges cannot directly be adopted. For one, each actor within the ecosystem has its own way of working that can hardly be standardized [13]. This results in many different practices applied across the ecosystem and, therefore, many different degrees of agility which can be difficult to align. Moreover, the actors do not belong to a single but instead to many different organizations which share different, possibly competing, relationships. For this reason, the actors do often neither share the same goals nor communicate in a fully open way. This makes the inter-team coordination even more difficult.

To our knowledge, the challenges of inter-team coordination beyond organizational boundaries are not yet sufficiently investigated in existing literature. For that reason, we raise the following research questions:

(a) How do agile teams within software ecosystems coordinate their efforts?
(b) Which inter-team coordination challenges do agile teams within software ecosystems face?

In order to achieve this, we conducted a case study within two large, industrial software ecosystems to investigate their processes and inter-team coordination. We elaborate the results along three dimensions that constitute the framing for our findings: (a) maturity of the ecosystem (b) phases within the agile lifecycle (c) openness/closedness of the ecosystem. We use this framing to map the conflicting interests between actors as well as the resulting challenges and implications to the dimensions. Therefore, the contribution of this paper is to unfold why certain conflicts arise in a particular situation or setting in order to increase awareness of other actors' mindsets, and to help practitioners understand certain challenges and possible trade-offs they, thereby, might be facing. Moreover, we were able to tie most of the challenges back to long communication paths and a lack of established processes, raising the need to extend existing agile practices.

The remainder of this paper is organized as follows: First, we explain the characteristics of software ecosystems in Sect. 2, followed by our case study design in Sect. 3. In Sect. 4 we present the results of our study, before providing an overview of related work in Sect. 5, and summing up and concluding our work in Sect. 6.

2 Characteristics of Software Ecosystems

One of the major differences between distributed teams in traditional organizations and software ecosystems is the fact that the teams or actors are not within the same company or organization but instead spread across several organizations, whereby each actor contributes different elements to the system or product. This entails various types of relationships between actors within an ecosystem. For instance, the actors can be competitors or share mutual benefits [12]. The complexity of relationships and dependencies increases with the number of parties involved in the ecosystem [13]. Moreover, the number of actors and their possibly competing relationships results in a lack of sharing data which has previously been observed in large organizations [15].

Even though iterative requirements engineering processes provide an increased flexibility and are already widely applied in software ecosystems, further challenges arise due to the ecosystem's various actors, the physical distance between them, and the complexity of dependencies within the ecosystem, which impede a common understanding among and alignment between actors [16–18]. For one, the interpretation and prioritization of requirements can differ highly between ecosystem actors because different stakeholders value different attributes when dealing with a requirement. Every partner contributes requirements to the ecosystem which might result in a requirement overload, causing complications in the prioritization process [19]. Additionally, the negotiation process of requirements is highly influenced by the amount of power and dependencies between actors [18]. An adequate understanding of the other actors' goals and business models is required in the requirements engineering process in order to satisfy existing stakeholders and attract new partners.

In this paper we analyze how the described characteristics and challenges manifest in the inter-team coordination of agile teams within software ecosystems.

3 Case Study Design

Case studies are a well-known research methodology to investigate and understand contemporary phenomena in their real-world context with no or little control by the researcher [20,21]. As our research questions aim at answering exploratory questions, we believe that this is the right methodology for our study, following the guidelines by Runeson and Höst [20].

Case Study Design. The research objective of our study was to investigate the inter-team coordination and its accompanying challenges across organization boundaries. Specifically, our study focuses on how teams in distributed organizations communicate with each other, what kind of information, feedback or data they share, how it is shared, and how they are making and communicating decisions that affect any of the other teams. To achieve this, we performed this case study in two large software ecosystems, *Ecosystem A* and *Ecosystem B*, which are established in the industrial and the healthcare domain, respectively. Each ecosystem originated in a large, industrial company and offers several services, mostly in terms of applications, to the companies' customers. In order to expand their offerings, they opened up their platform to internal as well as external partners developing applications on the platforms. Figure 1 gives an overview of the ecosystems' structures and actors. We chose the respective ecosystems for our study since the keystone as well as the partners work in agile teams and experience difficulties in their coordination.

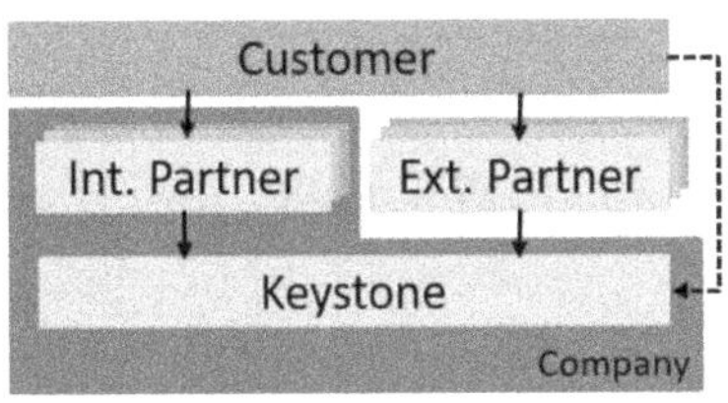

Fig. 1. Actors in ecosystems

Table 1. Description of ecosystems

Ecosystem	A		B		
# of platform devs	500–750		50–100		
# of internal partners	20–50		5–10		
# of external partners	100–200		5–10		
# of apps	20–50		10–20		
Interviewees keystone	DM	PO	PM		
Interviewees partner	SA		PO I	PO II	PO III

Data Collection and Analysis. We conducted semi-structured interviews with key stakeholders within the two ecosystems. Four product owners (PO), one product manager (PM), one demand manager (DM), and one software architect (SA) participated in the study. The demand manager is responsible for collecting and structuring requests from partners and customers before forwarding them to appropriate platform teams. Each of our interviewees belongs to a different, individual agile team within the respective ecosystem and was chosen as a key stakeholder to represents the views of their entire team. Moreover, all interviewees belonged to either the keystone who develops the platform (PM, DM, and one PO) or to a complementing player (three POs, SA) of an ecosystem, therefore providing views from both angles. One product owner, the demand manager, and the software architect belonged to *Ecosystem A* and the product manager and three of the product owners belonged to *Ecosystem B* (see Table 1 for a structured overview of the ecosystems and our participants).

All interviews included the following topics: communication structures, exchange of data and feedback with partners and customers, and decision making processes; though the interview guides were slightly adjusted to the specific roles. At the beginning of each interview the participants were given a brief introduction into the study and the structure of the respective ecosystem was shortly discussed in order to create a common understanding. Following this, the interviewees were asked for their permission to audio tape the interview, before the interviews were conducted. Each interview lasted between 45 min and one hour, and was transcribed and summarized afterwards.

Additionally to the interviews we derived further knowledge from two experts in this field. Both of them have been working in and with multiple ecosystems, including *Ecosystem A* and *Ecosystem B*, for several years, and shared their experiences in a couple of unstructured interview sessions. They provided additional insights on how the respective ecosystems are structured from a bird's-eye perspective in contrast to the team perspectives. Moreover, we discussed the findings of our interviews with them in order to support the validity of our study.

As a result, we achieve triangulation by **(a)** investigating multiple software ecosystems **(b)** interviewing multiple roles within the ecosystems **(c)** adding expert knowledge.

4 Results

One major difference between distributed teams in large organizations and teams within software ecosystems is that the actors within an ecosystem do not belong to the same company or organization and, therefore, do not necessarily share a common (business) goal. Since we wanted to understand why certain challenges occurred, we decided to first investigate the respective (differing) interests on the keystone's as well as the partners' side in order to locate potential sources of conflicts, before we focused on the analysis of the challenges. Hence, this section is structured as follows: First, we describe the dimensions used in our framework, followed by the conflicting interests, and concluding with the identified challenges.

4.1 Influencing Factors

During the analysis of our data we observed that our findings were highly dependent on three different factors: the phases of an *agile lifecycle* comprise different tasks that require different communication and coordination processes, and the *maturity* as well as the *openness* of an ecosystem influence the relationships between actors and, therefore, also the communication. These factors constitute the main dimensions of the models that include the results of our study, and are explained in detail in the following sections.

Agile Lifecycle. The common agile lifecycle includes an initial requirements definition and planning phase, followed by a development phase including integration and tests, a review and feedback phase, frequent releases, and a reprioritization phase before the next iteration begins [22]. Since all our interviewees work in agile teams, they all go through a similar agile lifecycle, experiencing different challenges in different phases. As the focus of our study is on coordination challenges, we neglected the technical phases (development and release) but rather focused on the planning, prioritization and feedback phase. We asked each interviewee about the phases they go through and, based on the literature as well as their answers, we propose the agile lifecycle in Fig. 2 that constitutes one dimension in our study.

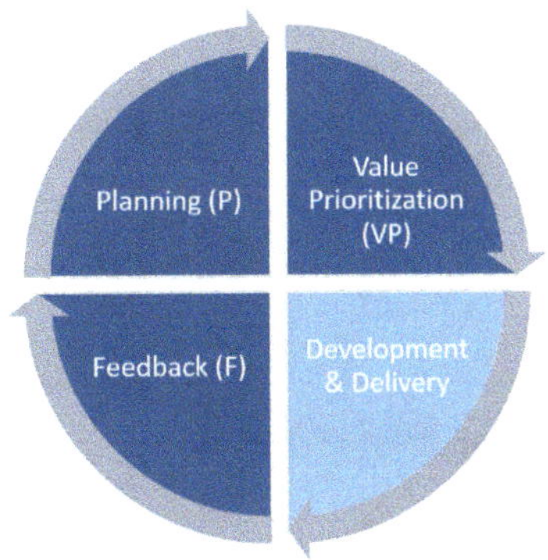

Fig. 2. Agile lifecycle

Maturity. Based on our interviews, we noticed that the maturity of the respective ecosystems plays a rather important role. Especially the communication between keystone and partners changes drastically over different phases of maturity. For instance, in the early phases of opening up a platform it is important to attract new and please existing partners, therefore the focus on communication is much higher than in later phases when the ecosystem is mature enough to attract partners automatically because of its success and the benefits for the partners.

One way to describe the evolution of a technology or an innovation is the s-curve. It describes the performance of a technology during different maturity stages from "pregnancy, birth, childhood, adolescence, maturity, and decline" [23]. Both ecosystems already have products on the market but regarding their maturity we would classify *Ecosystem A* as still being in the "birth" phase and *Ecosystem B* as being in the "childhood" phase. Specifically, *Ecosystem A* is still in the process of opening up their development to external partners while *Ecosystem B* is already established but still accelerating. For this reason, we define the second dimension as the maturity from "opening up" to "acceleration".

Openness vs. Closedness. Hartman et al. identified two different types of ecosystems, open and closed [24]. While closed ecosystems are still tightly coupled to and somewhat controlled by the keystone, open ecosystems are easily accessible for partners and can be characterized by their interchangeability of components and parties. However, ecosystems are not necessarily one or the other, they can also be in a hybrid stage [24]. This is relevant for our study since the communication and trust across ecosystem partners appears to be different for the two types. For instance, the actors in closed ecosystems are more interconnected than the actors of open ecosystems and, therefore, communicate more openly and share a higher level of trust. By tendency, *Ecosystem A* belongs to the category "open ecosystem" while *Ecosystem B* incorporates closed as well as open aspects. This is directly reflected in the characteristics of relationships that the keystone shares with different types of partners (both external & internal).

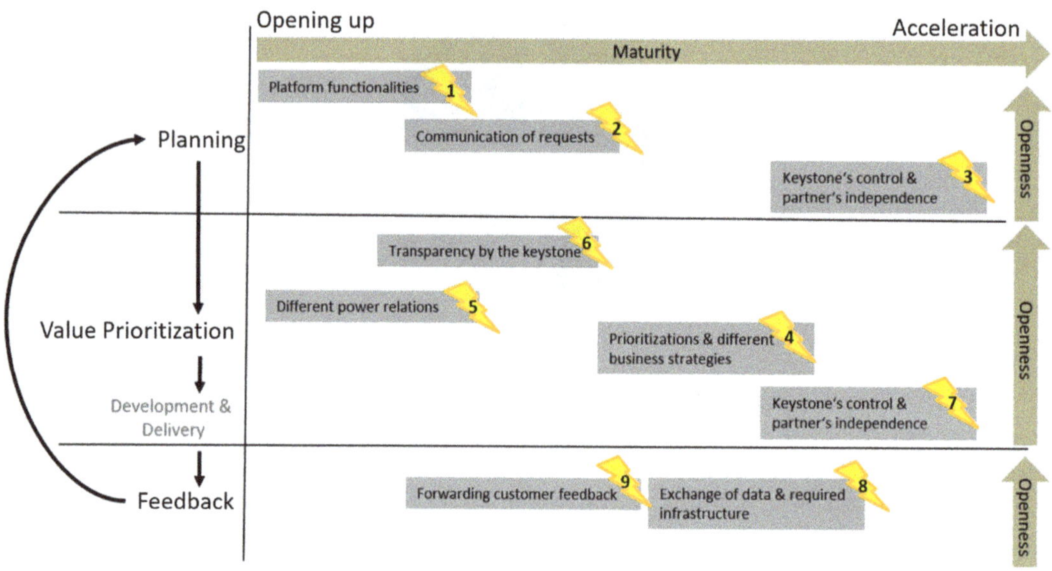

Fig. 3. Conflicting interests between different ecosystem actors

4.2 Conflicting Interests

Each ecosystem actor usually follows its own business strategy which can easily result in different interests that are hard to align and, therefore, cause conflicts between the actors. In order to analyze which opposing interests might lead to conflicts, and based on that even challenges, we extracted the interests of the partners as well as the keystone out of the interviews. Next, we mapped contrary interests that share a common link from both sides to each other which, therefore, constitute main drivers and crucial influencing factors for certain conflicts. Since not all interests and conflicts apply to all ecosystems or to all phases of agile development, we mapped the conflicting interests to different maturity levels, phases within an agile lifecycle, and the degree of openness (see Fig. 3). A more detailed description of the conflicts, interests of the platform and partners, and other influencing factors can be found in Table 2. All of the described results were derived out of the interview sessions of our case study. Overall, we identified nine conflicts that were caused by opposing interests on the partners' and the keystone's side. Three of the conflicts originated in the planning phase, four in the value prioritization phase, and two in the feedback phase.

Table 2. Description of conflicting interests between keystone and partners and the influencing factors in different phases

#	Conflict	Partners' Interests	Keystone's Interests	Ph	Ma	IF
1	Platform functionalities	Request specific partner functionalities	Provides the functionality that brings most value to the ecosystem	P	OP	O
2	Communication of requests	Expect fast & easy communication processes	Asks for well described requests	P	OP& A	O
3	Keystone's control & partners' independence (planning)	Become more independent	Keep control over the partners' customer interaction	P	A	C
4	Prioritizations & different business strategies	Follow own business strategy	Ensure the ecosystem's future	VP	OP& A	-
5	Different power relations	Want to be recognized by keystone	Wants to bind "important" partners to ecosystem	VP	OP	PR
6	Transparency by the keystone	Expect transparency (e.g. delivery timelines, commitments)	Wants to stay flexible/be able to reprioritize	VP	OP	O
7	Keystone's control & partners' independence (prioritization)	Obtain broad picture over all customers	Keep control over the partners' customer interaction	VP	A	C
8	Exchange of data & required infrastructure	Share customer feedback/data with collaborative partners	Low priority to provide infrastructure	F	OP& A	O
9	Forwarding customer feedback	Only benefit from forwarding feedback if it is directly connected to the partner's app/service	Needs the partners to forward requirements (if related to the keystone) of their customers	F	OP& A	O

Phases (Ph): Planning (P), Value Prioritization (VP), Feedback (F)
Maturities (Ma): Opening up (OP), Acceleration (A)
Influencing factors (IF): Openness (O), Closedness (C), Power Relations (PR)

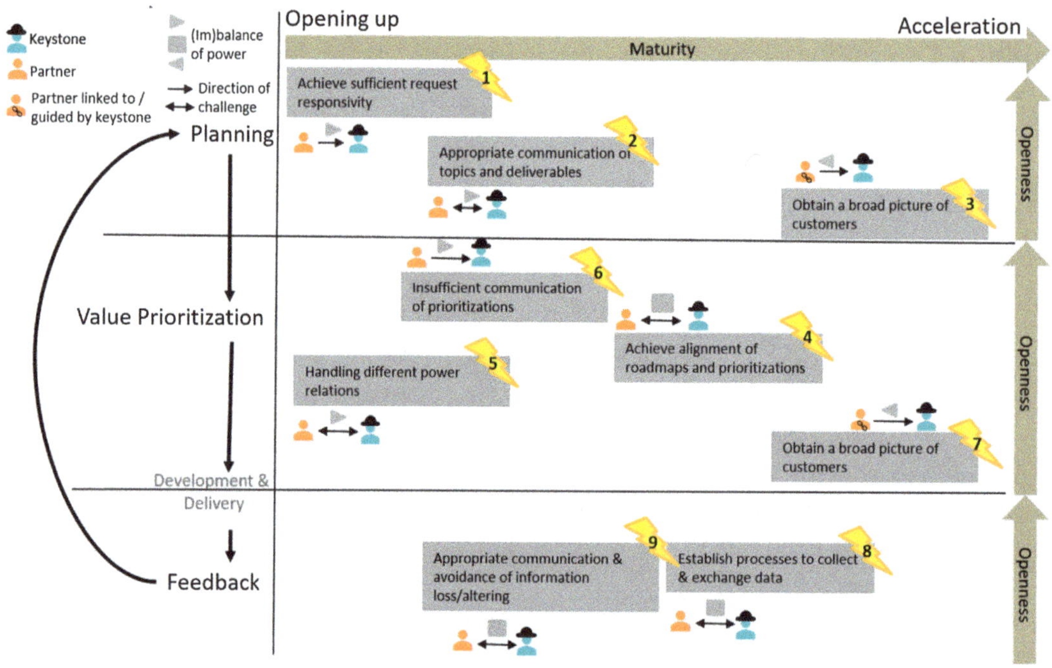

Fig. 4. Mapping of challenges to different settings

Planning Phase. Conflict #1 concerns the ***platform functionalities*** provided by the keystone and required by the partners. On the one side, the partners require the keystone to provide specific functionalities for their minimum viable product (MVP) while the keystone receives so many requests that it is difficult to take all partners into consideration so "[they] need to come to a point where [they] say what platform value creates the most value to the ecosystem and that's not easy because the ecosystem is so broad". For this reason, the keystone concentrates its planning efforts on the partners that bring the most value to the ecosystem.

The next issue (#2) is related to the ***communication of requests*** and the inconsistency of processes. Partners want to communicate their requests in an easy and fast way, and expect the keystone to respond to their requests, while the keystone "receive[s] quite small or tiny, tiny described requests" but "would like to receive more well described requests" from their partners. As there are no consistent processes available this often leads to misunderstandings of what the requirement actually is and, therefore, causes displeasure on both sides.

Moreover, the ***keystone's control and the partners' independence*** (#3) lead to conflicts, especially in closed ecosystems. While the partners want to be independent of the keystone in order to being able to optimize individual business interests, the keystone wants to keep control over the end-customers and the partners' interactions with these customers in order to ensure a coherent, overall business offering.

Table 3. Description of coordination challenges caused by divergent interests of actors within the ecosystem

#	Challenge	Description	Ph	Ma	IF	PR
1	Achieve sufficient request responsivity	P: Keystone not sufficiently reactive K: Keystone receives too many requests over a lot of different channels Why: many different communication channels, processes not well established yet	P	OP	O	P>K
2	Appropriate communication of topics & deliverables	P: Lack of transparency & lack of support -> leads to lack of trust K: Apps formulate high level user stories -> Keystone PM refines it -> potential misunderstandings Why: long communication paths, not all PMs have expertise in all areas -> easy to misunderstand	P	OP&A	O	P>K
3	Obtain a broad picture of customers (planning)	P: Partners get restrictions from keystone concerning customer interaction -> no broad overview on customer's needs K: Keystone wants to ensure an appropriate representation of the entire ecosystem in front of the customer Why: partners & keystone closely coupled, keystone does not want the customer to see the product in a non-ready state	P	A	C	K>P
4	Achieve alignment of roadmaps and prioritizations	P: Every ecosystem partner has own roadmap and prioritizations do often not match K: Challenging to consider all partners & decide what brings most value to ecosystem Why: no common business interests in software ecosystems	VP	OP&A	-	-
5	Handling different power relations	P: Keystone gives preference to certain stakeholders -> neglect "less important" partners Why: Not all partners can be treated the same K: Partners create pressure in order get their requests preferred -> How to decide which partner/customer is more important? Why: Keystone relies on "powerful" partners in opening up phase	VP	OP	PR	P>K
6	Insufficient communication of prioritizations	P: Prioritizations are not well communicated K: Challenge to handle trade-off between pleasing partners and maintaining flexibility Why: Keystone wants to stay flexible	VP	OP	O	P>K
7	Obtain a broad picture of customers (prioritization)	P: Limited communication between customers and partners -> not all customers included in prioritization process K: See challenge #3 Why: as a result of #3	VP	A	C	K>P
8	Establish processes to collect & exchange data	Partner & Keystone: No exchange of customer feedback within ecosystem, no direct Feedback channel / centralized way to store & access feedback -> information loss, "one-sided" feedback Why: off-the-shelf infrastructure can usually not be used, do both partners/keystone benefit by sharing?	F	OP&A	O	-
9	Appropriate communication & avoidance of information loss/altering	P: Insufficient communication of malfunctions by the keystone Why: communication channels for incident reporting must be established, more challenging in ecosystem K: Limited amount of information & information loss when communicating across multiple ecosystem partners Why: Multiple alterations due to long communication paths, feedback from end-customers communicated via partners	F	OP&A	O	-

Partner challenges (P), Keystone Challenges (K)
Phases (Ph): Planning (P), Value Prioritization (VP), Feedback (F)
Maturities (Ma): Opening up (OP), Acceleration (A)
Influencing factors (IF): Openness (O), Closedness (C), Power Relations (PR)
Power relations (PR): Partner > Keystone (P>K), Keystone > Partner (K>P)

Value Prioritization Phase. Conflict #4 concerns ***prioritizations and different business strategies***. As each partner follows its own business strategy, the keystone wants to ensure the ecosystem's future which leads to conflicts in the prioritization process since the different strategies can be difficult to align. One interviewee explains that they need to decide "from a platform point of view, what makes most sense, what is scalable, what is beneficial for a lot of customers [...] that's a challenge".

It is quite natural that some ecosystem partners are more important business partners to the keystone than others. However, this leads to ***different power relations*** (#5) as the important partners can create more pressure on the keystone than the others. Ultimately, the partners expect the keystone to be aware of them and their needs and to be treated (at least) equally to other partners, while the keystone wants to bind its important partners (e.g. defined by the number of customers, revenue etc.) to the platform.

Moreover, especially during that opening up phase, the ecosystem partners expect transparency of the keystone, e.g. concerning the prioritization of next steps, delivery timelines, or commitments. One of the interviewees states that he "would like to have more transparency how and on what basis decisions are made [...] because at the moment it's very non-transparent how [the keystone] decides what constitutes the biggest value for the overall project". However, the keystone avoids giving too detailed commitments and detailed timelines in order to stay flexible and being able to reprioritize. This leads to conflicting interests concerning the amount of ***transparency by the keystone*** (#6).

Analogously to and building upon conflict #3, the ***keystone's control and the partners independence*** (#7) create a conflict in the prioritization phase of closed software ecosystems. The partners would like to base their prioritization on a broad picture of all their customers while the keystone wants to keep control over the interaction with customers.

Feedback Phase. The partners would like to receive as much information on their customers as possible even if the data is collected by another partner. However, they are disinclined to share their data with competitors within the ecosystem but would be willing to do so with collaborative partners. On the other hand, the keystone perceives it as low priority to provide an infrastructure for sharing data across the ecosystem. This leads to conflicts concerning the ***exchange of data and the required infrastructure*** (#8) to do so.

Lastly, and related to the previous conflict, the handling and ***forwarding of customer feedback*** (#9) concerning other partners or the keystone also constitutes certain challenges since the partners only benefit from forwarding feedback if it is directly connected to the partners' apps or services. However, the keystone relies on the partners to forward platform-related requirements of their customers to them. Additionally, one interviewee explains that "feedback from customer visits are a tricky thing because the POs are going to the visits and we have a process described on how to feed back the feedback to the organization and also to me but that is still a little bit... some use it, some don't and some you have to chase to get their feedback for their customer" which is why they "need to turn that into a more automated, also tool-automated, process flow".

4.3 Challenges

Based on the previously extracted conflicting interests, all ecosystem related challenges faced by either the keystone or the partners were extracted out of the interviews. For each challenge we identified the following properties: The ecosystem's maturity, the phase within the agile lifecycle, other influencing factors, and causes for the respective challenge. Table 3 shows an overview of the detected challenges. In a next step, we mapped the challenges into a multi-dimensional model (see Fig. 4). The two main dimensions are the phases within the agile lifecycle (planning, value prioritization, and feedback) and the degree of maturity of the ecosystems. We added an extra dimension, the openness of the ecosystem, to each of the phases of the agile lifecycle because we identified challenges within these phases that were also strongly influenced by this factor. We identified two types of partners: partners that are closely coupled to or guided by the keystone and partners that are only loosely coupled to the keystone. Challenges between actors may be effective only in one or in both directions (arrows with one vs. two heads in Fig. 4). The power balance can be even or be dominated by one actor (indicated by a square or by triangles respectively).

Planning Phase. The first challenge results out of conflict #1 concerning the development of basis or new platform functionalities. The partners sometimes feel like the keystone is not sufficiently responsive and takes too long to deliver needed functionalities while the keystone receives too many requests over a lot of different channels which makes it difficult to respond to or handle the requests in a decent amount of time, as one interviewee explains "we keep on getting requests from everywhere [...] not everything can be taken up at the same time". The challenge is to ***achieve the right request responsivity*** (#1). Among others, this is caused by missing or not well established processes to handle such requests which, again, leads to many different communication channels.

Furthermore, both cases in our study perceived an ***appropriate communication of topics and deliverables*** (#2) between platform and partners as quite difficult as a result to conflict #2. The partners reveal that they would appreciate more transparency on the keystone's side in order to get a clear picture of what is possible to achieve. If this is not well communicated, this lack of transparency easily leads to a lack of trust. On the other hand, the keystone explains that they mostly receive high level user stories from their partners which have a high potential for being misinterpreted by the product manager who has to refine the user stories. Possible causes for this challenge are long communication paths across multiple stakeholders often implying information loss, and the fact that it is impossible for product managers to have expertise in all of the partners' areas which easily leads to misunderstandings, especially since the partner offering are "operating in a very specific domain which makes it difficult for most people to understand the topics".

Another challenge, closely coupled to closed ecosystems and related to conflict #3, is to ***obtain a broad picture of the end-customers*** (#3) due to keystone guidelines. In case partners and the keystone are very tightly coupled, partners who talk to customers are perceived as representatives of the entire ecosystem. For this reason, the platform wants to ensure an congruent representation of the ecosystem in front of the customers. In the particular case, the keystone has collaboration agreements with certain customers and the partners get instructions which partners they should talk to. However, this keeps the partners from getting a broad overview over all customers.

Value Prioritization Phase. As a result to conflict #4, it is challenging to ***achieve alignment of roadmaps and prioritizations*** (#4) as the actors within an ecosystem simply do not share a common business interest. This makes it difficult for the keystone to consider all partners and decide what brings the most value to the ecosystem. One of the partners states that "it is challenging because the keystone has its own roadmap, its own prioritizations and this can cause conflicts if the priorities or values do not match".

Quite the contrary to the previous challenge and related to conflict #5, this challenge addresses the difficulty of ***handling different power relations*** (#5) within the ecosystem. The partners feel like the keystone gives preferences to certain "important" customers and neglects the "less important" customers. One interviewee explains that he feels like "it depends on which partner has the greatest business potential". However, the keystone is simply not able to treat all partners with the same amount of attention because "[the partners] are always creating pressure" in order to get their requests preferred which naturally leads to the questions how to decide which partners are more important.

Conflict #6 concerning the amount of transparency by the keystone leads to an ***insufficient communication of prioritizations*** (#6), e.g. concerning the keystone's next steps, which causes displeasure on the partners' side. At the same time, the keystone faces the challenge how to handle the trade-off between pleasing partners and maintaining its flexibility.

As a result of challenge #3 and related to conflict #7, we observed that – due to the divergent viewpoints concerning the partners independence and the keystone's control – the partners face the challenge of ***obtaining a broad picture over all their customers*** (#7). The reason is that they are unable to include all their customers in their prioritization process due to the keystone's limitations concerning the customer communication. One of the interviewees even states that "It would be much better to run more statistics because I don't feel like this is a comprehensive picture".

Feedback Phase. Some of the interviewees reported on their interest in collecting and sharing customer data with certain collaborative stakeholders (conflict #8), however, so far there exist no established processes for software ecosystems to do so. The interviewees explain that they "would rather have direct feedback channels" or "centralized ways to store and access feedback" because off-the-shelf infrastructure can usually not be used for such kind of data sharing since fine-grained access to the data is not easy to control and legal or privacy issues need to be addressed. As a result, this leads to information loss and one-sided feedback. Therefore, the challenge is to ***establish processes to collect and exchange data*** (#8).

Lastly, both of our cases perceive the communication across stakeholders as insufficient and are under the impression that a lot of information gets altered or lost due to the (mis-)communication across multiple partners. This results in the challenge of an ***appropriate communication and avoidance of information loss and altering*** (#9). One of the interviewees revealed that the keystone does not immediately communicate malfunctioning platform features that the partners' features rely on to them because high priority communication channels for incident reporting in software ecosystems would need to be established first. On the other hand, the keystone suffers from limited amount of customer feedback and information loss since the chances for alterations are very high due to the long communication paths. One interviewee reports that "the more people you involve in between the more information gets lost". Moreover, the feedback from end-customers concerning platform features are often communicated via the partners. Especially in open ecosystems the keystone often does not have direct customer contact. This makes it challenging for the keystone to receive information on and to understand the real customer's needs.

5 Related Work

Previous research suggests that the application of agile practices is more difficult in large projects or organizations than in small teams [25]. As an organization grows it becomes challenging to keep an overview of all projects and groups within one organization [26]. Additionally, if the activities between them are not well communicated, it is hard to keep track of the existing dependencies. These factors often result in coordination challenges and additional coordination efforts [9,27]. For instance, an overarching figure or role, as well as appropriate methods, are required to coordinate the teams and address team-crossing challenges [11]. However, inter-team coordination in software ecosystems rises additional complications as the teams are distributed over several organizations who rarely share common goals or strategies nor a centralized control figure who coordinates them.

Moreover, it has been observed that an increased autonomy enabled by agile practices causes individual teams within a mutual organization to prioritize their own goals over the larger context [27]. Knowledge regarding the system is spread across the distributed teams and processes to share that knowledge need to be established [28,29]. Additionally, a global distribution of teams leads, among other challenges, to "reduced feelings of proximity when telecommunication is necessary, and difficulty in arranging frequent meetings due to time zone differences" [27].

Previous studies by Dingsøyr et al. [6] and Stettina et al. [30] indicate that most issues identified in agile large-scale software projects are related to processes as well as the people and their relationships. We observed quite similar results in our case study. Nevertheless, our results differ from the challenges of distributed agile teams in the way that the interactions between teams of a single organization are quite different to the interactions across organizations. In the latter case, single parties do not necessarily share a mutual larger context or even a common business interest which also impedes the sharing of knowledge. Moreover, the individual teams do neither apply or utilize unified processes nor can they be forced to do so since a central control figure does not exist in this context.

In order to improve the lack of visibility in large-scale projects, methods and solutions such as agile portfolio management, reporting or inter-team retrospectives have been introduced to connect the business strategy and the respective teams, to get an overview of all initiatives within a portfolio, and to address inter-team coordination challenges [6,10]. However, it has not been investigated yet how such practices could be applied across organizational boundaries. For instance, some actors can be reluctant to share their reports with certain other actors. Therefore, practices or guidelines would need to be established to coordinate the distribution of reports or to enable inter-organization retrospectives.

The complexity of (inter-)team coordination tends to increase with the size of the project and the number of teams involved (e.g. in multiteam systems). A shared mental model (e.g. concerning the work process, tasks, or awareness of who knows what), closed-loop communication, and trust are considered mechanisms that facilitate the coordination of multiple teams. Bjørnson et al. [7] investigated the practices that can be applied in order to implement these mechanisms. They identified, among others, formal as well as informal communication channels, specialized roles that rotate between teams, stand-up meetings, mini demos, and discussions in an open workspace as helpful tools to implement the mechanisms. In their case study, all teams are located in the same office and many of the proposed practices rely on the co-location of the teams, or at least on a shared common business interest and willingness to exchange information. These characteristics can usually not be observed in software ecosystems which makes it challenging to adapt these practices and mechanisms in this context.

Scheerer et al. [31] investigated different types of coordination strategies for multiteam systems. Each of their strategy types comprises three coordination types – mechanic (e.g. plans, rules), organic (e.g. mutual adjustment, feedback), and cognitive (e.g. cognitive similarity configurations) – that are applied to different kinds of extents, e.g. low, medium, or high. This work specifically focuses on multiteams that work on the same software product and while each team works toward an individual goal, they still share, at least to some extent, a mutual collective goal [31]. Rolling out a unified coordination strategy ecosystem-wide is very difficult to enforce since it would affect teams across several organizations, each of them pursuing their own goals and applying their own practices, without sharing a central control figure.

6 Conclusion

The research objective of our study was to elaborate the arising coordination challenges of agile teams within software ecosystems. Our findings indicate that many of the identified coordination challenges are either directly or indirectly related to long communication paths and a lack of well established communication processes, especially if information needs to be shared with other actors across organization boundaries. In contrast to distributed teams within one company, this is additionally challenging because of the varying, sometimes even competitive, relationships that influence the communication and the way data is forwarded or shared. For one, our participants perceived the responsivity as very slow and insufficient. Moreover, the deficient communication structures cause a lack of awareness and understanding of topics, deliverables and timelines between the keystone and its partners. The keystone is rather cautious when it comes to revealing its prioritizations and plans for the future which causes frustration on the partners' side. In addition to that, our results imply that on many occasions information gets lost or altered due to the multiple hops it has to pass. Our research provides evidence that there is a need to adapt or develop agile processes to facilitate and enable across-organization communication, coordination, and exchange of data.

Therefore, future work could be dedicated to solving the identified challenges and to investigate how agile practices would need to be adapted in order to fit across-organizational needs.

References

1. Cohen, D., Lindvall, M., Costa, P.: An introduction to agile methods. Adv. Comput. **62**(03), 1–66 (2004)
2. Alliance, A.: Agile manifesto, vol. 6, no. 1 (2001). http://www.agilemanifesto.org
3. Jørgensen, M.: Do agile methods work for large software projects? In: Garbajosa, J., Wang, X., Aguiar, A. (eds.) XP 2018. LNBIP, vol. 314, pp. 179–190. Springer, Cham (2018). https://doi.org/10.1007/978-3-319-91602-6_12
4. Leffingwell, D.: SAFe 4.0 Reference Guide: Scaled Agile Framework for Lean Software And Systems Engineering. Addison-Wesley Professional, Boston (2016)
5. Larman, C., Vodde, B.: Large-scale Scrum: More With Less. Addison-Wesley Professional, Boston (2016)
6. Dingsøyr, T., Mikalsen, M., Solem, A., Vestues, K.: Learning in the large - an exploratory study of retrospectives in large-scale agile development. In: Garbajosa, J., Wang, X., Aguiar, A. (eds.) XP 2018. LNBIP, vol. 314, pp. 191–198. Springer, Cham (2018). https://doi.org/10.1007/978-3-319-91602-6_13
7. Bjørnson, F.O., Wijnmaalen, J., Stettina, C.J., Dingsøyr, T.: Inter-team coordination in large-scale agile development: a case study of three enabling mechanisms. In: Garbajosa, J., Wang, X., Aguiar, A. (eds.) XP 2018. LNBIP, vol. 314, pp. 216–231. Springer, Cham (2018). https://doi.org/10.1007/978-3-319-91602-6_15
8. Begel, A., Nagappan, N., Poile, C., Layman, L.: Coordination in large-scale software teams. In: Proceedings of the 2009 ICSE Workshop on Cooperative and Human Aspects on Software Engineering, pp. 1–7. IEEE Computer Society (2009)
9. Bick, S., Spohrer, K., Hoda, R., Scheerer, A., Heinzl, A.: Coordination challenges in large-scale software development: a case study of planning misalignment in hybrid settings. IEEE Trans. Softw. Eng. **44**(10), 932–950 (2018)
10. Rautiainen, K., von Schantz, J., Vahaniitty, J.: Supporting scaling agile with portfolio management: case paf. com. In: 2011 44th Hawaii International Conference on System Sciences (HICSS), pp. 1–10. IEEE (2011)
11. Uludağ, Ö., Hauder, M., Kleehaus, M., Schimpfle, C., Matthes, F.: Supporting large-scale agile development with domain-driven design. In: Garbajosa, J., Wang, X., Aguiar, A. (eds.) XP 2018. LNBIP, vol. 314, pp. 232–247. Springer, Cham (2018). https://doi.org/10.1007/978-3-319-91602-6_16
12. Manikas, K., Hansen, K.M.: Software ecosystems - a systematic literature review. J. Syst. Softw. **86**(5), 1294–1306 (2013)
13. Bosch, J.: From software product lines to software ecosystems. In: Proceedings of the 13th International Software Product Line Conference, SPLC 2009, pp. 111–119. Carnegie Mellon University, Pittsburgh (2009)

14. Bosch, J., Bosch-Sijtsema, P.: From integration to composition: on the impact of software product lines, global development and ecosystems. J. Syst. Softw. **83**(1), 67–76 (2010)
15. Fabijan, A., Olsson, H.H., Bosch, J.: The lack of sharing of customer data in large software organizations: challenges and implications. In: Sharp, H., Hall, T. (eds.) XP 2016. LNBIP, vol. 251, pp. 39–52. Springer, Cham (2016). https://doi.org/10.1007/978-3-319-33515-5_4
16. Fricker, S.: Specification and analysis of requirements negotiation strategy in software ecosystems. In: CEUR Workshop Proceedings, vol. 505, pp. 19–33 (2009)
17. Knauss, E., Damian, D., Knauss, A., Borici, A.: Openness and requirements: opportunities and tradeoffs in software ecosystems. In: 2014 IEEE 22nd International Requirements Engineering Conference (RE), pp. 213–222 (2014)
18. Valença, G., Alves, C., Heimann, V., Jansen, S., Brinkkemper, S.: Competition and collaboration in requirements engineering: a case study of an emerging software ecosystem. In: 2014 IEEE 22nd International Requirements Engineering Conference (RE), pp. 384–393 (2014)
19. Karlsson, L., Dahlstedt, Å., Natt och Dag, J., Regnell, B., Persson, A.: Challenges in market-driven requirements engineering-an industrial interview study. In: Eighth International Workshop on Requirements Engineering: Foundation for Software Quality (2002)
20. Runeson, P., Höst, M.: Guidelines for conducting and reporting case study research in software engineering. Empir. Softw. Eng. **14**(2), 131 (2009)
21. Yin, R.K.: Case Study Research: Design and Methods, 5th edn. SAGE Publications, Thousand Oaks (2014)
22. Burger, R.: The ultimate guide to agile software development (2016). https://blog.capterra.com/the-ultimate-guide-to-agile-software-development/. Accessed 8 Jan 2019
23. Slocum, M.S.: Technology maturity using s-curve descriptors. TRIZ J. (1999)
24. Hartmann, H., Trew, T., Bosch, J.: The changing industry structure of software development for consumer electronics and its consequences for software architectures. J. Syst. Softw. **85**(1), 178–192 (2012)
25. Dybå, T., Dingsøyr, T.: Empirical studies of agile software development: a systematic review. Inf. Softw. Technol. **50**(9–10), 833–859 (2008)
26. Stettina, C.J., Schoemaker, L.: Reporting in agile portfolio management: routines, metrics and artefacts to maintain an effective oversight. In: Garbajosa, J., Wang, X., Aguiar, A. (eds.) XP 2018. LNBIP, vol. 314, pp. 199–215. Springer, Cham (2018). https://doi.org/10.1007/978-3-319-91602-6_14
27. Dikert, K., Paasivaara, M., Lassenius, C.: Challenges and success factors for large-scale agile transformations: a systematic literature review. J. Syst. Softw. **119**, 87–108 (2016)
28. Rolland, K.H.: Scaling across knowledge boundaries: a case study of a large-scale agile software development project. In: Proceedings of the Scientific Workshop Proceedings of XP2016, p. 5. ACM (2016)
29. Moe, N.B., Olsson, H.H., Dingsøyr, T.: Trends in large-scale agile development: a summary of the 4th workshop at XP2016. In: Proceedings of the Scientific Workshop Proceedings of XP2016, p. 1. ACM (2016)
30. Stettina, C.J., Hörz, J.: Agile portfolio management: an empirical perspective on the practice in use. Int. J. Proj. Manag. **33**(1), 140–152 (2015)
31. Scheerer, A., Hildenbrand, T., Kude, T.: Coordination in large-scale agile software development: a multiteam systems perspective. In: 2014 47th Hawaii International Conference on System Sciences, pp. 4780–4788. IEEE (2014)

Enterprise Agility: A Balancing Act - A Local Government Case Study

Leonor Barroca[1(✉)], Helen Sharp[1], Torgeir Dingsøyr[2], Peggy Gregory[3], Katie Taylor[3], and Raid AlQaisi[3]

[1] The Open University, Milton Keynes MK7 6AA, UK
leonor.barroca@open.ac.uk
[2] SINTEF, Norwegian University of Science and Technology, Trondheim, Norway
[3] University Central Lancashire, Preston, UK

Abstract. Austerity and financial constraints have been threatening the public sector in the UK for a number of years. Foreseeing the threat of continued budget cuts, and addressing the situation many local councils face, requires internal transformations for financial stability without losing the key focus on public service. Agile transformations have been undertaken by organisations wanting to learn from the software development community and bringing agile principles into the wider organisation. This paper describes and analyses an ongoing behaviour-led transformation in a district council in the UK. It presents the results of the analysis of 19 interviews with internal stakeholders at the council, of observations of meetings among senior and middle management in a five-month period. The paper explores the successes and the challenges encountered towards the end of the transformation process and reflects on balancing acts to address the challenges, between: disruption and business as usual, empowerment and goal setting, autonomy and processes and procedures, and behaviours and skills. Based on our findings, we suggest that behaviours on their own cannot guarantee a sustained agile culture, and that this is equally important for enterprise agility and for large-scale agile software development transformations.

Keywords: Agile transformation · Enterprise agility · Successes and challenges

1 Introduction

Agile approaches have reached a level of acceptance that has led many organisations to promote them to ever wider contexts than those initially envisioned of small projects and teams [1, 2]. Large-scale agile development is one such context, but agile is also being promoted outside the context of software development. Organisations are adopting agile principles outside of IT, hoping to cope with rapidly changing environments, and increase their capabilities for delivery and customer satisfaction; making organisations more agile is not always driven by the need to cope with agile software development at scale. Although there is no single agreed definition of business, organisational or enterprise agility [3] it is seen as a set of desirable qualities that

P. Kruchten et al. (Eds.): XP 2019, LNBIP 355, pp. 207–223, 2019.
https://doi.org/10.1007/978-3-030-19034-7_13

demand a transformation affecting the whole organisation. Such transformations are hard as they require a multi-disciplinary approach, and need to balance maintaining business-as-usual with significant and disruptive change. Approaches to achieve enterprise agility through business transformation [3] can be grouped into three categories: scaled-framework-driven (operational agility), business-driven (strategic orientation) and sustainable agility (cultural orientation). Scaled-framework-driven approaches include frameworks that have been used in software development environments to support large scale projects [1], e.g. DSDM, AgilePM, SAFe, LeSS; they address operational aspects to help with improving flow, value creation activities and delivery cycles. Business-driven approaches take a strategic view of agility considering how the business model can become more agile [4]. Sustainable agility [5] approaches take the view that the organisation culture is key in supporting the long-term objectives of a transformation. Approaches in this category view culture as the main focus of the transformation, with people's behaviours and values being central to its success and sustainability.

This paper explores the transformation of a local district council, in the UK. It was the first council to follow a behaviour-led approach focusing on cultural orientation, making it a unique case study for enterprise agility. Interviews were conducted with internal stakeholders and meetings were observed over a five month period. The council wanted to have an external view on how they were performing and how far they had travelled in their journey to be a more agile organisation; they also believed that understanding and changing organisational culture was an essential part of their transformation. The two research questions addressed were: RQ1: *What successes and challenges are identified towards the end of a behaviour-led transformation to become an agile organisation?* and RQ2: *What improvements suggested in the literature are applicable in this context?*

This work contributes to the growing area of enterprise agility when agile principles are applied in non-software development areas and organisations.

This paper is structured as follows: Sect. 2 introduces related work; Sect. 3 describes the method followed; Sect. 4 gives the context for the case study; the findings about the transformation are presented in Sect. 5, followed by discussion and conclusions in Sects. 6 and 7.

2 Related Work: Transformation Towards Enterprise Agility

Within the software agile community, there is a growing body of research into large-scale agile transformations and impact on the wider organisation [1, 2, 6, 7]. While the focus of this work is on transformations triggered by scaling agile software development, many of the challenges identified are not specific to software development; for example, change resistance, lack of investment, coordination challenges or hierarchical management and organisational boundaries [1].

Success factors in these transformations, are also mostly not software development specific as shown in the following categories [1]: management support, commitment to change, leadership, choosing and customising the agile approach, piloting, training and coaching, engaging people, communication and transparency, mindset and alignment, team autonomy and requirements management. While some of these categories are software-specific (e.g. choosing and customising the agile approach, piloting, training and coaching and requirements management) the others are not. Challenges [2] have also been identified that are software-specific (method, technology and ability-related) and non-software specific such as organisation, culture and motivation-related. Among the 11 categories of challenges identified by Uludag et al. [7] we also find two non-software specific categories: Culture & Mindset and Communication & Coordination. The former being about change, management buy-in and trust, and the latter about inter and intra-team communication in agile development teams and communication gaps with stakeholders.

Apart from scaling agile software development, enterprise, or business agility [8, 9] has become a desirable outcome for many organisations trying to survive in a continuously changing and competitive environment. It is the ability to adapt to change and continuously improve [10] that makes an enterprise agile. In a transformation process to achieve agility, organisations strive to develop capabilities to become adaptable and to develop a culture that will sustain the transformation in the long term. Teece [11] defends the need for dynamic capabilities to adapt to, and change in order to respond to a volatile environment. Dynamic capabilities are: sensing, i.e. identifying, developing and assessing opportunities and threats in relation to users' needs, using all available data to identify coherent patterns and imaginatively creating hypotheses about the future; seizing, i.e. mobilising resources to address needs and opportunities for which internal structures are needed to support flexibility and slack; and, transforming/shifting, i.e. continued renewal, for which organisations need to be very good at learning how to do new things [12].

It is not easy to establish a causal relationship between culture change and the development of these capabilities; however, it is recognised that an agile mindset needs to be promoted to sustain success over time [5], and that the organisational culture needs to be transformed to support the engagement of every person contributing to the work of the organisation [5, 13]. Carvalho et al. [5] propose an integration between organisational agility, organisational excellence, and organisational culture leading to sustainable organisational excellence and promoting adaptability. They highlight that the failure of many excellence programmes in organisations is due to neglect of how to sustain them in the long term. This continuous push for sustainability requires that:

"(1) senior leadership must be united in driving excellence, (2) the organisation, in a holistic perspective, must be committed and engaged, (3) the organisation strategy must be clear, defined and communicated, (4) the organisation must have process improvement ongoing activities together with self-assessment and (5) the use of information and data analysis must be a daily practice of the organisation." [10 cited in 5].

The role of senior leadership to achieve strategic agility is also addressed by Doz and Kosonen [4]; they propose an agenda constructed with a set of actions in three areas: strategic sensitivity, leadership unity, and resource fluidity. Increased sensitivity to internal and external environments, achieving true engagement and commitment of all, and making the required ingredients available will help foster a successful transformation.

There is a gap in the literature between research coming from a software development background and that coming from a business context. More cross-disciplinary learning is required between these domains. The work presented in this paper contributes to address this gap.

3 Method

We conducted a qualitative single-case case study [15, 16] to follow part of the journey for a local council that was undergoing a comprehensive transformation programme. We identified their successes and challenges, answering RQ1, and provided feedback to the council for continuous improvements, simultaneously addressing RQ2.

Data collection consisted of semi-structured interviews, meeting observations and studying official documents. Ethical permission was received from the University to conduct the study, and all participants consented to take part after reading an information leaflet. Data collection was conducted between January and May 2018. During this five-month period the research team observed and took notes of regular weekly meetings of the assistant directors, and carried out 19 interviews with employees in senior management roles. Of the people interviewed most had been employed at the Council throughout the transformation with only two participants having been recruited as a result of it. Each interview lasted around half an hour and was conducted by at least one of the first two authors plus the acknowledged researcher. All interviewees were asked about: their views of the transformation journey so far, the successes and challenges of the transformation and what they considered the next steps.

An inductive thematic analysis was undertaken to identify the main themes for the successes, challenges, and steps ahead [17]. The thematic analysis was carried out independently by two researchers, using the interview data and meeting notes, with the final analysis resulting from a comparison between both lists of themes. This final list was then discussed by the wider team. Literature on organisational culture and agility (such as that in Sect. 2) was used to help identify and structure potential areas of improvement highlighted through the empirical work. We also identified recommendations from this literature for the organisation to consider in their own context and decide whether and how to apply them.

For a more in-depth analysis focusing on the organisation's culture, we used the Agile Business Consortium's (ABC) Culture Development Matrix [18] (Fig. 1). The full matrix has seven elements, but we used six in our analysis because the Innovation & Learning element (omitted in Fig. 1) was not covered through the interviews.

Organisations can be assessed at 5 different levels (surviving, stabilising, secure, thriving and transformational) for each of the elements. Figure 1 shows the elements across the top row of the table, with the levels listed in the first column of the table. By mapping an organisation's behaviours against the relative development level in each element, a snapshot of readiness for transformation emerges, which can indicate a starting point for improvement.

4 Case Study

The council covers an area just outside greater London; it serves around 180 k residents, is the second largest district council (in the UK) and a major area for growth. The services provided by this council are: household recycling and waste collection, local planning and building regulations, housing advice, licensing (e.g. alcohol and entertainment, animal related, gambling, market stalls, sex establishments, taxis, etc.), environmental problems, benefits, council tax collections, community safety, public car parks and parks and community centres.

For the last decade this council has undertaken a top-down internal transformation, inspired by Simon Sinek's *Start with Why* [19]. Senior management had sensed the external environment and realised the need to achieve financial stability, given the threats to government grants for local authorities, while at the same time to continue to deliver improved services to their customers. It was a long transformation process that proceeded in stages and on different strands: commercially minded, community focused, customer and innovation, and financially fit.

The aim of this transformation was to achieve 'world-class support for those who need it' being 'the best place to work in the area with the best people'. It began in 2008 and had a number of milestones; trade unions were involved throughout. In 2008 the change programme was introduced by senior management to set managers on the road to cultural change; in 2010 this was one of the first councils to adopt a Cloud IT strategy; from 2011 onwards the total removal of the government grant by 2020 was foreseen and the need to change became a priority; in 2012 a new business model was deployed to explore opportunities in the market place; an ideas hub for the change process was created in 2013; and in 2014 the vision for moving into an income generating entrepreneurial culture took shape. In 2015 a new website was developed around residents' desires and needs with the digitalisation of services. In 2016, a new organisational structure was created.

Central to the transformation plan was a desire for all staff employed by the council to exhibit commercially-minded behaviours, and this underpinned the more practical milestones mentioned above. Most existing staff (320, excluding the CEO and 2 directors) went through a behavioural assessment exercise in the process of applying for jobs at the council – either in their original roles, or in new ones. The aim was for all staff employed by the council to adhere to the specified behaviours, rather than to change the behaviour of existing staff. Staff could apply for any job at any level, and some ended up being promoted several levels. As a result, around 70 people left the organisation (some through early retirement) and 100 new people were recruited. This behaviour-led programme resulted in a commercially-minded restructuring of the whole council based on the five behaviours shown in Figs. 2 and 3; big saving targets were also put in place. As a public service entity, the council cannot make a profit, so any surplus from commercial ventures must feed back into better service delivery.

AGILE CULTURE DEVELOPMENT MATRIX

Level	Purpose and Results (PR)	Agile Leadership (AL)	Well-being and Fulfilment (WF)	Collaboration and Autonomy (CA)	Trust and Transparency (TT)	Adaptability to Change (AC)
Transformational	A compelling, game-changing vision drives a passion to deliver	Leaders are selfless, supporting the needs of today and the vision of tomorrow	People achieve and are fulfilled at work and are vocal ambassadors for the organisation	A network of collaborative teams deliver change with an appropriate level of autonomy	Honesty, transparency and security allows knowledge sharing	Challenges sought with ideas rapidly tested. A strong operational core supports innovation
Thriving	Individual and team goals aligned to clear, long-term customer focused vision	Leaders take responsibility for their actions, admit personal limitations and act on feedback	People feel valued with a good work-life balance, sometimes over-loaded but don't feel threatened	Cross functional collaboration 'the norm' with cases of successful autonomous teams	Generally open and honest but under pressure old behaviours resurface, undermining trust	Reactive change is well managed and implemented although there is a tension with operational needs
Secure	Some alignment of targets with goals incorporating customer value	Leaders are task focused. They engage in discussion to obtain buy-in not genuine feedback	People enjoy working with colleagues and are active in decision making but don't always feel valued	Tensions between business as usual & improvements; responsibilities still functional & hierarchical	Most managers and peers trusted but decisions made behind closed doors	Small changes are managed in process; larger ones often imposed and therefore resisted
Stabilising	Predominantly Financial or Functional targets set with little alignment or buy-in	Leaders are authoritative and give orders but do not inspire	People keep their heads down and focus on delivering work to get paid	Functional silos exist with people tasked to deliver objectives rather than the common good	People don't feel valued and see some managers as manipulative. Information is not readily shared	There is a view 'if it is not broken don't fix it' so change is limited and seen as a risk
Surviving	Changes in direction and priorities are chaotic	Leaders prioritise fire-fighting and personal status	People feel demotivated and disengaged and cover up mistakes	Crisis mode prevails with unclear responsibilities and conflicting orders	A culture of everyone for themselves and knowledge is power so not shared	Changes are chaotic and uncoordinated, driven by immediate pressures

Fig. 1. Agile culture development matrix (adapted from https://www.agilebusiness.org/agile-culture)

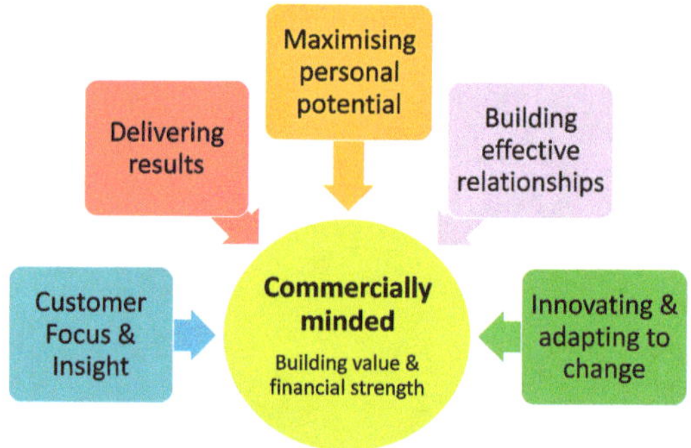

Fig. 2. The Council's Behaviour Framework (© Aylesbury Vale District Council 2017)

I act in a Commercially Minded way by:				
Customer focus and insight	**Delivering results**	**Maximising personal potential**	**Building effective relationships**	**Innovating and adapting to change**
I understand and am driven by providing excellent customer service. I look for opportunities and propose solutions to increase value for our current/ future customers and partners. I take time to 'see' our customer service through the eyes of the customer, informing and using appropriate data. I am driven by delivering value for our customers and am ambitious to ensure each customer receives the best service. I understand and work to meet the needs and expectations of our diverse population, ensuring we deliver all our services (statutory & non-statutory) in a commercial way. I take responsibility for each customer service interaction, seeking professional advice and input when required. I constructively challenge how we do things.	I am accountable and take responsibility for doing what I say I will do. I am motivated to achieve my personal best, knowing it will improve overall performance and maximise our commercial advantage. I look for and clearly voice my ideas to continually improve our processes and deliver commercially sound solutions. I analyse, manage and take calculated risks. I am financially aware, knowing how much it costs to serve my customers. I try to ensure there is a positive return on investment. I find and use appropriate data, considering wider Council implications to support and inform decision making. I make sure I understand our strategy and business model, using this to take the initiative and inform my actions.	I make commitments and take personal responsibility for delivering them. My ambition is to make the Council a success. I work with enthusiasm and desire to meet and exceed objectives and targets. I work to be the best I can be, identifying and filling gaps in my knowledge. I develop myself and others, updating my skills and expertise, whilst actively looking for opportunities to learn and apply knowledge. I listen and act appropriately to constructive challenge. I actively seek and act on feedback. I act with integrity, empowering myself and others to speak and act. I provide constructive feedback and challenge inappropriate behaviour.	I demonstrate and value the "One Team, One Council" approach. I work collaboratively with others to deliver our objectives and bring value for our customers. I share expertise, strengths and ideas. I build positive relationships, recognising that every interaction I have reflects on the AVDC brand. I am open minded and look for opportunities to work with other people in order that we can confidently build on each other's skills and expertise. I value organisational diversity, engaging and involving others with respect and empathy. I manage our supplier/ partner relationships to ensure best commercial value. I actively listen and communicate clearly and appropriately with others.	I look to do things more efficiently, understanding the commercial implications. I work with others to create, develop and implement ideas, supporting the production of proposals and business cases. I engage positively with change, focusing and reflecting on how the change will commercially enhance AVDC. I focus on finding solutions and keep trying until we succeed. I am forward thinking, being prepared to think on my feet whilst remaining flexible. I am outward looking, having an awareness of the 'market' in which we operate. I keep myself informed, up to date and seek out future ideas and trends. I make decisions aligned with our corporate strategy and policies. I use analytical and critical thinking skills to solve problems.

Fig. 3. Commercial Behaviours (© Aylesbury Vale District Council 2017)

This transformation focused on 'commercial' behaviours, but these behaviours map directly to the organisational culture factors that correlate with agile method usage described in Strode et al. [20]. These factors include, for example: 'the organization is results oriented', and 'the organization enables empowerment of people'. Only *Customer Focus & Insight* does not appear in Strode et al.'s list but it equates to 'customer collaboration over contract negotiation' in the Agile Manifesto [21]. So although employees at the council rarely spoke of an *agile* transformation, their goal was an agile organisation.

To sustain these behaviours, as well as the actions described above, the council implemented a new business model with a more commercial approach, reviewed every service, introduced charges for some non-essential services, and introduced new chargeable services.

5 A Transformation Towards Business Agility

5.1 Findings from the Thematic Analysis

Thematic analysis of the interviews, with meetings and documents as context, was used to answer RQ1: *What successes and challenges are identified towards the end of a behaviour-led transformation to become an agile organisation?* We found evidence for many positive elements of an agile culture as in Table 1; namely, that the organisation is results oriented, the management style is supportive and collaborative, the organisation values feedback and learning, social interaction in the organisation is trustful, collaborative, and competent, the organisation enables empowerment of people, and the leadership in the organisation is entrepreneurial, innovative, and risk taking [20].

Table 1. Successes

Themes	Quotations
A clear and inspiring purpose focusing on results to stakeholders	*I think we've done something incredible [..] all the money we make is about delivering customer services.) (our books are balanced [..] not just for this year, for the next four years [..] a huge amount of growth coming*
Supportive leadership	*We had to support each other [..] it's quite an enjoyable environment to work-in.[..] we've got a team doesn't wait to be asked to help people, it goes and helps other people when we see they need it*
A feeling of achievement	*It was monumental, what we did; It's really good.... Good stuff came out of it; our books are balanced [..] not just for this year, for the next four years [..] a huge amount of growth coming*
Commitment to transparency	*We try and be very transparent, or as transparent as we can be*
Need to be financially sustainable, not only commercial	*This bit of the organisation makes money and this bit of the organisation spends money, but that's ok; increase employment and deliver bigger benefits (trying to)*
Fluid, constantly changing, iterative	*And it did take us about three or four goes to get that messaging right with staff; you've got the same language being spoken across all of the groups; encourage innovation; while they are here (young people) how can we learn so much from them as well as they learning from us*
Collective ownership	*We all cover each other*
Restructuring, consolidating, learning	*We've learnt a lot about it we definitely need to get through our lessons learnt; We need to maintain the momentum it's how do we, it's about maintaining that momentum*

(*continued*)

Table 1. (*continued*)

Themes	Quotations
Strong team, supporting each other	*The team is pretty cohesive and we've all had to support each other ... If somebody struggling a little bit and not wanting to admit it, the rest of the team actually notice and go and give support; got to know some things about staff you didn't necessarily know about them before learning about other colleagues; And learning all of that sort of stuff together is quite good*
Good communication	*We sit together most of the time, we talk to each other every single day*

Analysis of the interviews highlighted challenges that were identified at the time of the interviews, the five-month period just after the main transformation (see Table 2).

Table 2. Challenges

Recruitment	*Behaviours vs skills/knowledge – some people who did really really well in their interviews but when they did the behaviours they didn't reach the benchmark, and the external benchmark is also higher than the internal one which is a bit of a contention*
Business as usual (BaU) vs transformation	*A lot of things fell through the cracks [..] we lost a lot of focus on the BaU delivery, the day to day delivery [..] the fact that we kept the services going is incredible [..] massive achievement in itself*
Loss of knowledge and experience	*That one person had all that knowledge [..] some things fell over [..] people leave and they have just taken 30 years of knowledge in their head*
Silos	*There is a definite difference between level 1 and level 2 [..] far more process driven (on level 1) [..] they probably perceive us as not doing very much [..] it has only gone worse since we have been through the review [..] even more siloed*
Internal processes and procedures	*[..] there is very much an attitude of get on and do it which I think is a double-edged sword [..] things are happening but it does mean that some of the processes and procedures aren't being followed or if they aren't existing processes and procedures people are creating them in the fly [..] sometimes we do things without having a solid robust procedure behind it [..] there is a risk that we started to see things that are happening and [..] we didn't even know we were doing that)*
Workloads	*Staff are very overloaded*
Leadership vulnerability and resilience to change	*We have a tendency, to, maybe, over-believe our own hype, and I think we've not been smart at bringing external organisations along with us [..] a lot of loose ends [..] everybody understanding what their responsibilities are [..] you've got to stop undermining the pro... [..] you've got to support the process [..] corporate challenging corporate [..] it causes tension [..] we need some clarity [..] (Associate Directors) they are still forming as a team*

(*continued*)

Table 2. (*continued*)

People	trauma, survivor guilt, pockets of unhappy people, frustration, resentment, old mindset, low morale	*At the lower levels[..] and those more specialist levels [..] for them [..] a little bit of resentment [..] they were put through this process [..] at the end of it they are still doing the same job [..] for them not much has changed. [..] a lot of people shut down and said thank god it is over*
	emotional journey, novel/unique, support	*we've never done anything like that before here; it's been a little bit of a bruising time the support was huge. And so staff were given time to absolutely prepare themselves for this transformation*
	old mindset	*there are people [..] who have gone back to what they are comfortable with [..] [..] people who passed the behaviours and then they haven't changed [..] the new framework hasn't landed*

5.2 Findings from the Agile Culture Development Matrix Assessment

The council wanted to achieve a deeper understanding of their culture after its most significant period of transformation, and to highlight areas that needed attention. We assessed our findings (Tables 1 and 2) against the Agile Culture Development Matrix (see Fig. 1). Based on this, the council scored as follows:

- Purpose and Results (Thriving to Transformational)
- Agile Leadership (Secure to Thriving)
- Well-being & Fulfilment (Thriving to Transformational)
- Collaboration & Autonomy (Secure to Thriving)
- Trust & Transparency (Secure to Thriving)
- Adaptability to Change (Secure to Thriving)

We identified, in particular, two areas for improvement towards a more agile organisation, Collaboration & Autonomy and Adaptability to Change, which are discussed below. For the former, the data underpinning two challenge themes of 'Silos' and 'Internal processes and procedures' indicated a lack of collaboration but also confusion around autonomy. For the latter, the theme of 'Leadership vulnerability and resilience to change' indicated an uncertainty about any changes to the leadership team. Looking back at the behaviour-led approach undertaken by the transformation (Fig. 3), the first area relates to Building effective relationships and the second to Innovating and adapting to change behaviours.

Collaboration and Autonomy

A transformational organisation is characterised by "a network of collaborative teams" and "authority is distributed with an appropriate level of autonomy" [22]. Our data indicates that the council does not meet either of these at this time. Although we found evidence of cohesive teams *the team is pretty cohesive and we've all had to support each other... If somebody is struggling a little bit and not wanting to admit it, the rest of the team actually notice and go and give support; got to know some things about staff you didn't necessarily know about them before learning about other colleagues; and learning all of that sort of stuff together is quite good*

it is unclear whether there is a network of collaborative teams and a clear understanding of responsibilities and priorities. Networked teams need to operate in the context of everyone working together, but also to an agreed way of working. One of the challenges raised through the interviews is the misalignment between autonomy for decision making (empowered teams, *get on and do it* attitude) and the lack of processes and procedures, with people creating them on the fly impacting the organisation's reputation.

There is a recognition of the need to maintain the momentum and revitalise, while also consolidating processes and procedures

[..] there is very much an attitude of get on and do it which I think is a double-edged sword [..] things are happening but it does mean that some of the processes and procedures aren't being followed or if they aren't existing processes and procedures people are creating them in the fly [..] sometimes we do things without having a solid robust procedure behind it

This also suggests that they didn't have an appreciation of what it is to be self-organising, i.e. people went off and made decisions without reference back to (or independent from) the core (a characteristic of the 'secure' assessment)

[..] there is a risk that we started to see things that are happening and [..] we didn't even know we were doing that

Adaptability to Change

A transformational organisation is characterised by having a strong core, i.e. a team of people that provides the stability to support the change [22]. There is definitely an ability to change as the council has gone through a big transformation and has come out of it successfully. However, it is too early to judge whether there is a strong core that can provide stability and flexibility to adapt and change, and internal challenges were identified (e.g. vulnerability of core team, leadership still forming as a team, …).

the organisation is still very reliant, I think, on the top team being very clear what it is trying to achieve.

We found examples of innovative approaches but we also found some concerns that 'the need to deliver today's results is an inhibitor to bold action' [22].

6 Discussion

In this section we discuss our findings in the context of the research questions, and highlight observations about the 'balancing act' we perceive.

6.1 RQ1: What Successes and Challenges Are Identified Towards the End of a Behaviour-Led Transformation to Become an Agile Organisation?

Table 1 provides a list of successes identified by our interviewees. Many of the factors for a successful transformation, highlighted by Dikert et al. [1], are reflected in those themes, namely:

- management support – *strong team supporting each other* (theme in Table 1);
- commitment to change – change was initiated by a very committed leadership in the council;
- leadership – a *supportive leadership* (theme in Table 1);
- training and coaching – all staff were well supported in going through the transformation and the behavioural assessments;
- engaging people – *collective ownership* (theme in Table 1)
- communication and transparency – *good communication* (theme in Table 1).

While Dikert et al.'s success factors focus on what needs to be in place in order for the transformation to be successful, our data was collected once the bulk of the transformation activity had taken place. But when interviewees were asked about successes of the transformation undergone, most talked not only about where they had got to, but also about the process itself; even the interviewees who had been recruited at the end of the significant transformation period were well aware of the process and referred back to it. Success factors for an agile transformation are also relevant to long-term sustained agility [5]. Carvalho et al. talk about agility enablers rather than success factors; enablers characterise agility in an organisation and some of our themes also appear as enablers, such as their organisational commitment and employee empowerment.

Some of the successes we encountered do not appear in Dikert et al's categories, in particular, the following themes (discarding the ones specific to the context of the case study)*: a clear and inspiring purpose focusing on results to stakeholders; a feeling of achievement; fluid, constantly changing, iterative; and, restructuring, consolidating, learning*. There are naturally differences when looking at agility from the perspective of software development and from the perspective of the whole organisation. We suggest, however, that the two perspectives are complementary and that the agile software community can benefit from understanding the wider perspective of the organisation. Lenberg et al. [23] stress the importance of organisational values in software companies, as successful transformations depend on organisation-wide aligned values.

Having undergone such a radical transformation, the local council is at a point where it can be considered successful as an agile organisation. The survival strategy adopted by the council was to undergo a behaviour-led transformation to become a commercially-minded organisation; however, the behaviours chosen are those of an organisational culture related to agile use [20]. An agile organisation is characterised by its capability of sensing and responding [4, 11], which was the aim of the council.

We also found challenges in two areas when mapping to the Agile Culture Development Matrix (Fig. 1), Collaboration & Autonomy and Adaptability to Change. The challenges encountered are not about the behaviours chosen, but rather about their implementation. The first falls within the Building effective relationships behaviour and the second under Innovating and adapting to change behaviour. Both of these behaviours were well accepted by interviewees but for both there were disconnects between the behaviour and practice; in the former, around the theme of *Internal processes and procedures*, and in the latter around the theme *Leadership vulnerability and resilience to change* (see Table 2). Only the first of these two themes resonates with a challenge in large-scale transformations [1]: Autonomous team model challenging. Although this challenge in Dikert et al. is about software teams it also emerged in the council: the lack of balance between the autonomy of teams and the broader goals of the organisation.

We concentrated on these two challenge areas as they were the most relevant to the council to assess and improve where they were, towards an agile culture.

6.2 RQ2: What Improvements Suggested in the Literature Are Applicable in This Context?

What can be done to implement intended behaviours better and to sustain what has been achieved? To address the first of the challenge areas, Collaboration & Autonomy, we drew on established frameworks to make suggestions for the council. Doz and Kosonen [4] developed a framework for strategic agility with 3 areas: strategic sensitivity, leadership unity, and resource fluidity. Of particular relevance to developing collaborative communities are actions suggested under leadership unity: dialoguing, surfacing and sharing assumptions and understanding contexts; and, aligning, rallying around a common interest. However, a balance needs to be struck between empowering collaborative communities and setting macro level goals while distributing authority. The fine tuning of this balance between autonomy and accountability requires the communities to have a clear strategy and clarity of purpose [24], and boundary conditions and expectations [25]; these help with establishing accountability within defined limits giving employees the freedom to decide how to achieve objectives.

Another balancing act has to be achieved between how much is left to autonomous teams and how much is documented in processes and procedures. Agile developers recognise that documentation is important for some projects, but are selective. Lessons can be learned from their practice to help achieve an optimal balance [26]; for example, checking whether and why documentation is needed, and for whom.

Addressing the second challenge area, Adaptability to change, and in particular the need for a strong core that provides stability, requires a succession plan, and relevant capabilities to be developed and supported [11, 12].

Sustaining agility is not mentioned as a challenge in large-scale agile transformations triggered by software development (e.g. [1]), but the need for sustainability is recognised as a challenge in organisational transformations (e.g. [5]). Further research is needed to understand why sustainability is not apparently an issue when software triggers the transformation.

6.3 The Balancing Act

The behaviour-led transformation undertaken by the council was intended to achieve a change of culture by only employing people who exhibit certain behaviours. It seems that this approach had a positive impact for the survival and financial sustainability of the council. But the challenges in their implementation require a balancing act between opposing forces:

- disruptive transformation activities while carrying on business as usual;
- empowering collaborative communities (resources) while setting macro level goals and distributing authority (responsibility) – a three-way balancing act;
- autonomy for decision making while defining and documenting processes and procedures that need to be followed, e.g. for regulatory reasons; and,
- adopting the desired behaviours while demonstrating the required skills.

We suggest that to achieve a successful transformation to an agile enterprise compromises have to be struck between these contradictory forces, with fine tuning actions to achieve the correct balance. The example of Spotify [25] suggests that to achieve the right balance between autonomy and accountability requires: a strategy and clarity of purpose, transparent boundary conditions, and expectations. This framework gives employees freedom to choose how they achieve objectives within exisiting constraints. But, is adopting and fine tuning the right behaviours sufficient to sustain a change in culture that can be sustained? Robinson and Sharp [27] discussed the relationship between behaviours (in their case XP practices) and culture and the difficulties in relating the practices adopted with the underlying culture. We suggest that achieving a change in culture through behaviours is not necessarily a guarantee for that change to be sustained. A continuous process of revisiting behaviours, learning lessons, and adjustment is under way in the local council and that is supportive of sustainability. But more research is needed to understand how agility and transformations can be sustained in the long term [28].

7 Limitations

There are limitations in the work presented here. The constraints of how the case study was conducted only allowed for a partial view of the local council with no access to staff below middle management. From our analysis, we also did not have enough data to consider all elements of the Agile Culture Development Matrix; to assess all the areas of the matrix would have required an organisation-wide consultation. Also, although we carried out the work after the main period of the transformation, the council has not stopped and changes have been happening since and will continue to happen.

The threats to validity [29] were addressed as follows: for internal validity, data was collected by three researchers who also carried out the analysis and discussed the data with the wider author set; for construct validity, the constructs emerged from the participants and were not imposed; for reliability, it is quite likely that the same results would emerge if conducted again with the same questions. As for external validity, the case study in this paper is a snapshot of a continuous journey; it is difficult to generalise what we found to other contexts.

8 Conclusions

The literature on large-scale agile transformations has been mainly focusing on software development transformations; concerns about the wider organisation are acknowledged but the assumption is often that these transformations are triggered by the digitisation of organisations. The case study in this paper presents a different angle: that of a local council that realises the need for transformation as the only way to survive and be financially sustainable. This was achieved successfully through 'commercially' oriented behaviours. The challenges encountered were about achieving the right balance in the implementation of these behaviours between: disruption and business as usual, empowerment and goal setting, autonomy and processes and procedures, and behaviours and skills. In this case study, behaviour change has led to evidence of an agile culture but a change in culture through behaviours alone is not necessarily a guarantee for that change to be sustained [14]. More effort is needed to achieve an appropriate balance, and work to maintain the behaviours and hence to sustain the change. These balancing acts were encountered in a transformation towards business agility, but they also need to be addressed by the agile software community. The focus on sustaining agility and on an organisation-wide perspective is important to both enterprise agility and to large scale software development agile transformations.

Acknowledgements. We would like to thank our collaborators at Aylesbury Vale District Council, UK. We acknowledge Daniel G. Cabrero's work in conducting the interviews. This work was supported by The Agile Business Consortium (http://agilebusiness.org).

References

1. Dikert, K., Paasivaara, M., Lassenius, C.: Challenges and success factors for large-scale agile transformations: a systematic literature review. J. Syst. Softw. **119**, 87–108 (2016)
2. Fuchs, C., Hess, T.: Becoming agile in the digital transformation : the process of a large-scale agile transformation. In: Thirty Ninth International Conference on Information Systems, pp. 1–17 (2018)
3. Karvonen, T., Sharp, H., Barroca, L.: Enterprise agility: why is transformation so hard? In: Garbajosa, J., Wang, X., Aguiar, A. (eds.) XP 2018. LNBIP, vol. 314, pp. 131–145. Springer, Cham (2018). https://doi.org/10.1007/978-3-319-91602-6_9
4. Doz, Y.L., Kosonen, M.: Embedding strategic agility: a leadership agenda for accelerating business model renewal. Long Range Plan. **43**(2–3), 370–382 (2010)
5. Carvalho, A.M., Sampaio, P., Rebentisch, E., Carvalho, J.Á., Saraiva, P.: Operational excellence, organisational culture and agility: the missing link? J. Total Qual. Manag. Bus. Excell. **15**, 1–20 (2017)
6. Paasivaara, M., Behm, B., Lassenius, C., Hallikainen, M.: Large-scale agile transformation at Ericsson: a case study. Empir. Softw. Eng. **23**(October), 2550–2596 (2018)
7. Uludag, O., Kleehaus, M., Caprano, C., Matthes, F.: Identifying and structuring challenges in large-scale agile development based on a structured literature review. In: 2018 IEEE 22nd International Enterprise Distributed Object Computing Conference (EDOC), pp. 191–197. IEEE (2018)

8. Overby, E., Bharadwaj, A., Sambamurthy, V.: Enterprise agility and the enabling role of information technology. Eur. J. Inf. Syst. **15**(2), 120–131 (2006)
9. Business agility. https://wiki.businessagility.institute/w/Main_Page. Accessed 10 Dec 2018
10. Conboy, K.: Agility from first principles: reconstructing the concept of agility in information systems development. Inf. Syst. Res. **20**(3), 329–354 (2009)
11. Teece, D.: Dynamic capabilities and organizational agility: risk, uncertainty, and strategy in the innovation economy. Calif. Manag. Rev. **58**(4), 13–36 (2016)
12. Reeves, M., Deimler, M.: Adaptability: the new competitive advantage. Harv. Bus. Rev. **89** (July/August), 134–141 (2011)
13. Shingo Institute: The Shingo Model, Logan (2018). https://shingo.org/mode
14. Brown, A.: Managing challenges in sustaining business excellence. Int. J. Qual. Reliab. Manag. **30**(4), 461–475 (2013)
15. Runeson, P., Host, M., Rainer, A., Regnell, B.: Case Study Research in Software Engineering: Guidelines and Examples. Wiley, Hoboken (2012)
16. Yin, R.K.: Case Study Research and Applications: Design and Methods, 6th edn. Sage Publications, Thousand Oaks (2018)
17. Braun, V., Clarke, V.: Using thematic analysis in psychology. Qual. Res. Psychol. **3**(2), 77–101 (2006)
18. ABC Agile Culture (2019). https://www.agilebusiness.org/agile-culture. Accessed 08 Jan 2019
19. Sinek, S.: Start With Why: How Great Leaders Inspire Everyone To Take Action, Portfolio (2009)
20. Strode, D., Huff, S.L., Tretiakov, A.: The impact of organizational culture on agile method use. In: 2009 42nd Hawaii International Conference on System Sciences, pp. 1–9 (2009)
21. Beck, K., Beedle, M., van Bennekum, A., et al.: Manifesto for Agile Software Development (2001). http://agilemanifesto.org/. Accessed 04 Jan 2019
22. ABC development matrix for agile culture (2019). https://agileresearchnetwork.org/wp-content/uploads/2019/03/agile-consortium-culture-DNA-Matrix-A2.pdf
23. Lenberg, P., Feldt, R., Tengberg, L.G.W.: Misaligned values in software engineering organizations. J. Softw. Evol. Process, 1–20 (2018)
24. Sutherland, J.: Agile can scale: inventing and reinventing SCRUM in five companies. Cut. IT J. **14**(12), 5–11 (2001)
25. Mankins, M., Garton, E.: How spotify balances employee autonomy and accountability. Harv. Bus. Rev. **95** (2017)
26. Ambler, S.: Agile/Lean documentation: strategies for agile software development (2018). http://agilemodeling.com/essays/agileDocumentation.htm. Accessed 09 Nov 2018
27. Robinson, H., Sharp, H.: XP culture: why the twelve practices both are and are not the most significant thing. In: Agile Development Conference, ADC 2003 (2003)
28. Barroca, L., Gregory, P., Kuusinen, K., Sharp, H., AlQaisi, R.: Sustaining agile beyond adoption. In: 44th Euromicro Conference on Software Engineering and Advanced Applications, pp. 22–25 (2018)
29. Runeson, P., Höst, M.: Guidelines for conducting and reporting case study research in software engineering. Empir. Softw. Eng. **14**, 131–164 (2009)

The Future of Agile

A Taxonomy of Software Engineering Challenges for Machine Learning Systems: An Empirical Investigation

Lucy Ellen Lwakatare[1(✉)], Aiswarya Raj[1], Jan Bosch[1], Helena Holmström Olsson[2], and Ivica Crnkovic[1]

[1] Department of Computer Science and Engineering, Chalmers University of Technology, Hörselgången 11, 412 96 Gothenburg, Sweden
{llucy,aiswarya,jan.bosch,ivica.crnkovic}@chalmers.se

[2] Department of Computer Science and Media Technology, Malmö University, Nordenskiöldsgatan, 211 19 Malmö, Sweden
helena.holmstrom.olsson@mau.se

Abstract. Artificial intelligence enabled systems have been an inevitable part of everyday life. However, efficient software engineering principles and processes need to be considered and extended when developing AI- enabled systems. The objective of this study is to identify and classify software engineering challenges that are faced by different companies when developing software-intensive systems that incorporate machine learning components. Using case study approach, we explored the development of machine learning systems from six different companies across various domains and identified main software engineering challenges. The challenges are mapped into a proposed taxonomy that depicts the evolution of use of ML components in software-intensive system in industrial settings. Our study provides insights to software engineering community and research to guide discussions and future research into applied machine learning.

Keywords: Artificial intelligence · Machine learning · Software engineering · Challenges

1 Introduction

Artificial intelligence (AI) has gained much attention in recent years. Software-intensive companies, such as Facebook [5], are increasingly employing machine learning techniques in development of intelligent applications. Machine learning (ML), as a rapidly developing branch of AI, provides the companies with key capabilities for improving and accelerating innovation in their offerings based on operational system data. The application areas of ML to real-world problems are vast and range from large use in recommendation systems of social [9] and e-commerce [10] services, to highly regulated products, such as autonomous vehicle prototypes. The development of AI-enabled applications in real-world settings is

P. Kruchten et al. (Eds.): XP 2019, LNBIP 355, pp. 227–243, 2019.
https://doi.org/10.1007/978-3-030-19034-7_14

non-trivial and the development process differs from that of traditional software. At present, there is a growing interest and need to understand how AI-enabled applications are developed, deployed and maintained over-time in real world commercial settings.

It is observed that three distinct approaches, namely requirements-driven, out-come driven and AI-driven, are used to create software [3]. AI-driven approach in operational commercial software is the least covered approach in literature. The development process of AI-enabled applications that employ ML techniques, including its subset deep learning (DL), involve creation of ML models based on data. When creating ML models, typically several experiments are conducted prior to selecting the final ML model. During ML model creation, learning algorithms are applied to a dataset to train and evaluate the accuracy and performance of created ML models. Although in academia much focus is given to theoretical breakthroughs of learning algorithms, empirical studies show that they constitute only a small part of the operational ML system [20]. As a consequence, several challenges are encountered in practice during development and maintenance of ML systems [6]. To address the problem, emerging evidence highlights the need to take into consideration and extend established software engineering (SE) principles, approaches and tools in development of ML systems [11,19].

The main objective of this study is to identify and classify engineering challenges for developing and deploying ML systems in real world commercial settings. Using a multiple-case study approach, we explore the development of seven ML components of commercial software-intensive systems. The main contributions of the paper are threefold. First, the paper provides a description of the development process of six AI-enabled applications across various domains. Second, it presents a taxonomy to depict evolution in the use of ML components in commercial software-intensive systems. Third, using the taxonomy a classification of most important challenges at each stage of the evolution in the use of ML components in software-intensive systems is presented.

2 Background and Related Work

The research area of this study is applied ML, wherein the focus is to create verifiable knowledge pertaining to the design of software systems that incorporate ML techniques [14]. In our study, the considered software systems not only incorporate ML techniques to real world problems but are in operational use in commercial settings. This is in contrast to application of ML techniques to activities of software development process in field of SE [23], such as fault prediction and localization in software testing, which also gives numerous benefits in practice [16].

There exists empirical studies [6] and experience reports [7,15,19,21] published across different disciplines that present an end-to-end development process and challenges of operational AI-enabled applications. In a field study of how intelligent systems are developed, Hill et al. [6] describe a high-level process that includes the following activities that are not necessarily sequential: *defining problem, collecting data, establishing ground truth, selecting algorithm, selecting features and creating and evaluating ML model.* Most of the challenges identified by the authors [6] at each activity of the ML process as well as cross-cutting issues are reported in other empirical reports [1,19]. For instance, the use of informal methods to manage dataset and common artifacts (trained models, feature sets, training jobs) during ML model selection experiments is a challenge that is commonly observed and presents difficulties to quickly reproduce and compare different experiments [18]. In addition to using agile approach for quick iterations [19], among the solutions proposed include using versioning in ML pipelines [22] and automating tracking of metadata and provenance information of the common artifacts [18]. However, some challenges are yet to be addressed, such as tracking provenance of complex final model that combines variety of models trained on different dataset [18] and data generated and processed through highly-heterogeneous infrastructure [13]. Concerning ML infrastructure several challenges are encountered, such as the ability to train models with large data volumes [5].

Using *technical debt* metaphor of SE, Sculley et al. [20] bring to awareness the different trade-offs involved, and require careful consideration, when maintaining ML systems overtime in real-world industrial settings. According to the authors [20], technical debt in real-world ML systems is attributed to maintenance problems of application code and issues specific to ML, such as data dependencies. ML systems have various sources of variability that need to be stabilized otherwise they can cause significant differences between ML models [8]. On the other hand, difficulties in debugging DL systems is currently one of the challenging topic that is gaining much focus in research [4]. Our study seeks to provide a taxonomy that can be used to consolidate the different challenges reported in prior empirical reports.

3 Research Method

For the purpose of this study we conducted an interpretive multiple-case study, following the guidelines by Runeson and Höst [17], to provide a deeper understanding of SE challenges for developing and operating ML systems in real-world commercial settings. The overall research design and process is described below.

3.1 Multiple-case Study Design

The multiple-case study research method was selected because it allowed us to explore SE challenges for developing ML systems in real-world settings both within and between cases. A case in our study pertains to a software-intensive system that incorporates ML component(s) developed at an organization.

Primarily we used semi-structured interviews to collect qualitative data. At the initial phase, we planned the study by describing the kind of data and practitioners that are relevant to the study. Based on the research objective and

Table 1. Description of domain of studied software-intensive systems, ML components, and roles of interviewees (*previous work)

Case	Domain	Use case of ML components	Interviewed experts	
			ID	Role
A	Automotive	Interpreting sensor data to understand the contained information at a high level	P1	Manager of DL organisation
B	Web	(i) Automating tagging of sentiments in online music library (ii) predicting quality of end product based on different measurements from machines, IoT devices of pulp processing and quality measures	P2	Data scientist
			P3	Head of data science team
			P4	Data scientist
			P5	UX lead
C	Web	Collaborative annotation of training data and predicting quality of annotations	P6	Co-founder
			P7	ML engineer
D	Telecom	Predicting failures at site to give insights into mobile network operations	P8	Project Tech lead
			P9	Senior researcher
			P10	Researcher
E	Web	Automating information extraction from out-of-office reply to optimize communication between sales reps and prospects	P11	VP data science
F	Web	Models of ML components of e.g., web search engine, are compared using important measures through A/B tests	P12	Data scientist, experimentation
			P11*	Principal data scientist

preliminary literature review, an interview guide was developed and reviewed in two iterations by the authors. The interview guide had a total of 18 questions structured in six sections. Background and context information of interviewee and ML system were inquired in the first two sections. Section three focused on the general development process of ML system. Sections four and five inquired in detail about data management, feature engineering, model building and deployment. Section six focused explicitly on perceived challenges of SE for ML systems. The interview guide was piloted with an external researcher prior to data collection. For the actual data collection, practitioners with experiences in developing real-world ML systems were sought from different organizations.

3.2 Data Collection

Our primary qualitative data collection process started by sending e-mails containing a short description of study's objective to different company representatives of Software Center[1] and others based on authors' personal networks. The email requested for their company's participation in the study and selecting suitable persons for the interview. Semi-structured interviews were conducted

[1] Software Center: https://www.software-center.se/.

with practitioners between August and December 2018. Altogether 15 interviews were carried out with professionals and allowed researchers to reach saturation of knowledge. Considering acknowledgment in literature (and our experiences when soliciting interviewees) that there are few experienced practitioners skilled in the area of intersection between ML and SE, the vast experience of our interviewees from different companies across multiple domains as shown in Table 1 is of great advantage to this study.

Three interviews were excluded from the study as they focused on the application of ML to the activities of software development process (see Sect. 2 for this study's research area). All interviews were face-to-face except for two interviews, which were done via teleconference. The duration of each interview ranged between 45 to 70 min. All interviews were recorded with interviewees' approval and were later transcribed for analysis. An opportunity for the follow-up questions was also agreed at the end of all interviews. After each interview session, a summary was written and discussed among authors. Secondary qualitative data was collected at a workshop held in December 2018 with practitioners where our initial research results were shared. Excluding researchers, the workshop had an attendance of 10 practitioners from different companies in automotive and telecommunications fields. Notes were taken by authors during workshop.

3.3 Data Analysis

Thematic analysis was used to analyse qualitative interview data. Interview transcripts were coded in NVivo by two researchers in two iterations. First coding iteration was done by coding the challenges using a set of six predefined high-level themes that depict the development of ML system. The six high-level themes were: *(i) data management and pre-processing, (ii) create model, (iii) train and evaluate model, (iv) model deployment, and (v) organizational issues.* First, the two researchers familiarized with the data and discussed the coding procedure at high level themes. Thereafter, the researchers coded separately a similar transcript in order to determine inter-rater reliability measure. A good agreement level was determined (overall Kappa value = 0.72)[2] and the researchers discussed disagreements when reviewing outputs of code comparison in NVivo. Coding for the rest of the transcripts proceeded by having each transcript coded by one researcher. Second iteration of the coding involved identifying challenges at each high-level theme. This was done through joint discussion between the two researchers. The notes taken during the workshop were reviewed and important aspects were taken into consideration in the reported taxonomy.

4 Case Study Findings

An overview of the cases and findings of the challenges from each case are presented. Several dimensions, such as learning task and source of training dataset

[2] Interpretation of kappa value in NVivo: Poor agreement (Below 0.40), Good agreement (0.40–0.75), Excellent agreement (Over 0.75).

[23], can be used to describe and differentiate ML systems. For each case, description of the software-intensive system incorporating ML component(s) is presented first and then followed by descriptions of the ML use case, source of training data, training and deployment of ML models. The ending paragraph of each case description presents a summary of the main challenges for developing ML system as perceived by the interviewed practitioners.

4.1 Case A: *Software for Automated Driving*

A joint venture company established by two large companies in automotive domain is developing software for automated driving (AD). DL models are used in development of software for AD where the main use case is perception. Perception is interpretation of sensor (e.g., camera and LIDAR) data to understand at a high level the contained information, such as presence of objects (e.g., pedestrians and vehicles) among other. DL organization consists of about 50 persons software engineers and ML experts responsible for training DL models, developing DL infrastructure and managing large data storage.

Large amounts of data are collected from the fleet of vehicles going on expeditions in different parts of the world. The collected data is transported and stored at a big data center where pre-processing methods are used to extract images that are to be annotated by an external company. ML experts use annotated data to train offline DL models. To quickly train DL models and rapidly iterate product development cycle, several graphics processing units (GPUs) are used. Software engineers develop different tool-chains, such as schedulers for training jobs, diagnostic and monitoring tools to the highly scalable DL infrastructure. Perception inference serves as a foundation and input to other layers of the system with decision and control are developed by other teams. These teams together with other stakeholders of DL organisation have specifications that give inputs to key performance indicators (KPI) used in model evaluations. The primary target for deployment of DL model in AD vehicle was GPUs, like the NVIDIA Drive Xavier [12].

While Case A poses issues and extreme requirements for storage and preprocessing of large data sets for creating DL models in automotive domain, one main engineering challenge perceived by the DL organization manager was difficulty in building DL infrastructure, as expressed below. This is in addition to problems related evolving requirement definition for AD vehicles, which affect model training and evaluations. At the time of the interview, there was limited support for quickly recreating the different training results.

> *There are no tool-chains you can download in an infrastructure with deep learning like this. And we realized after the mistakes and discussions with our new IT that they didn't really have the expertise to be able to deliver this to us. So we had to create new teams, which took the responsibility of creating both the infrastructure, but also the software tool-chain to be able to train deep learning networks within a reasonable amount of time.*

4.2 Case B: *AI Web Platform*

AI web platform is developed by a company that simplifies the development of ML applications. At the time of interview, the beta version of the platform had active customers using the platform from various industries. Two main use cases of ML focused on our study were for: (i) automatic tagging of sentiments in online music catalogue, and (ii) predicting quality of manufactured products (e.g., carton, cardboard, paper) based on measurements from different machines, IoT devices and microscopic images of wood fibres for pulp processing. AI platform clients typically know beforehand their ML use cases and have data available. Software developers in product team are developing the platform in collaboration with a data science team. The data science team, consisting of eight persons, communicate requirements to the product team, provides internal AI education and uses the platform to do projects with external companies.

In the studied ML use cases, a data scientist receives a training dataset, which is uploaded onto the AI platform. The training dataset is explored, curated and checked for quality on the platform. In the training set, tags initially applied by humans' (e.g., content managers) are assumed to be satisfactory to the client. Since the customer in the paper mill industry had efficient data pipelines for collecting various measurements from pulp processing and quality, data science team were able to get data from past several years. Using the training dataset, different ML models are built, trained and evaluated offline on the platform. For automatic sentiment tagging, the selected final DL model is deployed to a Kubernetes cluster in cloud infrastructure allowing among other, scaling. It exposes a REST API that can be called via JavaScript fetch from the online music catalogue application. At the time of interview, trained ML models of the output quality predictions of pulp processing had not been deployed in production but yielded feedback in form of report given to clients about features indicative of quality. The later was among factors considered in decision to buy a new machine.

In addition to challenges of developing AI platform, such as managing design trade-offs in customization of platform functionalities, other challenges concerned handling of data drifts in uploaded data, invalidation of models e.g., due to changes in data sources, and the need to monitor models in production for staleness.

> *You're trying to simultaneously build reproducibility, collaboration and ease of use at the same time you're trying to give people as much customization as possible. It's the difference between giving somebody a notebook where they can do anything they want and giving a higher level tool that has a lot of built-in functionality. It's there that I see most challenges*

4.3 Case C: *Collaborative Annotation Web Platform*

The collaborative annotation web platform is for creating training dataset of supervised learning used in the development process of customers' ML systems.

The company's clients are mostly automotive OEM companies. In addition, the platform incorporates ML model to predict reliability of an annotations. An annotation process designed by the company is collaborative through iterative development of annotation guideline that incorporates quick feedback between human annotators and the customer's stakeholders. Through the annotation guideline, customers express the desired outcome at an acceptable standard and level of error tolerance. At the time of the interviews, the company had seven employees.

The dataset from the customer is uploaded on the platform and a sample of it is given to both the customer and human annotators to annotate. This is done to determine uncertainty level using for example heat maps. Depending on the results, the customer gets an opportunity to improve annotation guideline thereby shortening the feedback-loop between customer and human annotators. Human annotators use the improved guideline to annotate dataset on the platform. While doing the annotations, meta-data is recorded e.g., time taken to annotate, number of clicks etc. From this data and reviews given by peers, a detailed Bayesian model is developed for each annotator to estimate the quality of the annotations and predict the probability that an annotator is able to produce what the customer wants. The model is running in a Google cloud environment and hooked to the platform through client calls that get executed whenever human annotators finish annotations.

Main SE challenges identified from Case C is the need for processes and tools for forming accurate and consistent annotations in large dataset, especially when the system has no self-labelling instrumentation. Furthermore, there are difficulties in negotiating interpretations and dealing with poor inter-rater agreement across a large group of annotators. Customers using the annotated dataset, often do not have other mechanisms to know if the annotations were done correctly.

> *"So the challenging part of creating large amounts of examples is that it's usually ambiguous. You have a distributed group of people and you need very low error tolerance, because if you're going to have production grade machine learning systems, their performance will be governed by the quality of the data"*

4.4 Case D: *Mobile Network Operations*

A large telecommunication company is enabling intelligent operations of networks by introducing ML techniques that help to predict issues at a source. For network operations centre (NOC) personnel, this allows them to automate and proactively evaluate, prioritize and take preventative actions on issues that might arise. ML use cases focused in this study are those from a project where a research team doing thought leadership at the company is involved and the main goal is to predict what can go wrong at a site (i.e., a building that has base stations, antennas, auxiliary power sources etc). Example of specific ML use cases, include predicting degradation of KPI e.g., latency and throughput, to facilitate remote troubleshooting; and predicting site's sustenance to power outage from auxiliary power e.g., using frequency of battery charging as input data. NOCs that are operated by the company are for about 400 client operator companies distributed in different locations.

Depending on the use case, and whether the team is allowed to move data, datasets of varying sizes are used to train models. In extreme scenario with a datasets of 3TB per day and where data is not allowed to be moved outside a country, federated learning is used. In federated learning an initial model is built locally and then it gets trained and improved at the edge. The training dataset is curated and features engineered by data scientists prior to training. ML models are trained while also residing in the CI-CD pipeline since the company supports many customers across different locations. When training the models care is taken not to mix data of different clients. The ML models are packaged as Docker images that are deployed on Kubernetes in the cloud and monitored for model usage and accuracy, in addition to CPU usage and memory, using a tool called Prometheus.

The main engineering challenges for Case D are related to data collection and model localization particularly in areas where data movement is constrained, as elaborated in quote below by the Tech Lead.

> *I think really the challenge is actually getting data and that is why we are investing so much in federated learning because in some cases the data cannot leave the country. And also in some cases the links that you have are not strong enough to carry the data that you want because they are used by other things. So that is really the key challenge here and that is why we are looking into the techniques such as federated learning and reinforcement learning so that we can improve on it.*

4.5 Case E: *Sales Engagement Platform*

Sales engagement platform primarily enables and optimizes communication between sales representatives (henceforth sales reps) and potential prospects. Sales communication occurs in natural language via different communication channels, including emails. The ML use case of focus was concerned with extracting automatically entities, such as date, using natural language processing (NLP) techniques from out-of-office emails. Specifically, for information extraction, emails are parsed and processed to understand the contained information, such as people, dates and best contact information from out-of-office emails. The information allows sales reps to take relevant actions, such as pausing sequences of automated steps. The data science team at the company consists of ten persons responsible for data analysis, ML, A/B testing and insights reporting.

All email communication done by sales reps is stored in a communication database out of which a few of these are labelled and form the validation dataset. Due to some factors, such as limited labelled data to train models, open sourced pre-trained models are used. Prior to extraction of entities, pre-processing steps, such as handling of different encoding, are conducted to get the email text. The step is followed by the entity extraction, which applies different pre-trained models to extract entities as well as construct relationship tree around the entities, for example to suggest the person with whom the phone number left in out-of-office email belongs. The pre-trained models are evaluated using the validation dataset and tuned to improve their accuracy in consideration of company's dataset. In addition, measures of actual user experience through A/B testing are gathered to provide feedback into the training of the model. Databricks tool is used to build and deploy the models, which are typically saved as a single library and are version controlled.

Prior to their recent use of the Databricks tool, the team faced challenges related to the lack of standardized approaches for reproducing model selection experiments quickly and scaling models in production.

> *We also needed to worry about scaling because the volume of messages differs a lot with time. Generally, on Monday sales people send hundreds of thousands of emails to new prospects. We had to either do it manually by deploying more copies of the model, and then bringing them down to not use-up resources, or leave the model and then there will be a queue. We did not do this manual approach and the queue would get to almost 24 hours long. So those emails will only get processed on Tuesday because of the volume.*

4.6 Case F: Online Experimentation Platform

An experimentation platform is developed by a large company to support various product teams in running trustworthy experiments, such as A/B tests. While the platform is also used by applications that do not incorporate ML/DL components, those that do use, such as web search engine, use it to compare trained models with important measures through A/B tests. The team in charge of the platform provide training and support to product teams to set-up, run experiments in addition to developing and maintaining the platform. The team consists of about consists of about one hundred persons, who among them are data scientists and software developers.

Experimentation platform consists of mainly four components namely experimentation portal, experiment execution service, log processing service, and analysis service. A good logging system that captures correct events, at correct time and identify targets is important for running experiments on the platform. This is because every product user is every single point in time in several experiments and logs need to be annotated with information of which experiments users in addition to using the data to (re)train models. Users can run their experiments on platform as per their requirement either with the help of some predefined templates or without templates by which they can eventually find a better performing trained model. This is important because the models are compared using measures that the business care for because users are using system functionality and not the models.

Among the challenges identified from practitioners of Case E are difficulties with complex and poor logging mechanisms as well as in designing experiments, including interleaving experiments often done in ML components and interpreting experiment results.

> *If product teams want to have good informative experiments they need to log the correct things. Logging in the past was done to understand if a product has crashed or not, or why it has crashed. This is not sufficient if you want to compute good business metrics in the end of the day*

5 A Taxonomy of SE Challenges for ML Systems

In this section, insights into SE challenges for ML system are presented using a taxonomy that depicts evolution of use of ML components in software-intensive system in industrial settings. The insights are based on the findings of our cross-case analysis and the literature presented in Sect. 2.

Based on the study, we have identified five evolution stages of the use of ML component(s) in software systems that follow a pattern wherein they are initially deployed for experimental (or research) purposes until maturing to function autonomously. This progression of stages in the taxonomy occurs at component basis. Essentially, model life-cycle activities (*assemble dataset, create model, (re)train and evaluate, deploy*) are performed at all maturity stages. The taxonomy is visualised in Fig. 1 and a summary of the challenges is given in Table 2.

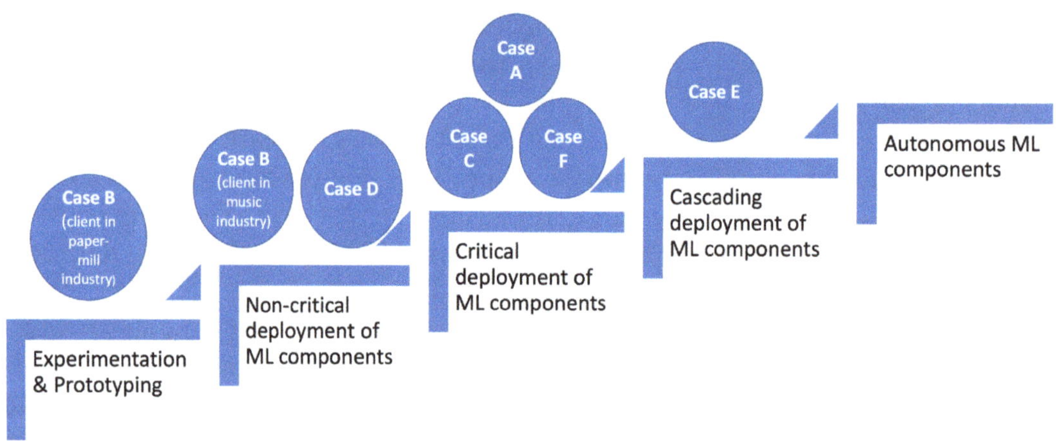

Fig. 1. Evolution of use of ML in commercial software-intensive systems

5.1 Experimentation and Prototyping

Initial application of ML techniques and creation of ML models in industrial settings is often for experimentation and prototyping. At this first step, different innovations and improvements to existing software-intensive systems are hypothesized through the use of ML techniques. There exists a vague description of ML problem or use case. However, critical decisions are made by designers about the learning algorithm, representation and training dataset. Decisions have profound effects on the success, or appropriateness, of ML components. In our studied cases, Case B's client from paper-mill industry belongs to this stage.

Existing data collection mechanisms and storage of software-intensive system are originally not set-up for ML systems. For example, poor logging and limited data cleaning mechanisms exist prior to the ML initiative. As a result, potentially large efforts are spent on data exploration, in addition to determining and formulating the problem of ML in the respective application domain. Difficulty in formulating the problem for ML is accounted for, among other, by the need to determine beforehand a benchmark or baseline against which ML model will be evaluated for accuracy and performance optimizations. While a variety of big data tools are used in data aggregation and structuring, different design decisions and trade-offs in model creation rely on inputs from domain experts, such as useful features. At this stage, models are not deployed but do provide valuable feedback to the experts about the direct impact of suggested features.

5.2 Non-critical Deployment

After gaining experience with initial use of ML techniques in respective application domain, ML model prototypes, or their revisions, are deployed on non-critical functions of the software-intensive system. Alternatively, inferences of ML components are inspected by human expert. At this stage, the hypothesized improvements through the use of ML are quantified in a production environment. As data pipelines for ML are being initiated, scarcity of labelled data and imbalanced training dataset challenge the creation of models. This is in addition to legal and privacy protection requirement challenges of accessing data. From our studied cases, Case B's client in music industry and Case D belong to this stage.

Data analysis and validation is an initial and critical activity for designers of ML components. Absence of critical analysis on training data results to training and serving skew, which describes differences in performance of ML model at training and deploy. The discrepancies are largely caused by differences in the handling of data distributions and pipelines during training and operations. Data sources or different fields in data e.g., in logs, may come from different components owned by other teams. Major changes to the values invalidate models trained on older data. Techniques and tools for monitoring and tracking data are crucial for developing ML systems, as supported in literature.

5.3 Critical Deployment

Successfully quantified improvements in stage 2 drive deployment of ML models to critical functions of the software-intensive system. For each critical function implementing ML component, designers take a separate account to their differences in system architecture and data distributions both at training and serving. At this stage, there is typically a co-existence of ML components with other software components developed using traditional techniques, as observed in Case A. Since ML components are developed at the same time as the product definition of the software-intensive system is evolving, the ability to track and adapt to the system changes and optimization objectives is necessary at training and evaluation. There is need to have an effective end-to-end ML pipeline that simplify and make it possible to quickly compare and reliably reproduce different results of model creation, training and evaluations. Case A, Case C and Case F belong to this stage.

For critical deployment of ML components, challenges in the implementation of the end-to-end ML pipeline comes with the need and difficulty in implementing an effective experimentation infrastructure. The experimentation infrastructure is used to evaluate performance improvements and effects of ML models with the use of metrics that are business-centric rather than algorithmic-centric. The ability to design and conduct several experiments on continuous basis is non-trivial. While experiments that are conducted online are exploring and exploiting the models, end-users are not to be affected and need to adhere to the stringent requirements of latency and throughput.

5.4 Cascading Deployment

At the next step is a software system that has cascading ML models whereby outcome(s) of one or more ML components serve as inputs to subsequent ML component. Cascading deployment of ML components was used in [10] to enable the elimination of irrelevant data items in earlier stages and discern relevant ones in later stages. According to the authors [10], the cascading deployment strategy achieves a balance, rather than a trade-off, with respect to effective ranking results from a large number of data items of Alibaba e-commerce and efficiency in terms of good user experience and savings in computational costs. From our cases, Case E, in addition to the studied use case, has models that detect the intent from prospect's email replies.

For the final model in the cascading deployment strategy, the challenge comes from the difficulty in tracking changes in models giving the input features and in performing a sliced analysis to the evaluation results. It is apparent that as the system scales to handle more models, it becomes difficult to identify the cause of poor performance for final system, for example due to undeclared consumers [20]. When final model performance results are not sliced, such as merely focus on accuracy on validation training set, according to [15] important effects are masked and can result in quality improving in one part but degrading in another.

5.5 Autonomous ML Components

At the final step is a system that incorporates ML components that have automatic processes (or minimal human intervention) of ensuring fail-safe outcomes,

Table 2. Summary of the challenges in evolution of use of ML components in commercial software-intensive systems

	Experiment prototyping	Non-critical deployment	Critical deployment	Cascading deployment
Assemble dataset	Issues with problem formulation and specifying desired outcome	Data silos, scarcity of labelled data, imbalanced training set	Limitations in techniques for gathering training data from large-scale, non-stationary data streams	Complex and effects of data dependencies
Create model	Use of non-representative dataset, data drifts	No critical analysis of training data	Difficulties in building highly scalable ML pipeline	Entanglements causing difficulties in isolating improvements
Train and evaluate model	Lack of well-established ground truth	No evaluation of models with business-centric measures	Difficulties in reproducing models, results and debugging DL models	Need of techniques for sliced analysis in final model
Deploy model	No deployment mechanism	Training-serving skew	Adhering to stringent serving requirements e.g., of latency, throughput	Hidden feedback-loops and undeclared consumers of the models

retraining and scalability of ML models. While we did not experience a case at this stage besides being expressed by practitioners as a future direction, concrete work in this direction is presented in existing literature, such as in online targeted-display advertising systems [15]. This stage also considers other learning strategies, such as active learning and reinforcement learning. Case A of our case study findings was considering active learning for automatic selective acquisition of training data and Case D was looking to explore reinforcement learning to eliminate efforts associated with model training and retraining.

For the alternative learning methods, such as active learning, some of the challenges are attributed to the lack of sufficient practical guidance for implementing the learning strategies [2]. Although, successful implementations have been demonstrated to obtain data and annotations automatically through the use of active learning, there remains great need to incorporate practices and tools for monitoring data sources and monitoring different sources of variability.

6 Conclusion

Developing, evolving and operating ML systems in real-world commercial settings is non-trivial. This paper explored engineering challenges for developing and operating supervised ML systems in real-world commercial settings. Multiple cases of ML systems from different application domain are presented, including description of their development process and perceived engineering challenges.

In an effort to energize and focus the discussion of ML systems on SE aspects besides the algorithmic issues, we have presented a taxonomy that depicts maturity stages of use of ML components in commercial software system and mapped the challenges at each stage. The challenges we have identified as most important require a lot of efforts to be managed, and in the future work we will refine the challenges with additional cases and explore possible solutions as well as provide guidance on how to move from one maturity stage to another. Furthermore, we acknowledge that our study has narrowly focused on the development process of ML components and that research into other SE topics, such as challenges related to software architecture are still of great interest and needed.

References

1. Arpteg, A., Brinne, B., Crnkovic-Friis, L., Bosch, J.: Software engineering challenges of deep learning. In: 44th Euromicro Conference on Software Engineering and Advanced Applications, pp. 50–59. IEEE (2018). https://doi.org/10.1109/SEAA.2018.00018
2. Attenberg, J., Provost, F.: Inactive learning? Difficulties employing active learning in practice. ACM SIGKDD Explor. Newsl. **12**(2), 36–41 (2011)
3. Bosch, J., Olsson, H.H., Crnkovic, I.: It takes three to tango: requirement, outcome/data, and AI driven. In: International Workshop on Software-Intensive Business: Start-Ups, Ecosystems and Platforms, pp. 177–192 (2018)
4. Hains, G., Jakobsson, A., Khmelevsky, Y.: Towards formal methods and software engineering for deep learning: security, safety and productivity for dl systems development. In: 2018 Annual IEEE International Systems Conference, pp. 1–5. IEEE, April 2018. https://doi.org/10.1109/SYSCON.2018.8369576
5. Hazelwood, K., et al.: Applied machine learning at Facebook: a datacenter infrastructure perspective. In: International Symposium on High Performance Computer Architecture, pp. 620–629. IEEE (2018). https://doi.org/10.1109/HPCA.2018.00059
6. Hill, C., Bellamy, R., Erickson, T., Burnett, M.: Trials and tribulations of developers of intelligent systems: a field study. In: Symposium on Visual Languages and Human-Centric Computing, pp. 162–170. IEEE (2016). https://doi.org/10.1109/VLHCC.2016.7739680
7. Kumar, R.S.S., Wicker, A., Swann, M.: Practical machine learning for cloud intrusion detection: challenges and the way forward. In: 10th Workshop on Artificial Intelligence and Security, pp. 81–90. ACM (2017). https://doi.org/10.1145/3128572.3140445
8. Lefortier, D., Truchet, A., de Rijke, M.: Sources of variability in large-scale machine learning systems. In: Machine Learning Systems (NIPS 2015 Workshop) (2015)
9. Lin, J., Kolcz, A.: Large-scale machine learning at Twitter. In: SIGMOD International Conference on Management of Data, pp. 793–804. ACM (2012). https://doi.org/10.1145/2213836.2213958
10. Liu, S., Xiao, F., Ou, W., Si, L.: Cascade ranking for operational e-commerce search. In: International Conference on Knowledge Discovery and Data Mining, pp. 1557–1565. ACM (2017). https://doi.org/10.1145/3097983.3098011

11. Murphy, C., Kaiser, G.E., Arias, M.: An approach to software testing of machine learning applications. In: 19th International Conference on Software Engineering and Knowledge Engineering, pp. 167–172. Knowledge Systems Institute Graduate School (2007)
12. NVIDIA: Nvidia drive hardware for self-driving cars. https://www.nvidia.com/en-us/self-driving-cars/drive-platform/hardware/. Accessed 11 Jan 2019
13. Polyzotis, N., Roy, S., Whang, S.E., Zinkevich, M.: Data management challenges in production machine learning. In: International Conference on Management of Data, pp. 1723–1726. ACM (2017). https://doi.org/10.1145/3035918.3054782
14. Provost, F., Kohavi, R.: Guest editors' introduction: on applied research in machine learning. Mach. Learn. **30**(2), 127–132 (1998). https://doi.org/10.1023/A:1007442505281
15. Raeder, T., Stitelman, O., Dalessandro, B., Perlich, C., Provost, F.: Design principles of massive, robust prediction systems. In: International Conference on Knowledge Discovery and Data Mining, pp. 1357–1365. ACM (2012)
16. Rana, R., Staron, M., Hansson, J., Nilsson, M., Meding, W.: A framework for adoption of machine learning in industry for software defect prediction. In: 9th International Conference on Software Engineering and Applications, pp. 383–392. IEEE (2014)
17. Runeson, P., Höst, M.: Guidelines for conducting and reporting case study research in software engineering. Empirical Softw. Eng. **14**(2), (2008)
18. Schelter, S., Böse, J.H., Kirschnick, J., Klein, T., Seufert, S.: Automatically tracking metadata and provenance of machine learning experiments. In: NIPS Workshop on Machine Learning Systems (2017)
19. Schleier-Smith, J.: An architecture for agile machine learning in real-time applications. In: International Conference on Knowledge Discovery and Data Mining, pp. 2059–2068. ACM (2015). https://doi.org/10.1145/2783258.2788628
20. Sculley, D., et al.: Hidden technical debt in machine learning systems. In: Cortes, C., Lawrence, N.D., Lee, D.D., Sugiyama, M., Garnett, R. (eds.) Advances in Neural Information Processing Systems 28, pp. 2503–2511. Curran Associates, Inc. (2015)
21. Tata, S., et al.: Quick access: building a smart experience for Google drive. In: 23rd International Conference on Knowledge Discovery and Data Mining, pp. 1643–1651. ACM (2017). https://doi.org/10.1145/3097983.3098048
22. van der Weide, T., Papadopoulos, D., Smirnov, O., Zielinski, M., van Kasteren, T.: Versioning for end-to-end machine learning pipelines. In: 1st Workshop on Data Management for End-to-End Machine Learning, pp. 2:1–2:9. ACM (2017). https://doi.org/10.1145/3076246.3076248
23. Zhang, D., Tsai, J.J.: Machine learning and software engineering. Softw. Qual. J. **11**(2), 87–119 (2003). https://doi.org/10.1023/A:1023760326768

Evolution of Scrum Transcending Business Domains and the Future of Agile Project Management

Richard J. J. Oprins[1(✉)], Helena A. Frijns[2], and Christoph J. Stettina[1,2,3(✉)]

[1] Leiden Institute of Advanced Computer Science, Leiden University, Niels Bohrweg 1, 2333 CA Leiden, The Netherlands
r.j.j.oprins@gmail.com, c.j.stettina@fgga.leidenuniv.nl
[2] Centre for Innovation The Hague, Leiden University, Schouwburgstraat 2, 2511 VA The Hague, The Netherlands
[3] Accenture B.V., Orteliuslaan 1000, 3528 BD Utrecht, The Netherlands

Abstract. The growing popularity of Agile management methods has led to their application to a number of areas inside, but also outside, the software development domain. However, despite many practitioner reports, research exploring whether and how Agile practices have been applied in domains beyond software development has been rather patchy with little empirical evidence. What is there behind the hype and how can other domains learn from it? To address this gap in the research, we present the findings of our study on the application of Agile management practices in other domains, including an outlook towards a potential expansion enabling Business Agility. To practitioners, this study presents examples of Scrum applied outside the software development domain including concrete practices applied. To researchers, it presents an empirical starting point for further exploration.

Keywords: Agile · Agile practices · Business agility · Change · Client orientation · Collaboration · Responsiveness · Retrospectives · Scrum outside software development

1 Introduction

In 2001, a meeting in a ski resort in Utah (United States) resulted in an agreement that changed the way software development would unfold, and which would, eventually, transform ways of working not solely in the field of management. This agreement was based on the practices of collaborative, self-organising efforts being undertaken by cross-functional teams who would not only consult with their customers and end users, but would also be self-reflecting, self-responsive and self-improving. This agreement is known as the Agile Manifesto [1], and it promoted 12 simple principles and four values. These principles were formulated as a direct response to the traditional waterfall methods of business planning and execution.

P. Kruchten et al. (Eds.): XP 2019, LNBIP 355, pp. 244–259, 2019.
https://doi.org/10.1007/978-3-030-19034-7_15

Given that Agility has come to be viewed in a wider context, as something more than a series of techniques, it is not surprising that many now consider it to be a fundamentally transformative management philosophy [2]. It is a dynamic process that has not only revolutionised software development, but is also equipping organisations and the people who manage them to respond quickly and appropriately in a world in which the pace of change is increasing exponentially day by day.

This article focuses on practical applications, examining how Agile practices have been implemented in domains beyond those related to software development. Using research findings, it also discusses what characterises those organisations that have applied Agile methods and, using empirical cross-case data and existing literature, it defines and describes the most commonly applied practices. Based on 18 interviews conducted with Agile practitioners from a variety of domains who are involved in business processes such as marketing, sales, communication and human resources, this article, through its analysis of the concrete impact of Agile methods, expands the current understanding of Agile project management methods, thus encouraging further exploration into future Agile implementation.

2 Related Work

While a lot of research work has been focused on expanding Agile methods within the software development and information systems domain [3,4], the application of Agile ways of working outside the IT sphere is relatively new. It is a subject that remains to be investigated, since exploration of Agile methods in different domains is supported only by scattered reports and by little empirical evidence.

One of the difficulties of identifying the application of Agile methods beyond IT is the expansion of information systems into other domains. For example, marketing is nowadays often driven by automation and supported by data engineers and software development teams (e.g. to automatically analyse and act upon responses from social media or automated mailing lists). This blurs the lines between marketing and software development. In one of the few contributions to the research, Conforto et al. [5] present a set of enablers for the application of Agile project management methods outside IT.

Further, due to their practical nature, Agile methods can be difficult to understand, and to delineate what is Agile and what is not is not an obvious undertaking [6,7]. While Agile project and portfolio management has an impact on the processes (practices applied in context), structures (roles and responsibilities) and culture (values and principles) in organisations [8], in this article we follow the advice of Laanti et al. [9] and focus on the behavioural components and specifically the Agile practices applied. We do so because Agile practices can be viewed as the most tangible elements of agility and as such can be easier to pinpoint by research participants. Even though a description of Agile practices can be found elsewhere [10,11] the most commonly applied Agile practices are [12]: (1) Iteration Planning; (2) Iterative Development; (3) Continuous Integration

& Testing; (4) Co-Location; (5) Stand-up Meetings; (6) Customer Access; (7) Customer Acceptance Tests; and (8) Retrospectives [11,12].

In the remainder of this section an analysis of the current state of knowledge is followed by a description of the gaps in the available literature, all of which led to the iteration of the research questions that formed the focus of our study. This research focused principally on (1) scientific and empirical contributions and (2) practitioner reports.

2.1 Scientific Reports

In our literature study we found studies conducted in the domains of Education, Sales and Manufacturing. The results are presented here.

Sales: Solingen, Sutherland, and de Waard [13] studied the application of Scrum in the sales domain, where Scrum rituals, such as short iterations, Sprint reviews, checking on progress and attending a daily stand-up meeting were adopted in relation to such activities. The application of Scrum enabled sales to become more predictable and revealed new ways of conducting sales with customers, thus exposing the relationships that existed between customer maintenance and referrals for new business. A study by Steenberg [14] revealed that Agile methods, when used to survey customer needs, provided invaluable feedback that could be used to improve client focus and to give sales teams insight into how their behaviour positively or negatively impacted clients, thus enabling the teams to quickly make changes and become more effective.

Education: Although the application of Agile methods is found in educational software development, some studies looked at Agile applications in teaching methods. Melnik and Maurer [15] studied the effect of XP practices on second-year academic students and their perception of the use of XP practices. They selectively adopted XP practices such as test-driven development; simple design; continuous integration; refactoring; pair programming; and collective code ownership. Based on the results, Melnik and Maurer concluded that Agile methods in the schools sphere must be specifically tailored to an educational context, in contrast to what took place in terms of industry. Several studies have looked at the use of altered versions of Scrum [16] and studied the impact of implementing Agile in research groups. These studies applied Scrum rituals such as daily scrum, sprint review and sprint planning. The use of Scrum had the effect of ensuring that faculty time was used more efficiently and that students improved their productivity. It helped students to be more involved and teachers to focus on helping and coaching their students which, in turn, helped them to propel the student's research forward. Students also started helping each other on their tasks and developed effective strategies to deliver their work on time. Stettina et al. [17] compared the impact of group sizes in relation to the use of Scrum rituals at universities, and in particular, analysed coaching and team routines. Coaching smaller teams took additional time, but improved the exchange of information and student satisfaction, all of which enhanced the maturity of the team.

Manufacturing: Studies analysed how the application of Agile methodology was evolving and looked at methods such as the application of Real Agile Manufacturing [18] and supply chain management [19]. Besides these studies, research was also carried out on the issues that should be considered when Agile is being fully embraced [19]. Manivelmuridaren [20] concluded that Agile manufacturing methods differed so markedly from traditional manufacturing that he described it as a paradigm shift. The results of these studies indicated that, overall, Agile methods of manufacturing change an organisation by placing the customer, and not the company, at the centre of the manufacturing process. To embrace the required changes, employers must build a flexible organisation that can move human and physical resources around very quickly, when needed. In another research case undertaken by Inmana, Samuel, Saleb, Green and Whittend, the analysts studied manufacturing organisations which had become more Agile by implementing just-in-time purchase and manufacturing processes, an approach which improved the operating performance of the firm [21].

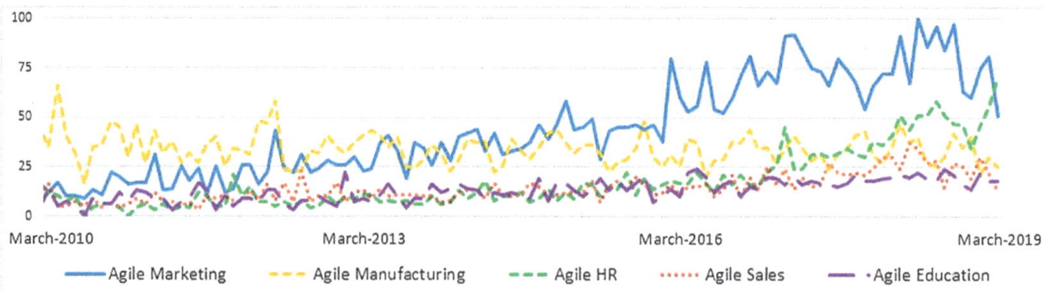

Fig. 1. Google search inquiries 2010–2019: Agile marketing (Blue), Agile manufacturing (Yellow), Agile HR (Green), Agile sales (Red), and Agile education (Purple) (Color figure online)

2.2 Practitioner Reports

Despite many practitioner reports and potential interest (see Fig. 1), we found little empirical literature on the application of Agile methods, especially in the domains of marketing, healthcare, finance and human resources. Most of the reports relating to these four domains consist of accounts of personal experiences recorded in specialist blogs, forum discussions and opinion pieces, and thus are not the result of scientific study but presentations of personal views.

Marketing: Drumont [22] has blogged about her experience with marketeers, who are constantly trying to become faster and more nimble in their responses. This is especially important in the digital domain, where the days of executing static campaigns that have been planned months in advance are gone. Another document describing the Agile way of working is a marketing manifesto [23].

Healthcare: King and King [24] describe the use of Scrum in a medical family practice, brought into play to improve the skills of professionals by being transparent and using feedback received from peers. Another interesting case study is that of the Dutch healthcare organisation *Buurtzorg*. They use Agile principles such as self-managing teams, client focus and the use of small teams to review and discuss cases and problems in order to improve their performance [25].

Finance: In a blog post, Hegarty [26] describes how Scrum methods have been implemented in relation to teams of accountants, with the use of story-maps, sprints and retrospectives.

HR: In the human resources (HR) domain, one article posted on the Scrumstudy website describes how HR teams can benefit from Scrum [27]. The absence of literature on Agile in HR has also been acknowledged by Gothelf in the Harvard Business School article 'How HR can become Agile and Why it needs to' [28].

2.3 Gaps in the Literature and Our Research Question

To summarise, while there are numerous practitioner reports pointing to the application of Agile methods in different domains, existing empirical research contributions are limited to manufacturing, logistics, sales [13], education [15,17] and research [29]. Based on the state of the literature, we thus posed the following research question: *In which domains can Agile management methods be found and what concrete practices/rituals have been applied to projects outside of the IT domain?*

3 Methodology

The subject of this research involves a new environment from which not much empirical evidence is available. To study this organisational phenomenon within teams using Agile as way of working, the authors decided to follow a qualitative research approach. The data was collected using semi-structured interviews with open-ended questions; initial questions were followed by the posing of additional questions, which emerged as a result of the information provided in the initial interviews.

Identification and Selection of Interview Participants: Interview participants and the list of final interviewees were selected on the basis of internet searches and the use of information and contacts via the researchers' personal networks.

Internet Search: After an initial literature review, the researchers, using Google and LinkedIn, identified potential interviewees through the application of such relevant search terms as 'Scrum', 'Kanban', 'XP' and 'Agile', especially in contexts outside software development; references to Agile methods in general were found in the fields of construction, human resources, manufacturing, marketing, education and sales. One criterion that necessitated the exclusion of a particular participant was clear proof that the individual did not possess the claimed expertise in applying these methods within his/her domain. The resulting pool of interviewees was chosen on the basis of familiarity with the implementation of Agile methods (such as Scrum); professional experience in non-IT domains in which Agile methods of working had been applied; and specialised knowledge of the application of Agile methods outside software development; and/or research conducted in this area.

Use of Personal Network: The researchers also identified potential participants from their own personal networks and these individuals were asked if they knew anyone with similar experience or if they had clients who might be interested in being interviewed.

Invitations to participate were sent to 37 people from 22 different organisations, along with the following screening questions:

1. Are you familiar with the application of Agile methods outside IT projects? If yes, in which domain?
2. Are there any people in your organisation who have initiated Agile methods in other departments/domains (for example in marketing, sales, business, communication, etc.) or in schools?
3. Can you refer us to any other people/organisations that have implemented Agile methods?

The resulting pool of participants was made up of (among others) managers, Agile coaches and consultants and researchers who had been or were currently involved in the application of Agile methods such as Scrum in contexts beyond the domain of IT (see Table 1).

Table 1. Overview of participants

Participant	Role	Agile exp. (in years)	Industry application of Agile methods	Domain application
1	Consultant	?	Local government and related organisations	Event management
2	Agile coach	?	Financial industry	Marketing
3	Agile coach	?	Financial industry	Marketing
4	Consultant, Agile coach	10 years	Manufacturing, Product Development, Transportation, Finance	Product development, R&D manufacturing, Procurement
5	Consultant	5 years	Finance	Marketing
6	Program Manager	6 years	Energy	E-commerce, Online sales
7	Consultant, Writer	>10 years	Administration	
8	PhD Student	1 year	Product development, Research	Research project
9	Public speaker	>10 years	Various	Marketing, Sales, Start-ups
10	Manager of methods, quality and technology	7 years	Food retail	HR
11	Consultant, Writer	>10 years	Various	Machine manufacturing, Sales and marketing
12	Manager Senior product owner	7 years	Financial industry Insurance	Sales Internet
13	Consultant	7 years	Financial industry	Marketing
14	Consultant	9 years	Energy, Manufacturing	Geology
15	Head of communication team	1 year	Education	Communication
16	Agile coach	5 years	Education	Schools
17	Marketing manager	3 years	Travel industry	Marketing
18	Consultant, (Scrum master) Writer	10 years	Telecom Software hosting	Customer Service, HR

Data Collection: The interviews were scheduled to fit the agenda of the respondents, took about 60 min and were held in the period between February and November 2017. Interview guides contained questions such as: *Do you have experience of implementing Agile methods/Scrum outside of IT in your organisation? Can you give us concrete example(s)? How and why did you start applying Agile methods/Scrum outside of IT? What practices/routines/rituals/ceremonies did you implement? What were the barriers to adoption?* Seven interviews were held via Skype, four by means of phonecalls and eight at face-to-face meetings. Audio recordings were made of the interviews with the participants' verbal consent. The audio recordings were transcribed by one of the researchers. The content of the transcribed interviews was sent to participants to make sure that the transcriptions did not misrepresent what they had intended to say. Participant 4 submitted four minor revisions, and participant 14 submitted two minor revisions. The transcribed interviews were anonymised for further textual analysis.

Data Analysis: During the course of this research, we interviewed 18 participants who worked in applying Agile management methods in the domains of marketing (6 cases); sales (2 cases); education (3 cases); human resources (2 cases); communication (1 case); event management (1 case); R&D (1 case), change management (1 case); and geology (1 case). As depicted in Table 1, the participants had on average about 5 years of relevant experience and worked in different industrial sectors, including finance, energy/utilities, education, the public sector and research. When adopting Agile methods across different domains, the vast majority of respondents indicated that they leaned on the Scrum framework as a starting point. The data was coded using an axial coding technique as described by Strauss and Corbin [30] resulting in a total of 144 pages of transcripts, over 18 h of recordings, and in total, 1089 codes.

The transcribed interviews were processed by one researcher. Two researchers analysed the transcriptions in search of results that would answer the following questions and which could be sorted according to the following categories: (1) methods used; (2) motivation; (3) change design; (4) success factors; (5) impact; and (6) practices. As it can be difficult to delineate what is Agile and what is not, we followed the advice of Laanti et al. [7] and compared the concrete practices applied.

4 Results and Discussion

The most commonly mentioned reasons given by participants to adopt Agile ways of working in their teams were: (1) external threats and fluctuating customer needs; (2) a lack of transparency about the value that was being delivered and how it connected to other organisational units; (3) the realisation that previously applied project management approaches did not work; and (4) the quest for increased employee satisfaction. As depicted in Table 2, the most applied practices were: structuring work in sprints (n = 15), daily stand-up meetings (n = 15), retrospectives (n = 15) and sprint planning (n = 14).

The most alternated practices were: daily stand-up meetings, sprint planning and the retrospective. The biggest reasons for alternation of practices among our cases were mobility (travelling team members prefer calls) and perceived usefulness. The success of Agile practices can be linked to Agile maturity as participant 18 points out: *"Scrum is introduced in many forms. This sometimes creates scepticism. Scrum was not always a success and this reflects on people's emotions. When rituals are removed and it didn't work, it is blamed on Scrum."*

The remainder of this section elaborates on (1) the domains of application and the concrete Agile practices applied across our cases; and (2) the basis of trends in the work field, discussing domains where one could expect to encounter the application of Agile management in the future.

4.1 Scrum Outside Software Development: Domains and Practices

In this section we discuss the six domains where we encountered the application of Scrum (marketing, sales, education, human resources, communication and geology) and which concrete practices had been applied. In several cases the rituals were altered or not used anymore. These changes varied from adjusting the time of the daily stand-up meeting to the decision to stop rituals. An overview of the rituals and practices we observed through the interview process can be found in Table 2.

Marketing: In marketing, the most applied rituals were the retrospective, mentioned by six out of the seven participants, followed by the use of iterations and the daily Scrum (stand-up) which was mentioned by seven respondents. Sprint planning was carried out by three out of the six respondents. Marketing had the most applications of an Agile way of working, but the rituals were not mentioned as frequently as in other domains. Participant 17 describes the application of cross-functional teams in the marketing department of a travel agency as follows: *"[..] the commercial department consists of four bases (Tribes: Core, direct, partner and passenger). These bases are responsible for the products, experience of the direct sales to the customer, service during the ticket sales, interfaces to third parties and the aftersales. [..] A Crew is a multifunctional team, product developer (product owner), content, communication and data specialist. Their goal is to create value in a benefit for a specific subject."*

Sales: We found four examples of sales departments changing their way of working to adopt an Agile approach. Almost all respondents mentioned that they implemented all the Scrum rituals, that is, they followed all the rules and processes described in the Scrum Guide [10]. One of the respondents mentioned that, after one implementation, the team was then free to alter how the rituals were implemented. This was based on the Shu-Ha-Ri principle, which states that a team first learns the rules and that later it can bend the rules. One respondent described a situation in a team where team members found it difficult to speak out: *"The team was not able to speak out about the previous sprint. They found*

Table 2. Agile practices across the identified domains

Participant #	Domain	structuring work in sprints	Daily Scrum (stand-up)	Retrospective	Sprint planning	Sprint review	Backlog	User stories	Definition of done	Co-located	Scrum master	Cross-functional teams	Empowering the team	Roadmapping	Dedicated product owner	Weighted shortest job first	Value owners
Participant 2	Marketing	●								●	●	●					
Participant 3	Marketing	●		⦸				○	●	●	●		●				
Participant 5	Marketing	●	⦸	●	⦸	⦸											
Participant 13	Marketing		⦸	●					●	⦸							
Participant 17	Marketing	●	●	●	●							●			●		
Participant 11	Marketing, Sales	●	⦸	●	○	○	●		●		⦸	●	●				
Participant 6	Sales	●	⦸	⦸	●	●	⦸	○			●						
Participant 12	Sales	●	⦸		⦸	●	●							○			●
Participant 8	Education	○	○	⦸	○	○											
Participant 16	Education	●	⦸	⦸	⦸	●						●					
Participant 14	Geology, Education	○	⦸	●	○	●	●							○			
Participant 10	HR	●	⦸	●	○	●	●	○								●	
Participant 18	HR	○	⦸	○	○	○											
Participant 1	Event Management	●	●	●	⦸	●	●	○	●								
Participant 4	R&D Measurement Instruments	○	⦸	⦸	⦸	⦸	●										
Participant 7	Change Management		⦸	⦸	●												
Participant 15	Communication	●	⦸	⦸	●		●	●		⦸					●		
	Totals	15	15	15	14	11	8	5	4	4	4	3	2	2	2	1	1

The ● symbol is used if a participant mentioned a ritual, the ○ symbol is used when the participant mentioned they implement rituals 'by the book' and there is evidence they used the specific ritual. The used and alternated rituals as mentioned by the participants are presented by the ⦸ symbol.

it hard to express themselves. This [The retrospective] was stopped" (Participant 6, Director Online Sales and Services, Program Manager).

Education: In education, we found that all participants implemented rituals such as a Sprint frequency, a daily Scrum, retrospectives, Sprint planning and Sprint reviews. The application of Scrum at schools was based on an altered version of Scrum and was implemented to enable students to organise their work. The rituals were shortened to fit in with student schedules. The teacher performed the role of Product Owner, but he/she also guided the process as the Scrum Master. Participant 16 described Scrum as follows: *"Students have more fun, results are better, [they] have ownership. Teachers can be a teacher again, have a coaching role, [feel] less pressure."* It can be assumed that applying Scrum in schools was successful, in that teaching staff subsequently adopted it; in addition, an added benefit was that, when students applied for jobs or when they continued their education, they were already familiar with Scrum and tended to apply to places where Scrum was used.

Human Resources: Two participants shared their experiences with Agile ways of working within the domain of human resources. Both mentioned that the application of Scrum formed the starting point, and was applied to a small-scale project. Scrum was implemented following the Scrum guidelines [10]. The daily Scrum ritual had to be altered, since the team was not at the same location every day. Participant 13 explained that they could not find a moment where they were all available at the same time. The solution was to have a planned conference call daily, so that the status of the project could be shared by the whole team: *"Because everyone was across the country, it became a daily phone-up to update everyone [about] the work at hand"* (Participant 10, Manager of Methods, Quality and Technology).

Communication: In the communication domain, only one example of Agile ways of working was found. This team used Agile to create an overview of the tasks at hand (transparency). They then started working in iterations (Sprint frequency), and had a daily Scrum, a retrospective and a Sprint planning session. The retrospective was stopped because of the lack of follow-up by the team. Respondent 15 explained this in the following way: *"Reflection happened, but not in an orderly matter. They did make a mark if something went wrong, but did not [provide a] follow-up on how to improve. There was a feeling this would only cost [more] time"* (Participant 15, Head of the Communications Team).

Success in implementation took place when room for making errors was factored in and when the surrounding teams were involved in the process. An additional success factor involved the crucial element of starting with people who were enthusiastic about applying Scrum. These people would then spread the news about the success of Scrum throughout the organisation.

Geology: In the domain of geology, the application of Scrum was two-dimensional. First the team searched and made calculations related to drilling operations and secondly they started drilling. To prevent errors being made during the drilling process, the first part of the process (research and calculation) is done using an Agile way. Working with a backlog, daily stand-up meetings and retrospectives, respondent 14 explained the team could work efficiently and when research was going nowhere they could stop early in the process. This made the team effective by reducing the time prior to the drilling phase.

4.2 Domains Where Agile Methods Could Be Applied in the Future

This section explores potential applications of Agile management methods in domains where they have not yet been tried. Based on the findings from this study, we provide a trajectory of where we expect Agile management methods to be explored in the future; these tentative explorations would involve experimentation and additional research studies; in other words, the approach taken needs to involve both academic and professional/business applications.

Firstly, we compared the shared characteristics identified across our cases with the enablers presented by Conforto et al. [5] and organised them along the dimensions of *Structure, Process, Culture and Nature of work* as presented in Table 3. The main enablers on the intersection as discussed by our participants and literature were: *Team-based work, Continuous improvement, Learning organisation and Customer involvement.*

Secondly, in order to understand potential fields that are ripe for Agile applications, we looked at the current reports on work trends involving both the academic and professional domains, such as those provided by the European Trade Union Institute [31]; Accenture [32]; and PwC [33], as well as academic research [34,35]. The workforce trends commonly discussed in these reports are linked to digitisation, flexible work arrangements and work taking place in ecosystems, and the importance of a work/life balance. This section focuses on the impact of digitisation as the trend that is commonly acknowledged as having the biggest potential future impact. Specifically, the categories of Frey and Osborn [34] have been used to guide the discussion. In their article [34], Frey and Osborn present their views on the probability of computerisation. The domains they mark as less likely to be automated are domains where Agile methods could be applied. Jobs in domains that require creativity and those which are based on (cross-functional) teams are less affected by computerisation.

When looking at the findings of Frey and Osborn, it becomes apparent that there are some domains representing jobs that are not threatened by automation. Because Agile management methods are team-based methods, it is interesting to look at creative work fields that fit the criteria iterated above, especially those with high employment and the low probability of computerisation. As many manual tasks will be automated in the future, the human workforce fulfilling creative tasks will be expected to work more effectively in the future. Further, looking more in depth, skill sets of *empathy and support, management and leadership, and science and engineering* will require a major increase in the future according to labour market reports [36]. This shift towards creative work could open up further demands for Agile methods in other domains.

We picked four categories from Frey and Osborn [34] on the basis of two factors: (1) future occupational employment, and (2) low probability of computerisation. These two factors meant that a human workforce was required, and thus these categories shared characteristics of Agile management as discussed above.

In the *management, business and financial* category, the authors foresee a further application of Agile in the domains of change management, business development and Agile project and portfolio management in general. Furthermore, many organisations today are shifting their focus from being process-centred to being people-centric by changing previous management styles into those that involve leadership and collaboration [37]. The emergence of frameworks and methods that specifically focus on such domains as design thinking, lean start-ups, growth hacking, beyond budgeting and so on are all providing the impetus to change these domains and make them Agile.

In the *computer, engineering and science* domains, in addition to software development and engineering, which were the domains where Scrum was originally applied, the authors foresee an application of Agile methods to engi-

Table 3. Enablers for use of Agile methods outside software projects

		Structure					Process		Culture							Work type					
Participant / Source	Domain	Team based	Multidisciplinary teams	Product or service orientation	Self-managing teams	Preference for co-location	Continuous improvement	Development in Sprints	Learning organization	Strong executive support	Acceptance of Agile methodology	Collaborative culture	Decentralized decision making	Entrepreneurial culture	Customer involvement	New product or service development	Collaborative work	Creative work	Supplier involvement	Allows for flexible feedback
Conforto et al [5]		●	●	●	●	●	●						●							
Participant 2	Marketing	●	●			●		●	●									●		
Participant 3	Marketing	●				●			●		●	●					●			
Participant 5	Marketing		●		●		●	●	●		●	●	●				●			
Participant 13	Marketing	●			●				●	●	●				●					
Participant 17	Marketing	●	●	●	●	●	●		●	●	●				●	●			●	●
Participant 11	Marketing, Sales	●		●			●	●	●	●		●		●					●	
Participant 6	Sales	●	●		●	●	●	●		●	●	●			●	●	●			
Participant 12	Sales		●	●	●		●	●	●	●	●		●		●		●		●	
Participant 8	Education																			
Participant 16	Education	●		●				●	●	●	●				●				●	
Participant 14	Geology, Education	●		●			●		●						●	●		●		●
Participant 10	HR	●		●	●		●		●						●			●		
Participant 18	HR	●	●					●	●	●					●					
Participant 1	Event Management	●					●			●	●				●			●		
Participant 4	R&D Measurement Instruments		●			●	●	●		●	●				●	●	●	●		
Participant 7	Change Management	●	●		●		●		●	●		●	●		●	●				●
Participant 15	Communication	●		●			●		●	●	●				●					

neering. Many engineering disciplines have developed more flexible development and prototyping technologies, thus allowing for more flexible and more iterative feedback. While 3D printing and programmable logic facilitate faster industrial design and hardware development cycles, Agile and iterative management might prove useful only in the design stages of a construction project (such as building a bridge). Potential applications can also be found in the growing demand for data science projects, research projects in general, as well as in architecture.

Besides the case involving the use of Scrum in relation to education that was presented here, it is envisaged that the use of Scrum can foster enhanced student engagement (participant 16); in addition, we foresee an application in the design and coordination of educational programmes and in team-based course assignments in the domains of *education, law, community service, arts and media.*

In the healthcare practitioners and technical domains, there are examples of an Agile way of working being applied to make organisations or domains more responsive to their surroundings. Some examples involve community care in the Netherlands, a domain which is being changed by a new way of working (as applied by Buurtzorg [25]). Medical care in the Netherlands is changing towards a structure of self-supporting entities. This presents a challenge in relation to regional hospitals. Several hospitals have responded by shifting their focus towards the patient [38]. By using multidisciplinary teams at the first-aid post, an expert is immediately available because he/she is part of the team. This makes the care provided more effective for the patient. Earlier applications of this approach can be found in the domain of clinical operating teams [39] which, while needing to stay close to medical protocols in the operating theatre, need to adapt to the local needs of a particular patient and learn from those.

5 Limitations

Bias and Participant Sampling: The pool of participants was made up of (among others) managers, Agile coaches, consultants and researchers. Those interviewed were chosen based on their expertise in the topics under discussion. However, since they performed leadership or consulting roles in the application of Scrum, this could result in biased answers, especially when participants were asked about the perceived success of the implementation of Agile methods within their organisations. Furthermore, using Google and LinkedIn as the basis of a web search when looking for participants may have led to a biased sample, as these searches offer personalised results. Moreover, the majority of the participants were part of the researchers' personal network. While this allowed for targeting potential participants based on perceived expertise, it could make replication of the results of the study difficult.

Reliability: Only one person per discussed implementation was interviewed with the exception of one case, in which two participants were interviewed. Cross-checking claims by interviewing another person within the organisation could make the results more reliable. During interviews, some participants were found to take examples from previous experience on software development teams. When talking about Agile methods, it may be difficult for participants to separate their experience outside the software development context from their experience within IT. We tried to mediate this issue by reminding the participant during the interview that the main focus was on applications outside software development, if we noticed that a participant gave an example that clearly related to software development. However, we cannot guarantee that this solved the issue completely, as we asked participants questions about their experiences which they had to answer based on memory and interpretation.

6 Conclusions

Based on interviews with 18 experts, we came to a number of conclusions involving the use of Scrum and of Agile methods in general. Firstly, we identified those organisations applying Scrum in six domains (marketing, sales, communication, education, human resources and research projects). Secondly, we present, based on our cases and the enablers as identified by Conforto et al. [5], characteristic enablers for the successful application of Scrum in non-IT environments. Thirdly, we identified the most applied practices that were used in successful Agile implementation outside of IT (iterations in short frequencies; daily Scrum (Stand-ups), retrospectives, Sprint planning, Sprint review and backlogs). And fourthly, we identified four fields where, potentially, Agile methods could be applied (management, business and financial; computer, engineering and science; education, legal, community service, arts and media; and healthcare, practitioners and technical).

In addition, we found that companies and departments were often inspired by the success of Scrum in IT environments, and that while participants perceived that retrospectives were important, this ritual was often neglected [8]. Finally, we conclude that there is a strong potential for Agile project management expanding into domains yet untouched by this management method (including in domains not mentioned in this study). As organisations are inspired to implement Agile methods, we would like to invite researchers and change agents to actively apply Agile project management to new domains through action research and experiments, thus breaking down barriers to the future global expansion of Agile methods and techniques.

Acknowledgments. We thank all the participants for generously contributing to this study. We would like to also especially thank Nina Kojevnikov PhD. for her review, comments and critical notes.

References

1. Beck, K., et al.: Manifesto for agile software development (2001)
2. Conboy, K., Fitzgerald, B.: Toward a conceptual framework of agile methods: a study of agility in different disciplines. In: Proceedings of the 2004 ACM Workshop on Interdisciplinary Software Engineering Research, pp. 37–44. ACM (2004)
3. Dingsøyr, T., Nerur, S., Balijepally, V., Moe, N.B.: A decade of agile methodologies: towards explaining agile software development (2012)
4. Abrahamsson, P., Conboy, K., Wang, X.: 'Lots done, more to do': the current state of agile systems development research (2009)
5. Conforto, E.C., Salum, F., Amaral, D.C., Da Silva, S.L., De Almeida, L.F.M.: Can agile project management be adopted by industries other than software development? Proj. Manag. J. **45**(3), 21–34 (2014)
6. Conboy, K.: Agility from first principles: reconstructing the concept of agility in information systems development. Inf. Syst. Res. **20**(3), 329–354 (2009)
7. Laanti, M., Similä, J., Abrahamsson, P.: Definitions of agile software development and agility. In: McCaffery, F., O'Connor, R.V., Messnarz, R. (eds.) EuroSPI 2013. CCIS, vol. 364, pp. 247–258. Springer, Heidelberg (2013). https://doi.org/10.1007/978-3-642-39179-8_22
8. Stettina, C.J., Hörz, J.: Agile portfolio management: an empirical perspective on the practice in use. Int. J. Proj. Manag. **33**(1), 140–152 (2015)
9. Laanti, M., Salo, O., Abrahamsson, P.: Agile methods rapidly replacing traditional methods at Nokia: a survey of opinions on agile transformation. Inf. Softw. Technol. **53**(3), 276–290 (2011)

10. Schwaber, K., Sutherland, J.: The scrum guide. The Definitive Guide to Scrum: The Rules of the Game (2016)
11. So, C., Scholl, W.: Perceptive agile measurement: new instruments for quantitative studies in the pursuit of the social-psychological effect of agile practices. In: Abrahamsson, P., Marchesi, M., Maurer, F. (eds.) XP 2009. LNBIP, vol. 31, pp. 83–93. Springer, Heidelberg (2009). https://doi.org/10.1007/978-3-642-01853-4_11
12. Williams, L.: What agile teams think of agile principles. Commun. ACM **55**(4), 71–76 (2012)
13. van Solingen, R., Sutherland, J., de Waard, D.: Scrum in sales: how to improve account management and sales processes. In: 2011 Agile Conference, pp. 284–288. IEEE (2011)
14. Steenberg, R.: The impact of measures when optimising sales processes using scrum, February 2016. (Working Paper)
15. Melnik, G., Maurer, F.: Introducing agile methods in learning environments: lessons learned. In: Maurer, F., Wells, D. (eds.) XP/Agile Universe 2003. LNCS, vol. 2753, pp. 172–184. Springer, Heidelberg (2003). https://doi.org/10.1007/978-3-540-45122-8_20
16. Hicks, M., Foster, J.S.: Score: agile research group management. Commun. ACM **53**(10), 30–31 (2010)
17. Stettina, C.J., Zhou, Z., Bäck, T., Katzy, B.: Academic education of software engineering practices: towards planning and improving capstone courses based upon intensive coaching and team routines. In: 2013 IEEE 26th Conference on Software Engineering Education and Training (CSEE&T), pp. 169–178. IEEE (2013)
18. Jin-Hai, L., Anderson, A.R., Harrison, R.T.: The evolution of agile manufacturing. Bus. Process. Manag. J. **9**(2), 170–189 (2003)
19. Agarwal, A., Shankar, R., Tiwari, M.: Modeling the metrics of lean, agile and leagile supply chain: an ANP-based approach. Eur. J. Oper. Res. **173**(1), 211–225 (2006)
20. Manivelmuralidaran, V.: Agile manufacturing-an overview. Int. J. Sci. Eng. Appl. **4**(1), 156–159 (2015)
21. Inman, R.A., Sale, R.S., Green Jr., K.W., Whitten, D.: Agile manufacturing: relation to JIT, operational performance and firm performance. J. Oper. Manag. **29**(4), 343–355 (2011)
22. Drumond, C.: Agile marketing: fad or future of marketing? (2016). Accessed 1 July 2016
23. Ewel, J., et al.: Marketing manifesto (2018). Accessed 22 Aug 2018
24. King, E., K.V.: Success story: agility and health care, 2 February 2018
25. Gray, B.H., Sarnak, D.O., Burgers, J.S.: Home care by self-governing nursing teams: the Netherlands' Buurtzorg model (2015)
26. Hegarty, C.: Breaking departmental silos: scrum in finance, 9 June 2011
27. SCRUMstudy: How HR teams can benefit from scrum, 27 December 2013. Blogpost: http://blog.scrumstudy.com/how-hr-teams-can-benefit-from-scrum/
28. Gothelf, J.: How hr can become agile (and why it needs to), 19 June 2017. Blogpost on HBR.org: https://hbr.org/2017/06/how-hr-can-become-agile-and-why-it-needs-to
29. Zhang, H., Easterday, M.W., Gerber, E.M., Rees Lewis, D., Maliakal, L.: Agile research studios: orchestrating communities of practice to advance research training. In: Proceedings of the 2017 ACM Conference on Computer Supported Cooperative Work and Social Computing, pp. 220–232. ACM (2017)
30. Strauss, A., Corbin, J.M.: Basics of Qualitative Research: Grounded Theory Procedures and Techniques. Sage Publications, Inc., Thousand Oaks (1990)

31. Degryse, C.: Digitalisation of the economy and its impact on labour markets (2016)
32. Accenture: Workforce marketplace: invent your future (2018)
33. PwC: Workforce marketplace: invent your future (2017)
34. Frey, C.B., Osborne, M.A.: The future of employment: how susceptible are jobs to computerisation? Technol. Forecast. Soc. Change **114**, 254–280 (2017)
35. Katzy, B.R., Stettina, C.J., Groenewegen, L.P., de Groot, M.J.: Managing weak ties in collaborative work. In: 2011 17th International Conference on Concurrent Enterprising (ICE), pp. 1–9. IEEE (2011)
36. Accenture: It's learning. Just not as we know it (2018)
37. Nerur, S., Mahapatra, R., Mangalaraj, G.: Challenges of migrating to agile methodologies. Commun. ACM **48**(5), 72–78 (2005)
38. Kim Bos, J.W.: NRC article: reward for less care, 23 September 2017. https://www.nrc.nl/nieuws/2017/09/23/beloond-voor-minder-zorg-12248867-a1574534
39. Stettina, C.J., Groenewegen, L.P., Katzy, B.R.: Structuring medical agility. In: HEALTHINF, pp. 614–617 (2011)

Author Index

www.ingramcontent.com/pod-product-compliance
Lightning Source LLC
LaVergne TN
LVHW082122200926
848484LV00008B/1995
* 9 7 8 1 0 1 3 2 7 3 2 5 4 *